W9-DBP-083

THE
BUFFALO

(U.S. Bureau of Sport Fisheries & Wildlife)

THE
BUFFALO

Francis Haines

ILLUSTRATED

Thomas Y. Crowell Company

NEW YORK

ESTABLISHED 1834

Grateful acknowledgment is made for permission to use material from the following sources:

Columbia University Press, New York, *Gold Rush*, by J. Goldsborough Bruff, edited by Georgia W. Read and Ruth Gaines, 1949, pp. 17, 18, and 25.

William W. Whitney, California Historical Society, *The Journal of Madison Berryman Moorman*, edited by Irene D. Paden, 1948.

Apollo Edition 1975

Copyright © 1970 by Francis Haines
All rights reserved. Except for use in a review, the
reproduction or utilization of this work in any form
or by any electronic, mechanical, or other means, now
known or hereafter invented, including xerography,
photocopying, and recording, and in any information
storage and retrieval system is forbidden without
the written permission of the publisher.
Published simultaneously in Canada.

Manufactured in the United States of America

L. C. Card 76-94794

ISBN 0-8152-0380-2

Contents

Acknowledgments

PICTURES WERE OBTAINED through the courtesy of the following:

Mary K. Dempsy, Montana Historical Society, furnished photographs of Montana Buffalo.

Beatrice Boone, Office of Conservation, U.S. Fish and Wildlife Service, sent the pictures of the modern herds.

Mary S. McLanahan, The Walters Art Gallery, Baltimore, supplied photographs of the paintings of Alfred Jacob Miller.

John C. Ewers and William Truettner, of the Smithsonian Institution, furnished the photographs of the pictures by George Catlin.

THE
BUFFALO

During the 1800's, George Catlin traveled in the West and devoted his talents to recording on canvas the dress, features, and customs of the Indians. Here, he shows a winter buffalo chase. (Oil on canvas by George Catlin, Smithsonian Institution)

1

Man and Buffalo in North America

Here each hunter sprang in haste from the tired animal he had ridden, and leaped upon the fresh horse he had brought with him. There was not a saddle or bridle in the whole party. A piece of buffalo robe, girthed over the horse's back, served in place of one, and a cord of twisted hair, lashed around his lower jaw, answered for the other. Eagle feathers dangled from every mane and tail, as marks of courage and speed. As for the rider, he wore no other clothing than a light cincture at his waist, and a pair of moccasins. He had a heavy whip, with a handle of solid elk-horn, and a lash of knotted bull-hide, fastened to his wrist by a band. His bow was in his hand, and his quiver of otter or panther skin hung at his shoulder. Thus equipped, some thirty of the hunters galloped away to the left, in order to make a circuit under cover of the hills, that the buffalo might be assailed on both sides at once . . . at that moment each hunter as if by a common impulse, violently struck his horse, each horse sprang forward, and, scattering in the charge in order to assail the whole herd at once, we all rushed headlong upon the buffalo. We were among them in an instant. Amid the trampling and the yells I could see their dark figures running hither and thither through clouds of dust, and the horsemen darting in pursuit.

While we were charging on one side, our companions attacked the bewildered and panic stricken herd on the other. The uproar and confusion lasted but a moment. The dust cleared away, and the buffalo could be seen scattering from a common center, flying over the plains singly, or in long files and small compact bodies, while behind them followed the Indians, riding at furious speed, and yelling as they launched arrow after arrow into their sides. The carcasses were strewn thickly over the ground. Here and there stood a wounded buffalo, their bleeding sides feathered with arrows; and as I rode by them their eyes would glare, they would bristle like gigantic cats, and feebly attempt to rush and gore my horse.

This vivid account of a Sioux buffalo hunt in southeastern Wyoming was written by a young Harvard graduate, Francis Parkman, who spent the summer of 1846 with the Oglala band of Sioux. The type of hunt he describes was repeated, with infinite minor variations, hundreds of times each year for nearly two centuries on the Great Plains.

With its great size, vast numbers, and wide distribution, the buffalo was in sheer mass the largest game species ever known to mankind, and it exerted a profound influence on man from his first arrival in North America until the destruction of the herds in the late nineteenth century.

A mature bull, his massive head and shoulders covered with long, curly hair, is an impressive sight. He stands as much as seven feet tall at the shoulder, and in good condition weighs up to 2,000 pounds. Two curved horns project from the mass of hair above his weak eyes. His hindquarters are small and tapering, covered with short, light-colored hair and terminating in a short tail with a wisp of long hair as a tassel. The cows are built on the same pattern as the bulls, but on a smaller scale. They stand five feet tall at the shoulder and weigh from 700 to 900 pounds.

The buffalo is a gregarious animal, living in small bands containing from five to fifty animals of both sexes and all ages. In time of danger they form a compact mass and present a united front to their enemies, the younger animals in the middle of the band. Until the advent of man the buffalo bands had little to fear from predators. The packs of wolves that prowled around the herds killed off the weak, the sick, and the crippled, but seldom dared to attack the united band.

[2]

When the first hunters appeared, the plains were stocked with larger species of buffalo, now extinct. With only spears, darts, and later, bows and arrows, the hunters had a difficult time bringing down these huge, tough animals in open country. Their most effective hunting method was fire, used to stampede the animals over a cliff or into a ravine.

A marked change in climate about 25,000 years ago melted the ice sheet in the middle west, exposing large new areas of pasture land. As the pasture increased, for some unknown reason all the species of larger buffalo died off, leaving the open country to be occupied by the smaller buffalo of modern times, which came up from Mexico to fill the empty spaces. These buffalo multiplied and spread until at their peak they numbered about 40 million head and occupied nearly half the North American continent.

As the buffalo herds increased, new tribes of hunters were moving in from Siberia through the Alaskan corridor and on south to the plains. Most of them settled in small farming villages on the fringes of the buffalo country and went out on the plains each summer and fall to follow the buffalo herds for a few weeks and secure meat for winter and hides for robes.

A few small bands of Indians lived out on the plains among the herds the year around and did no gardening or farming at all, depending on meat from the buffalo supplemented by some small game and whatever fruit and nuts they could gather in the draws and along the streams. During the winter they sought shelter in a valley or canyon, hoping some buffalo would drift near their camp. All these bands of buffalo hunters suffered from hunger each year while buffalo by the thousands pastured just beyond their reach.

Then came the dramatic flowering of the picturesque plains culture, stemming from an abundance of food and a resulting rapid increase in population. The horse, introduced in North America by the Spanish, was the magic factor that brought the hunters from bare subsistence to abundance almost overnight, for this new servant enabled them to kill buffalo in large numbers at any time of the year.

The plethora of fresh meat supplied the energy and the ease of hunting furnished the leisure hours that enabled the men to devote much of their time developing the stylized war games and elaborate religious ceremonies that gave such color to the plains culture of the nineteenth century.

The Indians secured their first horses, starting about 1640, from Pueblo Indians who had become disgruntled with their Spanish masters in New Mexico and run off to join the wild tribes in the buffalo country. The runaway with his tame, well-trained horses soon instructed his new friends in the use of horses and all the complexities of horse culture, and in about ten years had developed them into a horse-using tribe. Then they, in turn, could spare a few of their old, gentle horses for other tribes farther to the north and east. Thus the horse culture of the Spanish spread throughout the entire Great Plains area in about 120 years.

Although in most tribes the horses were first used as pack animals, the Indians soon discovered that a fast, well-trained horse was of inestimable value in hunting buffalo and keeping the camp supplied with fresh meat for most of the year. As the supplies of meat and robes flowed in, the men had more leisure time but the work of the women increased greatly, until a married woman needed an old mother, a widowed aunt or two, and perhaps even two or three co-wives to help her with the work.

With horses to carry goods and people from place to place, the bands gained greatly in mobility and new patterns of conduct became necessary. It took just two or three days for a camp to become a mess and for the horses to eat all the grass for a mile or two in every direction. Then the tipis and camp gear, the bales of dried meat, and the piles of buffalo robes were loaded onto the pack string and the whole village moved to a fresh, clean spot with new grass for the herds. Usually a large band broke up into several small groups, each with its own camp a mile or so apart from the others, for the better handling of the horses.

The adjustment of an Indian tribe to nomadic living among the buffalo herds is well illustrated by the Comanches, who came out of their canyons and valleys in the Colorado foothills and took over a large part of the western plains from central Kansas south into Texas, and sent raiding parties deep into Mexico. The Blackfeet moved down from a small area in central Alberta until they held the land as far south as the Sun River in central Montana. The Sioux moved west from the Minnesota lake country, partly drawn to the buffalo plains, partly pushed by the better-armed Crees and Chippewas. In time the Sioux claimed all the Dakotas as their hunting grounds and encroached westward into the Crow country in Montana and Wyoming.

On the eastern edge of the buffalo country the tribes living in the woodland fringe raised corn as their staple food, and usually made two hunting excursions each year after meat and robes. After these tribes secured horses, they continued to live in their permanent farming villages and to raise crops, but they were able to spend more time among the buffalo, going farther to the west, where the hunting was better. They could carry back much larger supplies of dried meat and buffalo hides. Since these people left most of their possessions in the villages when they went hunting, they did not need as many horses as did the roving Plains tribes.

Three hundred miles to the west of the Montana buffalo country a number of small tribes lived in the Columbia Basin. They were a sedentary people in little fishing villages, dependent on the salmon runs for most of their food. Once they secured horses, they began to cross the mountains on long hunting excursions among the buffalo. For thirty years their movement to the east was impeded by the hostile Blackfeet until smallpox reduced the fighting capacity of that tribe. Of these western tribes the Flatheads, Coeur d'Alene, and Nez Percé were the most successful at buffalo hunting. About a third of each tribe became seminomadic, spending two or three years at a time east of the mountains, but salmon continued to be their most important food.

A disturbing new factor came to the plains when the covered-wagon trains began to roll toward Oregon and California in the 1840's. At first the little trains were more of a curiosity than a danger to the Indian tribes. Then came the California gold strikes, and the trickle of wagons swelled rapidly into a rolling flood. Each year brought new gold strikes, new boom towns, and more people. From the first big gold strike in 1848 until the last one in 1865 the Overland Trail was crowded each year with the fortune hunters.

Indians along the Platte soon realized that the wagon trains were more than just a nuisance. The travelers killed off or drove out the buffalo, pastured off the grass on a wide strip all the way to the mountains, and brought in diseases that each year wiped out large portions of the tribes near their route.

Finally the trail divided the buffalo country into a northern and a southern segment. The vast herds had once roamed freely from the Dakotas south into Kansas and back, but now their movement was blocked by this wide, dusty strip, which the herds shunned. The continuing invasion of the Indian country stirred the tribes to active resistance and brought on a period of bloody fighting that did not end until the buffalo had been exterminated, the fighting power of the hostile tribes broken, and the remnants herded onto reservations.

The rapid growth of the west coast and the mining towns in the Rockies hastened the construction of the first transcontinental railroad, the Union Pacific. Then came other railroads, the Kansas and Pacific, the Santa Fe, both into the heart of the buffalo herds. They furnished cheap transportation for western products seeking eastern markets, and high on the list of marketable goods were buffalo hides. Eastern tanneries could handle any quality of hides the hunters could ship them. The buffalo herds were mowed down by the blazing guns of thousands of eager hunters.

Army officers looked at the slaughter and approved, for once the herds were gone the Plains Indians would be more peaceful. The cattlemen were pleased too; every buffalo killed made room for one more longhorn steer. The farmers came west in droves, eager to plant wheat once the fields were safe from the trampling herds.

The Plains Indians put up a spectacular fight for their hunting grounds, their buffalo herds, and their old ways. For a decade, 1866–76, wars raged over the whole plains country, with army columns vainly chasing the elusive red men. The army finally started attacking the Indians in their winter villages, slaughtering the families, burning the lodges, destroying the food. The fighting Indians of the Great Plains gave up when the buffalo herds were gone. They had to surrender or see their families starve.

By 1900 only a few hundred buffalo were left. They were held in very small numbers in zoos or were captives on western cattle ranches, except for one wild herd in the woods of northern Alberta. Then several groups interested themselves in the preservation of the species, the most effective being the Canadian government, which added to its wild herd by securing some of the American captives. Soon the United States government joined in, establishing the National Bison Range in western Montana and putting a small herd in Yellowstone Park. Many other small herds were started from surplus stock from these government herds.

With good ranges, plenty of food, and protection from hunters, the buffalo herds grew rapidly. In twenty years it was evident that the number of buffalo that could be raised was limited only by the amount of pasture land that could be set aside for their use. The buffalo had been saved from extinction.

[6]

2

Prehistoric Bison in North America

ABOUT 40,000 YEARS AGO primitive hunting tribes from Asia moved across a land bridge into Alaska, perhaps the first men to reach North America. They were trailing herds of large grass-eaters—mammoth, musk oxen, moose, and a dozen or so species of large bison. The herds found a favorable environment in the new land and prospered over a long period.

These were not the first bison to reach the American west. At least one cousin had preceded them by 200,000 years or more; a skull of the species, exposed by recent erosion in sedimentary strata in northern California, is the oldest and largest reported in North America. Presumably this giant species vanished long ago, replaced by smaller, more agile bison.

The hunters from Asia came across at about midpoint in the last ice age, when, over a few thousand years, the great Wisconsin ice sheet receded along its western edge, leaving an ice-free corridor from the Yukon Valley of Alaska across the Rocky Mountains and southward along the foothills to the southern plains. During this period large ice sheets covered northern Europe and several other areas of the globe. The oceans were lowered more than 200 feet as moisture became trapped in the ice. When the oceans shrank, a wide land bridge joining

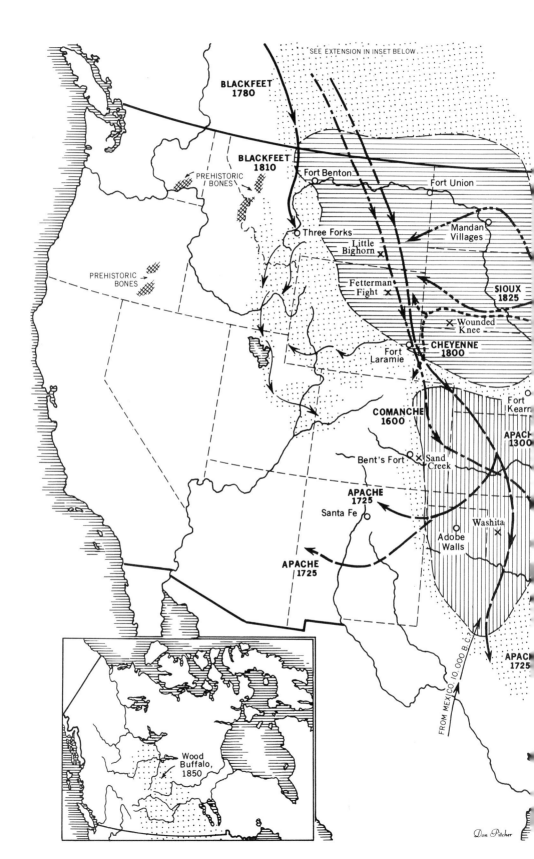

SEE EXTENSION IN INSET BELOW.

BLACKFEET
1780

BLACKFEET
1810

PREHISTORIC
BONES

Fort Benton

Fort Union

Three Forks

Mandan
Villages

Little
Bighorn

PREHISTORIC
BONES

Fetterman
Fight

SIOUX
1825

Wounded
Knee

Fort
Laramie

CHEYENNE
1800

Fort
Kearn

COMANCHE
1600

APACH
1300

Bent's Fort

Sand
Creek

APACHE
1725

Santa Fe

Washita

Adobe
Walls

APACHE
1725

APAC
1725

FROM MEXICO, 10,000 B.C.(?)

Wood
Buffalo,
1850

Don Pitcher

	Greatest extent of the Buffalo, A.D. 1600
	Lines of Buffalo travel, A.D. 1000 to A.D. 1600
	Northern Herd, 1850
	Southern Herd, 1850

INDIAN MOVES

	Blackfeet
	Cheyenne
	Apache
	Comanche
	Sioux
	Shawnee

× Red Settlement
○ White Settlement

○ Red River Settlements

○ Pembina

SIOUX
1700

CHEYENNE
1700

EASTERN LIMIT OF BUFFALO, 1800

SHAWNEE
1740

OMANCHE
1725

Small Isolated
Herd, 1686

MIGRATIONS OF THE BUFFALO
AND THEIR HUNTERS

N

| 0 | 100 | 200 | 300 | 400 |

Scale of Miles

Alaska and Siberia was uncovered, an inviting highway for migrating animals. Then the ice sheet expanded again, closing off the corridor for another 10,000 or 15,000 years. About 25,000 years ago it began melting away again and opened the corridor east of the Rocky Mountains by 16,000 B.C.

As the migrating herds moved southward to the Great Plains they were followed by the primitive hunters, armed with crude spears and clubs—poor equipment for attacking large, healthy animals. And so the pursuers looked for the old and crippled, or those unfortunate enough to be trapped in bogs or drowned in rivers. At times they managed to stampede a small herd over a cliff or into a swamp; even crude weapons were effective against trapped or crippled victims.

Over a period of centuries the moving herds and the hunters following them reached the southern Great Plains, where they found food in abundance. The hunters also found a bewildering variety of species new to them—giant sloths, giant beavers, mastodons, horses, tapirs, camels, and many others. While any of these animals would furnish an ample supply of meat for a band of hungry men, they were all large, tough, and hard to kill.

However, man had one dread weapon effective against even the largest and fiercest animals: fire. In the fall, when the plains were covered with a mat of dried grass and the animals were in prime condition for butchering, a well-placed fire, fanned by a favoring wind, could stampede several animals to their destruction, furnishing enough meat to feed the hunting band throughout the winter.

Over all the plains the hunting fires were set each fall, some of them burning unchecked for days and blackening thousands of acres. With each small hunting band setting even one or two fires a year, and lightning adding a few more, the entire plains area suffered millions of burned acres each year. Such recurring fires were an important factor in keeping the grasslands free from encroaching shrubs and trees, and in pushing back the forests along the eastern edge of the plains. The Shawnees used this method to keep several thousand square miles of Kentucky free from forests in the eighteenth century.

Through all this time the ice sheet was melting, each year exposing large new areas for grasses. These two factors, the hunting fires and the melting of the ice sheet, probably aided by other factors not yet identified, gave central North America the largest pasture lands known. The open lands stretched from the Canadian forests southward to the

Gulf of Mexico and from the Rocky Mountains eastward almost to the Mississippi River. Fingers of the prairie country extended eastward across the Mississippi, across Illinois, Indiana, and Ohio to the western ridges of the Alleghenies.

Then came a puzzling development. With conditions seemingly more favorable than ever for the grazing herds, many of the large species disappeared entirely, while similar species flourished and multiplied. The mastodon and the giant sloth suffered a rather swift destruction, while remnants of the horse herds lived on for several thousand years before succumbing.

Since the only identifiable new factor at this critical period was the appearance of man and his fires, some geographers suggest that the extensive burnings might have triggered the catastrophe. Large, slow animals such as the mastodon and the giant sloth would be especially vulnerable to fire, but this explanation does not account for the killing off of the tough, agile wild horses, while the larger, clumsier, more stupid bison not only survived but thrived to an astonishing degree (although all other species of the bison did disappear in the widespread disaster).

Traces of the vanished bison have been found all across the United States from New Jersey to California, with the fossil remains usually estimated as about 40,000 years old. So far none of the bones identified as belonging to these vanished herds have been found in association with early artifacts. But this is negative evidence that does not really prove anything, since hunters of this period stripped away meat at the site of a kill and seldom bothered to carry large bones back to their caves.

About the time the herds were facing destruction, the route from the Yukon Valley to the Great Plains reopened as a result of the continued melting of the ice sheet. More hunting bands came across Siberia into North America, bringing with them a new weapon more effective against large game: the heavy dart projected by an atlatl, or throwing stick. The darts, four to six feet long and stone tipped, could be thrown with some accuracy for a hundred yards or so, and at fifty yards could inflict a serious wound on an animal struck in the intestines. Many thousands of years later other migrants from Siberia brought bows and arrows. Hence any bison remains associated with artifacts left by hunters using atlatls would be much older than remains left by hunters using bows and arrows. So far all the bison remains found with artifacts have been of the period of the atlatl or later. With the refined method of dating remains by carbon 14, it is now possible to place early kills in accurate sequence.

Near Folsom, New Mexico, in about 15,000 B.C. hunters using the atlatl and darts killed twenty-seven bison in one place. The species found here has been named the Taylor bison. It was somewhat larger than the modern bison.

At Big Sandy Creek in southeastern Colorado a large kill of bison was made about 6500 B.C. All of these animals are classed as *Bison occidentalis*. In northwestern Iowa the skull of another *B. occidentalis* was found at a village site and dated 6471 B.C. In this case the skull had probably been brought to the village for use in some sort of religious rite.

There is some question whether the *B. taylori* and the *B. occidentalis* are not actually the same species. At any rate, they are closely related and are considered to be extinct, although some geographers believe it is possible that the extant wood buffalo in northern Alberta is actually the *B. occidentalis*.

Wood buffalo have been protected for nearly a century and the herd has increased during that period, but it is probable that they have crossbred with the plains buffalo for the last sixty years. Hence it is considered impossible to secure an animal known to be a specimen of the true wood buffalo that could be compared in detail with the skeletons of the *B. taylori* from the Folsom kill and the *B. occidentalis* from the Big Sandy Creek kill.

During the period when many species of large grass-eaters were destroyed, the modern bison was common in Mexico, as shown by the many fossil remains. It is possible that the conditions that killed off the animals on the plains did not occur in Mexico, or perhaps the Mexican bison had a biological edge that enabled it to survive. When the northern grasslands were left almost empty and the Mexican pasture changed to desert scrub with the changing climate, these bison moved north and filled the vacant spaces.

Over many thousands of years, between about 10,000 B.C. and A.D. 1000, the natural increase of the modern buffalo filled the plains. Eventually the necessity for more pasture forced the animals on the outer edges to move beyond the plains and occupy marginal lands on the east and the west. The eastward-moving herds crossed the Mississippi into northern Illinois, then into Indiana and Ohio. Some of them turned south and crossed the Ohio River into Kentucky and northern

Tennessee, finally reaching the tidewater regions of the Carolinas and Virginia. On the west the herds found rather easy passes through the Rockies and across the continental divide in both Montana and Wyoming. On the western slope of the divide they occupied the Bitterroot, upper Snake, Bear, and upper Colorado valleys.

These marginal herds were small and scattered compared to the dense masses that filled the plains. They had not even filled their new pastures before their further growth was stopped rather abruptly by the arrival of white settlers with their guns and horses. The settlers and the Indian tribes attacked the herds in the east with guns, while the Plains Indians secured horses and greatly increased their annual kill on the plains. Horses were also used for buffalo hunting by the Columbia Basin tribes west of the divide.

Imaginative writers, visualizing the movements of these many herds and ignoring the hundreds of years involved, have developed the theory that the thousands of buffalo, moving in orderly columns on regular migrations, trampled out a vast network of broad trails the length and breadth of buffalo land and that these trails were later taken over by the Indians and still later became wagon roads and highways for the early settlers.

The writers support their premise by pointing to the pattern of well-beaten trails leading to salt licks and water holes in buffalo country. Sometimes these trails were worn down as much as six or seven feet below the surface of the surrounding land where they crossed a small swell or dropped down a bank. However, there are some fundamental errors in this concept, stemming from a lack of knowledge of the buffalo as a grazing animal.

The buffalo herds, depending entirely on grass for food, had to be on the move constantly seeking fresh pastures. In their search for grazing land they wandered rather aimlessly, often going from good pasture to poor for no apparent reason. At times they became frightened and started running. Then all the other buffalo in sight might start running too, until thousands were off on a wild stampede. As they ran they usually merged into a compact mass and galloped until they became exhausted. They trampled any small objects in their path but often were crippled or killed from running into large obstacles.

Except when stampeding, the progress of the herd was slow. Each animal needed several hours of grazing each day, and several more of standing or lying down to digest its food. About once a day the herd would go down to the water to drink, but they could go two or three days without water.

When the herds were moving across the country, unless they were stampeding, they spread out on a broad front, as much as fifty miles across, with each small band scattered over a few acres and separated from the other bands by about a quarter of a mile in all directions. While moving in this manner, and grazing as they went, a herd would not leave any definite trail. The buffalo bunched up and moved in a column or compact mass only when their route was constricted by natural barriers. Thus when the buffalo approached a narrow mountain defile or a canyon, they came together and proceeded as a column until they reached the end of the passage, but as soon as they regained open country they again spread out on a broad front and the well-marked trail ended abruptly. Herds going to water or to salt licks followed the same pattern. Well-marked trails led some distance from the water's edge, but faded once good grass was reached.

And even when the herds crossing ranges were forced into mountain passes, they left no well-beaten path if the pass was fairly wide and covered with grass. Such broad passes used a great deal by buffalo were the Bozeman Pass between the Yellowstone and Gallatin watersheds, and the Reynolds, Monida, Deer Lodge, and South passes across the continental divide, the first four in Montana, the fifth in Wyoming. The early settlers found no well-beaten trails in these passes, and had to lay out their own wagon roads.

Buffalo trails were generally unsuitable for development into roads. George Washington noted in his journal: "At the crossing of this creek (Sandy Creek, West Virginia) Mccullock's path, which owes its origin to buffaloes, being no other than their tracks from one lick to another and consequently crooked and not well chosen, strikes off from the new road." And early hunters on the plains observed that buffalo trails usually were crooked even when there were no obstacles in the way.

Many of the early white explorers and hunters thought the buffalo were migratory animals, moving along definite routes with the changing seasons, northward in summer, southward in winter, but they could not agree on which direction the herds moved at any given time, nor where the migration paths could be found. Other observers were equally convinced that the herds did not migrate, for the buffalo would have beat out broad roads over their regular routes.

The Indian hunters were intelligent observers of the animal life around them and they paid particular attention to the buffalo, which furnished them with meat and hides so necessary for their basic living. With their very lives depending on a thorough knowledge of the buffalo and its habits, one would assume the Indians would know the precise movements of the herds, but in hundreds of years of hunting buffalo the Plains tribes were never able to discover a definite pattern for the herds. They learned that the buffalo were scattered over the entire range throughout the year and that a herd might be found at almost any place at any time. This uncertainty about the movements of the herds led the various tribes to develop elaborate dances and other ceremonies designed to lure the animals to the proper spots on the tribal hunting grounds.

Even when the herds had established well-marked trails leading to good fording places on a river, the next time they wanted to cross they often ignored that place and chose a new crossing a few miles away. Perhaps they did not remember the old crossing, or just did not care to look for it. Hence even the trails leading to good crossings were not used consistently, and no trails at all were trodden out across the broad expanse of the open plain.

Cattle on the open range, when left to their own devices, follow a pattern of behavior similar to that of the buffalo, except that they are smarter than the buffalo and less apt to get into trouble by trying a new, difficult place. The only time range cattle follow trails in open country is when they are being guided by stockmen.

The driving of cattle herds and wagon trains through the western grass country left behind distinct ruts that are plainly visible a century later. Once the grass sod is broken and the underlying soil eroded, the scar may heal but it will not disappear. Where the buffalo trampled out trails to water or left wallows on the open plain, the marks remain until the land is plowed, but in all the wide ranges in eastern Montana, untouched by a plow, where the buffalo ranged in large herds for thousands of years, there is no trace of a buffalo highway.

When they drove buffalo from higher, bare ridges down into snowdrifts, Sioux hunters could easily spear the floundering beasts. (Oil on canvas by George Catlin, Smithsonian Institution)

3

Early Hunters on the Great Plains

THE ROVING BANDS OF HUNTERS who moved down from Alaska about 40,000 years ago left few traces of their passage. An occasional camp spot can still be found, usually near a good source of chipping rock for making weapons and tools, and in good game country. The waste chips of stone and the fragments of artifacts broken in the making are easily recognizable as made by human hands.

Sometimes the hunters found sheltering caves in good game country and lived in them over a long period, leaving their traces in the form of artifacts of stone. The garbage dumps, covered and preserved by drifting dust, may still hold some of the more durable remains of their food—bones from animals, pits from fruits, and seeds and stalks from plants. The sites of fire pits may be marked by charcoal fragments left from cooking fires.

Scant as these remains are, they tell a good deal about the level of material culture reached by these primitive people, as well as something of their diet, but nothing whatever of their physical characteristics. Only much later, when people came to settle in one place and learned to bury their dead, can enough skeletal material be found to identify the physical types.

Once the migrant bands established themselves on the southern plains, they had to find sheltered places where they could wait out the winter storms. A desirable location would lure them back year after year, until they found it advantageous to build small earth-covered lodges at the site. Strewn around the lodges were many discarded items, such as worn-out tools and broken stone artifacts. Sometimes, too, good knives, spear points, and the like were lost in the dirt. Many of these lodge sites have been excavated since World War II, giving a much more detailed picture of these early people and their activities than had been available earlier. Dating the village sites by the carbon-14 method, developed since 1950, has helped a great deal in establishing the time sequence for the sites. They vary from 6741 B.C. in an Iowa village to many fifteenth- and sixteenth-century villages in Kansas.

These primitive hunters lived in the heart of the buffalo country, yet their refuse heaps contain very few buffalo bones. The bones of several kinds of smaller animals are more common.

There is a simple explanation for the absence of buffalo bones: The animals were large, and had heavy bones. When one was killed, the meat was stripped from the bones and carried to the village, usually quite a distance away. From one adult animal the meat would weigh from 400 to 900 pounds, and there would also be the heavy green hide to carry, another 75 to 150 pounds. With this large load of desirable parts, no one wanted to carry home the heavy, rather useless bones, unless a skull might be needed for some religious rite or a new shoulder-blade hoe was wanted for the garden patch. When buffalo bones are found in a village, they are usually either a skull or a shoulder blade, neither of which would be carried home for the meat on it.

Bones of small animals are more plentiful in the old villages since their entire carcasses could be carried quite easily. Even a horse, deer, or antelope could be cut into two or three parts for easy handling. Thus their bones might be much more common in the village excavation than buffalo bones, but the villagers probably ate a hundred pounds of buffalo meat to one pound of smaller game.

It is a mistake to picture these early hunters on the plains wandering in small nomadic bands, entire families carrying all their belongings and trailing the buffalo herds 365 days a year, with a large train of dogs carrying the extra packs. This picture has come down to us from the early European visitors to the plains, who usually met the wandering bands in late summer or fall when the people did indeed follow the herds. However, Pedro de Castañeda, with Coronado's expedition in

1541 in the Texas Panhandle, who left the earliest written account of these plains people, mentions that the buffalo hunters were "dressing skins to take to the pueblos to sell since they go to spend the winter there."

Tough and hardy as these people were, they had to seek shelter when the blizzards blew in from the north with their driving snow and bitter cold. The small skin tipis and few scant robes the people could carry would not keep them from freezing to death on the open plains. Even the larger tipis of later times, with their inner linings and floors covered with robes, needed to be pitched in a sheltered spot during a storm. If a band could not visit a farming village for the winter, it would settle in a canyon or deep valley where there was some protection from the storms and timber for firewood.

In the late summer, wild plums, seeds, nuts, rose hips, and a variety of berries—buffalo berries, service berries, and choke cherries—were ripe for harvest. Young rabbits and fat prairie dogs were plentiful along the draws and on the flats. In this time of plenty the hunters learned to feast on the fresh fruit and small game, hoarding the seeds, nuts, and rose hips against the "starving time" of winter. Because these hoards would not be needed for months, and the heavily burdened people did not want to carry all that extra weight each time they moved camp during the fall hunt, they stored the food reserves in caches near a good spot for a winter camp, sheltered from the sweep of the north wind, perhaps in a thicket near a stream. In later times, when the women learned to pound the berries, form them into small cakes, and dry them in the sun, these too were added to the winter stores.

When the food caches were opened in the winter, the seeds were placed on large, flat stones and ground fine by rubbing them with smooth river stones from the gravel beds. The numerous grinding stones found at the various camp sites indicate that many bushels of seeds were ground in this way, for the stones have the patina that comes only from hundreds of hours of being rubbed on hard-coated seeds.

Once the harvest was gathered and stored, the band turned to the serious task of killing a large number of buffalo, at least one for each person, and more if the hunting went well. For the big fall hunts they either surrounded small groups of buffalo and attacked them with spears or used fire to drive a herd over a cliff or into a ravine. While the fire was more deadly, often herds would not be found in the right position for such a drive. The "surround" was easier to stage, but more dangerous and less dependable. It also provided better robes, unsinged and not battered by a fall onto rocks.

In either case, a successful drive produced a large number of carcasses, often more than could be used before the meat spoiled. The dead buffalo had to be skinned and cut up quickly into large chunks so that the meat could chill in the night air. The next day it was cut into thin strips or slabs and placed on wooden frameworks to keep it out of reach of the dogs. The dry air rapidly sucked out the moisture while a small smoldering fire furnished smoke for a preservative and a little heat to hasten the drying. At a large kill much of the meat spoiled before it could be processed.

A successful hunt provided about a hundred pounds of dried meat for each man, woman, and child in the band, and one new hide for each. The hide still weighed thirty pounds or so after being dried for several days. It was physically impossible for the people to carry all this weight in addition to their regular camp gear, even with the help of many dogs. The dogs, of course, ate the same kind of food the people ate, so their number had to be limited. Hence it made sense to cache the dried meat and the new hides near the seed caches until winter set in.

Once the hunters had established a permanent site for a winter camp they were no longer true nomads, for they now had a fixed abode, a lodge or a cave, where they lived for some months each year. Their lodges were round, built of timber and covered with a layer of grass and reeds, then a layer of dirt for warmth. Such shelters would last for several years, and their sites are still recognizable after a few thousand years. The outer circle, with decayed wood in the post holes, and a fire pit with some charcoal are the most obvious signs of these ancient structures.

The hunters gradually learned how to raise a few crops, perhaps borrowing farming methods from their neighbors in the woodland fringe to the east or from the Pueblos along the rivers in New Mexico to the southwest. They planted small patches of corn and beans, and later, squash and sunflowers. The corn, beans, and sunflower seeds were easily stored for winter use and served as a valuable food supplement during the hungry months when game was scarce.

In the spring the leafy new plants were attractive to deer, rabbits, prairie dogs, and other animals, and had to be protected until they were about half grown and became less appetizing to the foragers.

Then they might be left untended for two or three weeks with little danger until they began to ripen—and the animals reappeared. After they were harvested, the crops were put into the caches, leaving the villagers free to roam the plains on the trail of buffalo until the snows came. The fall hunt might last as long as three months.

The yearly routine of the seminomadic buffalo hunters from one spring to the next began with small bands searching for buffalo as soon as the snows melted. They needed some fresh meat even though they might still have some stored foods. At this time of year only the buffalo bulls were fit for food, and they were in poor condition after the long winter. Better meat could be found along the streams when carcasses came down on the spring floods.

In the warm spring sunshine the villagers dug up their little garden patches in the soft alluvial soil near the streams. With dibble sticks and buffalo-shoulder-blade hoes they prepared many small circles, about two feet across, for the seeds, leaving all the rest untilled. Then the hunters packed up and left for the plains, to be gone a month or so on the early summer hunt, leaving the very young, the very old, and the invalids to care for the crops, with the hardest work being done by a few sturdy women. The rest of the women went on the hunt.

By early summer when the hunters moved out to the plains the new grass was high. The buffalo cows were still lean and scrawny from nursing their new calves, but the bulls were again sleek and fat. Over most of the plains the warm weather and frequent rain made it difficult to dry meat. The bull hides were practically bare of wool, and of no use for robes. The hunters lived on fresh meat while they stripped the hides of hair and tanned them for leather, or left them untanned as rawhide, to be made into thongs, moccasin soles, and parfleches (the so-called "Indian suitcases," made by folding damp rawhide into container shape and allowing it to dry).

When the crops were ripe the hunters returned with a little dried meat, some tanned hides, and rawhides. They harvested the crops, put them in storage, and went off again on the long fall hunt, taking everyone along. Now the cows were in prime condition, with their hides covered with thick, fine wool, almost a fur. Their meat was the best, and the carcasses yielded plenty of fat, especially the two fine strips of back fat so prized by all the hunting tribes. A few of the bulls might be killed in the fall hunts too, but frequently they were feeding at a distance from the cows and were ignored by the hunters. The calves were killed though, for they were very good to eat and their thin hides were needed for clothes.

Back from the hunt, the village prepared for winter, bringing in fire-wood and patching the dirt covering of the lodges. When the storms came they stayed close to the lodges, although between storms, especially during a chinook (a warm winter wind from the west), the hunters went out for a few miles in all directions looking for fresh meat of any kind.

If a herd of buffalo had chosen the same valley for their winter range, the hunters fared well, taking fresh meat back to the village. In times of poor hunting everyone subsisted on the food reserves. Although they seldom were in serious want, they called this the "starving time."

Throughout the year it was a comparatively easy task for a hunter to find buffalo on the well-stocked plains, but killing one of these large, tough animals was not so easy. The crude spear of the early hunter could inflict a fatal wound only if he was close to his quarry and able to choose his point of attack, and it was difficult to approach the animal on the open plain, for it lived and fed in small, closely knit groups, each led by an alert old cow. And if the hunter did manage a close approach, the buffalo could easily move out of reach or might even turn and kill him. In either case there was no meat for the families.

A single thrust of the clumsy spear, with its heavy, crude point, could kill a buffalo quickly if it pierced the rib cage and struck either the heart or the lungs, or if it entered the throat, severing the jugular vein or windpipe, but these blows could not be struck unless the spear was held firmly in both hands and aimed carefully. Such an attack could be made only against a trapped or crippled animal.

A large target, and one vulnerable to a thrown spear, was the paunch. Here a wound could produce internal bleeding, which might cause death in a few hours. If the spear could be driven forward beneath the ribs to pierce the diaphragm, the lungs collapsed and death came in minutes. The hunter's best chance for such a blow required him to get within a few feet of his victim, and this could best be done by allowing the buffalo to come to him. Each day the buffalo approached the watering places to drink, usually along well-trodden trails. The hunter hid in the tall grass near the trail and a few feet downwind so that his scent would not be detected. When the buffalo filed by, a well-thrown spear could inflict a fatal wound on one of them, preferably a young cow near the end of the line.

A lone hunter could also be successful if he found an animal trapped in a bog or mudhole, or crippled by a fall. Often when a large herd stampeded, it left several dead or crippled in its wake as the herd in its mad rush encountered obstacles in its path. While the cripples were easy to kill, the hunter had to find them before the wolves did. But the people could not depend on such chance finds; they needed a reliable source of meat, resulting from a planned course of action.

The fire drives were of this sort. A fire could be used on the plains almost any day from midsummer to late fall, but it required a brisk favoring breeze and a herd of buffalo in position upwind from some obstacle, such as a rimrock or a steep ravine. The hunters formed a line several hundred yards farther upwind and set a row of fires in a wide arc reaching halfway around the herd. As the frightened animals dashed in terror from the wall of wind-driven flame, they left a heap of dead and crippled animals at the foot of the cliff or in the bottom of the ravine, ready for the butchering crew.

When winter storms drove the snow across the plains, often the higher ground was left bare while deep, soft drifts formed in the hollows. When the buffalo sought the bare ridges with the exposed grass, they might be stampeded into the drifts, where they floundered helplessly in the deep snow as hunters on snowshoes speared them.

Smooth ice on a lake or river was deadly to buffalo. They sprawled around, unable to regain their footing. If the ice was thin, the whole herd might break through and drown, to be harvested in due time by the hunters.

Here is an eyewitness account of a buffalo kill on smooth ice: "The slipperiness of the ice was turned to good account the other day by the Indians, as they drove a band of buffalo cows so that they had to go out on the ice of the lake, where of course they fell and stumbled, and could make no progress, while their pursuers, approaching on foot, with ease killed the whole, to the number of fourteen."

At another time, along the Missouri, Charles Mackenzie reported that the buffalo broke through the river ice:

At times the Indians would congregate in great numbers and continue to drive large herds to the banks of the Missouri, and by gradual approaches, confine them into a narrow space where the ice was weakest, until by their weight and pressure, large squares of ice, some of fifty yards, would give way and vast numbers of the animals were plunged into the river and carried under the solid ice to a *mare* (opening) a little below, where they again emerged, floated and were received by crowds of women and children, provided with the proper hooks and instruments to haul them on the ice, which, in a short time, became strewn with dead carcasses.

Each year large numbers of dead buffalo were carried down the rivers by the spring floods. Some had broken through the ice during the winter and drowned, others had been swept away while trying to swim the flooded streams. One man, John McDonnell, on May 18, 1795, counted over 7,360 dead buffalo along a stretch of the Saskatchewan.

When the carcasses came floating down on the flood, some of them were rather ripe, but the early hunters probably thought the carcasses both tender and nourishing even though they had turned green. In later years fur traders reported, with some revulsion, seeing Indians harvesting and feasting on drowned buffalo along the Missouri.

After the first hunters had been on the plains for 20,000 years or so, new waves of migrants from Asia brought in a new hunting weapon, the atlatl, sometimes called the spear thrower. With this instrument a skilled hunter could throw a stone-tipped dart some four to six feet long to a distance of 150 yards, and use it with some accuracy at 50 yards. The atlatl dart, with its finely chipped point, penetrated much deeper than the old spears, and opened up new styles of hunting.

Two or three hunters would take their atlatls and darts, disguise themselves with wolf skins, and creep up on a band of feeding buffalo. The animals paid little attention to them, seemingly unafraid of a few wolves skulking nearby. When the hunters were within range, they rose up and threw their darts, dropping quickly to the ground in hopes that the other buffalo would not start to run but would continue grazing while the wounded animals slowly died.

In the fall hunts, when the hunters needed to make a big kill, they used the surround, which needed fifty or more people for best results. Women and older children could help in this method. The group would fan out and slowly approach a small band of buffalo feeding on the edge of the main herd, and quietly surround it, keeping a hundred yards or so away. This had to be done on a windless day lest the buffalo become alarmed by the scent. During this season the bulls usually grazed in separate bands a few miles away from the cows and calves.

Once the people were in position they advanced very slowly until the old cow who was the leader noticed them and became restless. With no scent to warn it, the short-sighted buffalo usually did not notice anything wrong until the hunters were within about thirty yards. When the old cow started toward the center of the herd, away from the people she had sighted, the people on the opposite side would advance quickly, alarming the cows on their side and starting them toward the center before the herd could begin any general movement in one direction.

If the action was timed accurately, the buffalo would become confused and huddle for a few moments in a compact group. At this point all the hunters threw their darts, wounding as many animals as possible before one of the herd dashed through the enclosing ring, followed by all the rest. A successful surround of this kind might net ten or more buffalo, enough to keep the hunting band busy for several hours with the butchering.

If the hunters were lucky, the fleeing buffalo would run away without disturbing the main herd, a quarter of a mile away. Then the hunters could hope to stage another surround in the same locality in a day or so, when they had the first kill taken care of.

A few thousand years after the atlatl came to the plains, new migrants from Asia brought in the bow and arrow, but the hunting patterns changed very little on account of this new weapon. Only when horses came to the plains in the seventeenth century was the hunting pattern significantly altered.

When meat was scarce every edible scrap was salvaged, and a hungry man would eat any particle he could chew and swallow, including all of the organs, intestines, and odd bits. When a large kill was made and there was more meat than could be used, he took only the choicest morsels, which on a buffalo in good condition always included the two strips of back fat. The tongue, even on the old bulls, was always saved.

In handling a buffalo carcass, the first step was to remove the hide if it was to be saved. The fresh hide from a large bull might weigh 150 pounds, and from a large cow, 100 pounds. These were too heavy to be handled in one piece, so they were taken from the animal in two pieces, being first split down the belly, then down the back, from neck to tail. The buffalo was placed in a prone position, with his legs spread out, for this operation. Then practically every morsel worth saving could be gleaned without having to move the heavy and awkward skeleton.

The two halves of the skin, spread flesh side up, received the chunks of meat as they were removed from the carcass. A large cow in good condition would produce about 500 pounds of meat, and a very large bull, 900 pounds. This included the back fat, tongue, and heart. The liver, kidneys, lungs, paunch, small intestines, and sweetbreads were all saved, but were not classed as meat, for they could not be preserved by drying but had to be eaten within a short time. When meat was scarce the lungs and any blood in the body cavity were also saved. Frequently the skull was opened and the brains taken for food. When a large kill was made and there was much more offal than could be used, most of it was left untouched in the body cavity, for the handling of just the meat took all the time and energy of the butchering crew.

The hides of younger animals were usually removed in one piece. In the mid-sixteenth century, Castañeda observed that the hunters in Texas slit the hide down the back, rather than down the belly as was done in later times. When the belly slit is used, the hump of the animal makes it difficult to keep the carcass belly up, so the head is twisted back against the shoulder as a prop. Some white hunters in the nineteenth century even severed the head so it could be used to greater advantage as a prop. The hides of these smaller animals were usually reserved for clothing.

The Plains Indians devised many ingenious ways to use the various parts of the buffalo for nearly every daily necessity. One list secured from the Blackfeet in the late nineteenth century contained nearly a hundred different uses, and a more thorough survey might have extended the list by another score.

Buffalo hides tanned with the hair on were used as wraps and blankets, and are usually called robes to distinguish them from the hides tanned into leather without the hair or those dehaired but left untanned. Robe-tanned hides were used to make outer garments for winter on the northern plains, a practice common among the Blackfeet. Soft-tanned hides, usually smoked over a fire of smoldering damp rotten wood to make them dry soft and pliable after a wetting, were made into dresses for the women and girls, leggings, shirts, and breechclouts for the men, and moccasins for everyone. Worn-out lodge coverings, well smoked and heavy with grease, were also cut up for clothing, especially moccasins.

Summer skins from the bulls were often left untanned after the hair had been removed. When the skins dried, they became the hard, tough rawhide of a dozen uses, such as moccasin soles, belts, all sorts of lashings, and indestructible, waterproof containers for supplies.

Buffalo horns were shaped into spoons, cups, and ladles. The long shaggy hair from the head was braided into rope. The short soft hair was used for stuffing game balls. The tail with the tuft of hair left on the end became a fly whisk, or the skin from the tail could be made into a knife sheath with the hair tassel for a decoration.

Buffalo bones were used for making long awls and hide scrapers. Rawhide could be braided into rope, which was drawn back and forth through the eye socket of a skull to remove the hair and soften the rope. Rib bones made sled runners, pieces of bone were shaped into small counters for gambling games—and these uses do not exhaust the list by any means.

In the historic period many new uses for buffalo products were found; for example, almost all the horse gear used on the plains was made from buffalo hides or hair, and early travelers wrote down Indian recipes for many savory buffalo dishes and methods of preserving the meat for future use.

4

The Buffalo's Life Cycle and Distribution

A SHIPWRECKED SPANISH EXPLORER in southern Texas in 1530–35 later returned to Spain and told this story:

> Cattle [buffalo] come as far as this. I have seen them three times, and eaten their meat. I think they are about the size of those in Spain. They have small horns like those of Morocco, and hair long and flocky, like that of the Merino. Some are lighter brown, others black. To my judgment, the flesh is finer and sweeter than that of this country. The Indians made blankets of those that are not full grown, and of the larger they make shoes and bucklers. They come as far as the coast and in a direction from the north, and range over a district of more than 400 leagues. In the whole extent of the plain over which they roam, the people, who live bordering upon it, descend and kill them for food; and thus a great many skins are scattered throughout the country.

So wrote Álvar Núñez Cabeza de Vaca after five years as a castaway among the Texas Indians. He is the first European of record to make an eyewitness report of the American buffalo. The description given in Antonio de Solis' history of the conquest of Mexico, and attributed to one of Cortes' men, was apparently inserted about a century after the event. It did not appear in any of the original accounts.

Pedro de Castañeda, traveling with Francisco Coronado on the Texas plains in 1541, had a much closer acquaintance with the buffalo:

Their faces are short and narrow between the eyes, the forehead two spans wide. Their eyes bulge on the side, so that when they run they can see anyone who follows them. They are bearded like large goats, and when they run they carry their heads low, their beards touching the ground. From the middle of the body toward the rear they are covered with very fine wooly hair like that of a coarse sheep, and from the belly forward they have thick hair like the mane of a wild lion. They have a hump larger than that of a camel, and their horns, which barely show through the hair, are short and thick. During May they shed their hair on the rear half of the body, and then look exactly like a lion. To remove their hair they lean against small trees found in some of the gorges and rub against them until they shed the wool, as a snake sheds its skin. They have a short tail with a small bunch of hair at the end, and when they run they carry it erect like a scorpion. One peculiar thing is that when they are calves they are reddish like ours, but in time, as they become older, they change color and appearance. Excellent garments could be made from their wool, but not bright colored ones, because the wool itself is a dark red.

The buffalo appears to be an ungainly animal, with an enormous head, heavy high shoulders, and skimpy hindquarters. Actually, the thick growth of long, curly hair over the head, neck, and shoulders makes them appear more massive than they are, while the rear half of the animal has very short hair. The true shape can be observed on an animal with the skin removed and on a six-month-old calf, which has grown its hump but which still has short hair over the whole body.

A full-grown bull may measure as much as 6.5 feet to the top of the hump, and in good condition will weigh over 2,000 pounds, but the average height of the adult bull is about 6 feet, and its weight 1,600 pounds. An average bull will measure 12 feet from the tip of the nose to the root of the tail. He will usually reach his full size at six or seven years of age.

The cow is definitely smaller, with a height of 5 feet, a length of

7 feet, and will weigh from 700 to 1,200 pounds. She produces her first calf at the age of three or four.

All adult buffalo have dark brown, almost black, hair on the fore-parts. The shorter hair on the hindquarters varies in color from a brown in the fall to a washed-out brownish yellow, almost a buckskin, in the spring.

The calves during the first few months look very much like those of domestic red breeds, but darken over the next two years, when the hindquarters fade to the adult color.

A buffalo will dress out about the same as domestic beef, with a trimmed carcass at about 50 percent of the live weight. An early fur trader who each year bought about 150 cows and many bulls and calves kept records of the average weights: usable meat from a large bull in good condition, 800 pounds; average cow, 400 pounds; two-year-old heifers, 200 pounds; yearlings (killed in the winter, these would be long yearlings, 18 to 20 months old), 110 pounds.

The breeding season for buffalo extends from about mid-July to the end of August, and the gestation period is about nine and a half months. In Texas calves start arriving in early April, while in Canada they come two or three weeks later. Calves are nursed for nearly a year, the mothers weaning the young in the spring about the time the next calf is due. Buffalo milk is rich in butterfat, just the supplementary nourishment needed in the cold winter on the plains by calves too young to store up an ample supply of body fat of their own.

Buffalo are considered as adults in their fourth year, but they continue to grow for the next two or three years. They live to about twenty years of age in protected pastures, with some living more than thirty years.

Buffalo never learned to paw the snow away to expose grass for winter feed as range horses do. Perhaps their split hooves hinder such pawing. When the snow is light and fluffy, the buffalo can nose it away, but when a crust of ice forms or the snow packs, the animal soon gets its nose all raw and bloody in attempting to feed. Fortunately on the plains the wind usually keeps a good deal of the high ground blown bare.

Before the buffalo were driven back from the marginal ranges of their domain, they had occupied about a third of all North America, adapting themselves to a wide range of climate and terrain, but they always needed good grass for pasture. They preferred the Great

Plains, where they could find excellent grass the year around, with some shelter from winter storms in the valleys and in the narrow belts of timber along the streams. They did quite well in the prairie country too, and in open woodlands of either scattered pines or deciduous trees with patches of grass. They avoided the dense coniferous forests with their heavy duff of decaying needles and heavy underbrush. Such places had no food for the buffalo, which is not a browsing animal.

The heavy coniferous forests of Canada limited the northern range. Along the foothills of the Rockies, where the timber was more open, small herds lived to the northern limits of Alberta. On the south was another vegetation barrier, the chaparral thickets of southern and southwestern Texas, which were as effective in stopping the spread of the herds as any mountain barrier. The eastern limit was the tidewater of the Atlantic Ocean, while on the west the many ridges of the Rocky Mountains loomed as a formidable wall, breached in only two places: at South Pass in southern Wyoming, and along the upper Yellowstone and Missouri rivers in southwestern Montana.

Buffalo found a rather easy passage up the Yellowstone and across Bozeman Pass into the Three Forks country of Montana. From there they could go north to Clarks Fork of the Columbia River, but they were commonly found only as far as the western end of Deer Lodge Valley. Small bands did penetrate farther downstream into Bitterroot Valley; their bones have been found there, and local Indians tell stories of them. There has been but one recorded kill of a buffalo beyond Deer Lodge Valley, a stray bull at Horse Plains in 1853, 150 miles down Clarks Fork.

In prehistoric times some buffalo penetrated the mountains and reached the Columbia Basin, and possibly as far west as the mouth of the Snake River. The herds were not able to establish themselves permanently, and were killed off by hunters.

From the upper Missouri drainage, at the head of the Madison and Beaverhead rivers, wide passes enabled the herds to cross the continental divide with no trouble. These passes led the animals into the upper Snake Valley in southeastern Idaho, where their westward movement was blocked by desert scrub, recent lava flows, and deep canyons. One small gap between the mountains and the lava flows could be passed under favorable conditions. That some buffalo did pass through here is evident from their presence in southeastern Oregon at two different periods, perhaps 3,000 years apart. Skulls of the more recent herd have been found in the mud at Harney Lake, where they were seen in 1826 by Peter Skeene Ogden, a factor for the Hudson's Bay Company. There is no evidence that either of these herds lived more than a few years in the Oregon country.

Buffalo from the upper Snake Valley and from South Pass filled the valley of the Bear River and spread south between the Wasatch Range and Great Salt Lake. There they were hemmed in on the west by the desert, on the south by canyons, and on the east by the Colorado mountain mass, but they were in good range country in the valleys around Grand Junction, Colorado, and to the north. This herd became established and lasted until the late nineteenth century.

From Minnesota eastward the northern boundary of the buffalo range was approximately a line from the Falls of St. Anthony to the southern tip of Lake Michigan, then following a small northern bulge into Michigan between Lake Michigan and Lake Erie, then along the southern shore of Lake Erie, the Niagara River, and Lake Ontario about to Oswego, New York. The line then went south to the mountains and followed the main ridge of the Alleghenies into West Virginia and eastward to the Potomac River and Chesapeake Bay.

In Texas the southern limit of the range was close to the Gulf coast. As it swung north, it kept close to the outer edge of the woodlands through Arkansas and Missouri to the Missouri River, then down the north bank of that stream to the Mississippi, down its east bank to the Ohio, and up the north bank of the Ohio to the mouth of the Tennessee. The Tennessee River was the southern boundary across that state to Chattanooga.

The buffalo found in the Carolinas and southeastern Georgia appear to have come from the north, from the herds that had gone up the Great Valley into Virginia and so passed the last of the mountains. One small band was reported far from the rest—in the extreme southwestern tip of Georgia in 1686. They seem to have been strays and probably were killed off in a short time, for there is no further mention of them.

Within this vast area the buffalo roamed in uncounted millions. Several people have attempted in various ways to arrive at a reasonable total, their results varying from a low of 30 million to a high of 200 million. Since the grazing lands did not appear to be overstocked when the first white explorers visited them, perhaps the lower figure should be taken. But whatever figure is taken, it is only a guess, and an error of 10 or 20 million would have little significance now.

While the total buffalo population was enormous, the individual bands were small. One of the hide hunters of the 1870's, Frank Mayer, left records on the size of the bands he encountered in his several years of hunting, during which he brought to market over 10,000 hides, almost all of them from animals he found in small bands. He said that a band of more than sixty was most unusual, and he never saw a band of over two hundred. Bands of about fifteen were the most common, with some being as small as three. This hunter killed all or almost all the animals in more than a thousand separate bands.

For a large part of each year there would be no bulls with the band. The bulls might be feeding within a mile or less, but they were not regular members of any group, which consisted of a few cows with their current crop of calves, and the yearlings and two-year-olds from the previous two crops. One of the cows would be accepted as the leader on whom the rest depended for guidance. She went where she liked, and the rest followed. She chose the time to go to water, and when to move to new grazing. In time of danger she led the dash for safety, but when she got into trouble the others did not know what to do. They just milled around her in hopeless confusion.

When the country was covered by herds scattered as far as the eye could see, the number of buffalo was beyond counting, but a trained observer could take a quick count of the bands close by and make a considered estimate of the rest. General Isaac I. Stevens remarked on the unending herds when he and his party were in northern Dakota conducting a survey for a transcontinental railway. These men were all experienced observers.

July 10, 1853. About five miles from camp we ascended to the top of a high hill, and for a great distance ahead every square mile seemed to have a herd of buffalo upon it. Their number was variously estimated by the members of the party—some as high as half a million. I do not think it any exaggeration to set it down at 200,000. I had heard of the myriads of these animals inhabiting the plains, but I could not realize the truth of these accounts till today, when they surpassed anything I could have imagined from the accounts which I had received.

Grazing animals such as buffalo cannot remain in large, closely packed herds for any length of time or they will soon starve. Hence the small herds were usually found scattered over a wide expanse, with several hundred yards of open space around each band. Travelers could pass through these open spaces without stampeding the herds, and might take days to make the passage. Coronado, on his visit to the buffalo country in 1541, reported, "I came upon plains so vast that I did not reach their end, although I marched over them for more than three hundred leagues [about a thousand miles]. On them I found so many cattle it would be impossible to estimate their numbers for there was not a single day until my return that I lost sight of them." This march through the buffalo country lasted three months, and led from just east of the Pecos River into the Texas Panhandle and north to the Great Bend of the Arkansas. The buffalo seen each day were new animals, except for the few occasions when a herd stampeded in the direction of the line of march.

A person today attempting to visualize such herds would need quite an imagination. He might start by visiting the bison range in western Montana and see what a far-ranging herd 700 animals make when they are grazing. Then he could take a map of North America and fill it with dots, each one representing a herd, fifty here, a hundred there, and perhaps a thousand at a time in the heart of the Great Plains, until he has put in 40,000 dots. But no matter how he approaches the task, the tally of the great animals will be in the tens of millions.

Disguised in wolf skins, Catlin and a guide creep close to an unconcerned buffalo herd. When unable to smell their enemies, the nearsighted, dull buffalo made easy targets. (Oil painting by George Catlin, Smithsonian Institution)

Indians surround and slaughter buffalo. Hunters aimed at the buffalo's side, behind the last rib and a third of the distance from backbone to belly, where a weapon could more easily penetrate the intestinal cavity. (Painting by A. J. Miller, The Walters Art Gallery)

5

Horses for the Buffalo Hunters

BEGINNING 4,000 YEARS AGO wild horsemen poured down from the Iranian Plateau south and west into the fertile Euphrates Valley, to the consternation and terror of the farming villages along the river. Ever since that time wild tribes from the grasslands of the world, dashing about on their spirited mounts, have captured the imagination of sedentary people. With horsemen dominating the wide expanse of the Asiatic Steppes and the grasslands of North Africa, European explorers and traders from the Atlantic seaboard were not surprised to find equally wild horsemen occupying the grassy Great Plains of the American west.

During the first half of the nineteenth century travelers usually assumed that the Plains tribes must have used horses for many centuries. The Indians all the way from the eastern edge of the prairies to the Cascade Range, 2,000 miles to the west, and from the Gulf of Mexico to the Canadian forests all had large horse herds and a colorful, highly developed horse culture, complete with trappings, gear, methods of training, and many legends. All of this would indicate a long period of development.

Then historians, delving into the records of early Spanish and French explorers west of the Mississippi, found that the horses had come to the Indians from the Spanish colonies of New Mexico. The highly developed horse culture of the Plains had been borrowed bodily from the Spanish, and had then been enriched with a few gaudy Indian trappings.

Excavations of fossil deposits throughout the west have uncovered a large number of bones and many complete skeletons of horses that ranged the region for a few million years but were wiped out by a mysterious disaster 15,000 years ago. Hence when the Spanish brought horses to the plains in the sixteenth century, not even a trace of horse lore remained among the Indian tribes. Because the horse played such an important part in the lives of the Plains Indians, and especially in their buffalo hunting, details of its introduction and rapid spread throughout the whole western country are of importance to anthropologists and historians.

Francisco Coronado, searching for the fabulous Seven Cities of Cibola and their reputed treasure hordes, traveled east from the Rio Grande Valley of New Mexico to the Texas Panhandle, then north into Kansas. Thus in the summer of 1541 he brought the first horses of modern times into the buffalo country. The Querecho Indians in northern Texas, who lived entirely off the buffalo, were not greatly impressed by the mounted Spanish band, strange as it was, and of imposing numbers (the chronicler of the expedition listed 1,500 people, most of them Indians from Mexico; 500 cattle and 5,000 sheep—the traveling commissary; and 500 horses). This same year, 1541, remnants of the expedition led by Hernando De Soto reached the Trinity River in Texas, on the southeastern edge of the buffalo country, with a small herd of horses.

About a hundred years ago imaginative armchair historians began speculating on the possibility that horses from the two expeditions escaped onto the Texas plains, where they reverted to a wild state and increased over the years until there were thousands of wild horses at hand for the Indians to catch and tame. This idea was given good standing by Clark Wissler, dean of American anthropologists, but it collapsed quickly when subjected to critical evaluation by people who knew both the difficulties in attempting to develop a horse culture from scratch, and the trials and dangers that horses would undergo on the western ranges.

There are three important considerations that rule out this romantic possibility. First, Coronado had, at the most, three mares in his entire

[3 7]

horse herd, and it is doubtful that any of them were taken east of the Rio Grande. De Soto had none. The Spanish did not use mares for military work, and this was definitely a military expedition. The possibility that even one of the mares escaped onto the Texas plains is remote indeed. Second, there is no record of any number of horses escaping at one time. The only losses of any account were of horses killed in chasing buffalo. Third, there was not a sign of any horse in this open country, wild or tame, mentioned by Spanish travelers for the next 140 years, and no wild herds are mentioned until after the Indians of the area had been using horses for thirty years.

Even highly intelligent Indians could not catch, tame, and train wild horses, and develop the complicated gear needed for handling the animals in only a century or so when it required the combined resources of a few million people and 4,000 years to accomplish the same results in the Near East. For the Indians to accept horses as rapidly as they did, and to use Spanish gear as far north as the Canadian plains, they had to have tame, gentle, well-trained horses from the start. They also had to have many samples of horse gear to copy. These well-broken horses could have come at first only from the Spanish colonies in New Mexico, and the first of these colonies was not established until 1599, fifty-eight years after the Coronado expedition. Even with horses on the Rio Grande by 1599, no contemporary document mentions Indian tribes in the area using horses until 1659, sixty years later.

On modern ranches, where well-fed stock horses are used only for a short period each working day and are hauled to and from work in a truck, a rancher handling several hundred head of stock on a well-fenced range can manage with just a few trained saddle horses. On the Spanish frontier, conditions demanded that the rancher and his vaqueros spend a major part of each working day in the saddle, with each man using several horses a week.

The seventeenth-century rancher depended on his horses to transport both people and supplies. Pack strings supplied the sheep herders on the open range, for the flocks had to be tended twenty-four hours a day 365 days a year, and spent several months of each year miles from the home ranch.

The herds of cattle needed constant attention, and could be handled only by men on horseback. These rather fierce Spanish cattle could easily outrun any man on foot who tried to drive them, or might just as likely turn and kill him. And finally there were the horse herds, composed of brood mares, the young stock, and spare riding horses, which needed supervision lest they go astray, be stolen by wild Indians, or wander into the crops in the unfenced fields.

The horse herd had to be quite large for the ordinary stock ranch. The working horses were fed no hay or grain, but subsisted entirely on natural forage. They required two or three days of rest after each working day, to replenish wasted tissues and to store up reserves for another working day. A horse could work hard only about half a day twice a week, if it was to be kept in good condition. Thus an active vaquero might need a saddle string of six regular horses, with two special mounts for the more demanding work, such as roping. He usually had a couple of green horses, broncos, just starting their training. All these horses would be needed when the rider was working on a roundup or trail drive.

When the rancher traveled cross-country he usually took along two or three men for protection and companionship. Each rider required several mounts for an extended journey, so even a small group of three or four men might start out with a string of twenty horses, changing mounts each morning and noon, driving two or three pack horses along with the loose horses, and using new pack horses each day. In addition to all these riding horses and pack animals, they took a few draft animals for cultivating the fields and for small hauling jobs.

To keep up this large number of working horses, the rancher needed about an equal number of brood mares. Since range-raised horses grew rather slowly, they were not usually broken to the saddle until they were four or five years old. This meant that the mares would have with them the new colts, the yearlings, the two-year-olds, and the three-year-olds. In addition, all the riding horses and pack horses resting up between jobs would be out with the herd.

Thus for each full-time rider at the ranch there would be about twenty horses out to pasture at all times, and these had to be herded constantly, as did the cattle and sheep, to keep them out of the cultivated fields during the growing season and to protect them against thieves and straying. In colonial days it was physically impossible to fence the pastures, or even the larger plowed fields, in the desert and range country, for there was no suitable timber within miles.

It is obvious that raising, breaking, handling, and using horses kept the Spanish ranchers busy. About a fourth of their total effort was spent producing and training the horses necessary for taking care of the herds that produced the working horses. In order to get his work done, the rancher turned to the local Indians for help with the stock, especially around the stables and corrals. They took care of the saddle stock, saddling and unsaddling, watering, and cutting out the horses needed for each day's work. Although it was against Spanish law for any Indian in New Spain to ride a horse, the Rio Grande Valley was far removed from the viceroy at Mexico City, and the need for horsemen was great. Ranchers often ignored minor breaches of this law around the home place, and many permitted the Indian helpers to ride out for range stock and to help with the horses and camp chores on a long cross-country trip.

The young men from even the sedentary Pueblo tribe became restive under their bonds and rebelled against the constant labor demanded of them. With the Spanish holding all the Pueblo villages, a rebel had no place to hide and no place to run, unless he went out to one of the wild tribes to the north or east, across miles of open country. In that case, he needed a horse to ride, and, if he did not want to get caught, he also took the fastest mounts in the stables, leaving the slower animals for his pursuers.

The fugitive might be killed by the wild tribe, but more often he was welcomed. With his well-trained horses and his experience in using the animals, he could teach his new friends a great deal about horses in a short time. As soon as the wild tribe became accustomed to the horses, they could go out and steal a few more, begin a herd, and in five or ten years become a tribe of skilled horsemen.

In the colonial archives there are many accounts of runaways. At times a whole family made its escape to join an Apache band. In addition to teaching the Apaches about horses, they also gave instructions on how to improve their gardens, lodges, and pottery.

Even when they had gentle animals and good instructors, many Indians were a little dubious of the large, strange creatures. The Flatheads tell how one of their hunting bands managed to capture a gentle mare from a Shoshoni camp after hiding and watching for several days how the horses acted and how they were handled. Even so, they kept their distance for a time, forming a ring of men around the mare and marching along. In a day or so they ventured to pet her, then to use a lead rope on her, and so take her home. Even though these were brave and intelligent men, if they handled a tame horse like this, it is difficult to imagine that they would ever attempt to catch even a foal from a wild herd.

Nez Percé tradition says that their first animal, a white mare in foal, was bought from the Shoshoni. Before anyone tried to ride her, the whole band spent many days sitting around and watching her every move, learning her habits, the kind of feed she liked, and how she rested.

A rather timid band of Sanpoil learned to ride their first horse by having one person lead the horse slowly, while the brave rider balanced himself with two long sticks, thrusting them against the ground on either side. These incidents are cited to show that a tribe needed both a gentle horse and an instructor if its members were to learn quickly.

In each band the bold young men learned to ride first, then taught their younger brothers. In about ten years, when these men were the respected warriors of the tribe, all the fighters and many of the others would have learned to ride. As long as the band could secure more horses this transition worked rather rapidly.

Each tribe was friendly with one or two others farther to the north and east. When a tribe had secured enough horses for its own use, it would trade a few to these friends and teach them horsemanship, and so the horses spread throughout the plains.

The whole movement was speeded up by the Pueblo Revolt of 1680, when the village people drove out or killed the Spanish colonists. The Spanish fugitives retreated hastily to the south, leaving most of their livestock in the hands of the rebels, who then began to fight among themselves. Several Apache bands that had helped in the revolt now took a large number of horses as their share of the booty. Then other wild tribes began raiding the herds and took most of the rest. Some horses had been traded off to ransom Pueblo Indians who were held as prisoners on the plains, and more went in exchange for buffalo products—meat and robes. In two or three years many thousands of horses reached the Indians in the Great Plains, and the horse frontier moved rapidly to the north and east across the buffalo country.

In 1685 horses were reported among the tribes in southern Texas. Five years later they were seen at the mouth of the Colorado River in Texas and on the Red River near the Texas-Arkansas border. Charles C. DuTisne, a French trader, found horses in Oklahoma in 1719, Etienne Venyard Sieur de Bourgomont, another French trader, reported them in eastern Kansas in 1724, and they approached the Mandan villages in Dakota by 1739. By 1770 horses had reached the northeastern limits of the grasslands: the Sioux country in western Minnesota.

Buffalo-hunting tribes soon learned that the best of their horses could outrun a buffalo on the open plain, and they made changes in their hunting patterns to take advantage of this. They could kill a few animals any time they found a herd. In a short time the tribes were living better, with more meat the year around. A band with a few good horses could kill an ample supply of fresh meat at almost any season, and could get a large surplus in the fall to dry for the hungry time.

With horses to carry the people and their packs from place to place, a band could follow the wandering herds for a hundred miles or more. Their pack horses carried in the meat from the kill and transported the dried meat from camp to camp. This allowed the band a wider choice of good camping spots.

A camp for the winter could be in the best timber patch along a stream, for the hunters could ride out to hunt between storms. The tipis were made larger, with good liners and rugs on the floor to keep out the cold. Many packs of dried meat fed them through winter storms, and in times of real distress, when hunting failed and all the dried meat was eaten, a few of the pack animals could be butchered to stave off starvation.

The ample diet and easier living conditions produced healthier people. More babies were born, and more of them were raised to maturity. In many tribes the introduction of the horse led in a generation or so to a rapid increase in the population.

Even a small band of Indians consumed an enormous quantity of meat when that was all they had to eat. When fresh meat could be secured, about ten pounds each day for each man, woman, and child was considered desirable. When the buffalo were near and in good condition, a band of a hundred people would eat all the meat from two or three animals each day; two or three hunters on good horses could kill a week's supply in a single run. When hunting was good, not every scrap of meat was used. Often the less desirable parts of a small kill went to the camp dogs. After a large kill, the wolves cleaned up the remains of the carcasses.

When the buffalo were not in good condition it took more of them to supply the meat. Then it might require from seven to ten buffalo for each person, or more than 2 million each year to feed all the buffalo-hunting tribes. This was still only a small portion of the annual birth rate, which averaged one calf a year for every five animals of both sexes and all ages in the herd, or 6 million new calves a year in herds totaling 30 million.

The buffalo chase was exciting, dangerous, and efficient. For this the rider had to have a horse that was swift, strong, brave, and intelligent, a real buffalo horse. Since buffalo have poor eyesight, horsemen could usually approach them slowly upwind within a quarter of a mile before they became alarmed. Then they took off at full speed, and a good horse could catch them in a half a mile. If the horse did not catch the herd in two miles, he was considered too poor a horse for the chase, but might be used as a spare to ride up to the vicinity of the herd while the good runner was led.

Once the horse caught the herd, he had to have the courage to plunge into the dust and confusion of the jostling, galloping beasts, work his way through the rear fringe of old, slow bulls, and place the hunter within a few feet of the chosen animal.

Such a horse was a treasure to be guarded. A few of them in the village herd of several hundred could mean the difference between easy living or short rations for the whole group. On rare occasions when a good buffalo horse was sold, it might bring the price of ten, twenty, or even fifty ordinary horses—and be worth every bit of it. It had to be guarded at all times against thieves from other tribes. At the first sign of enemy scouts or thieves near the camp, the buffalo horses were caught and picketed near the master's tipi and fed with grass plucked by the little girls. In time of extreme danger, the horses would be taken into the tipis for the night, even though the women and girls had to sleep outside to make room.

Once the hunter had a good horse, he needed a weapon that would kill efficiently at close range. This was usually a short bow, which could be handled well on horseback, and a quiver of a dozen or so arrows, each with its owner's individual mark. On the southern plains some hunters preferred a slim lance with a long, slender point, perhaps because good cane for lances was plentiful but good wood for bows was scarce. Either weapon was deadly in the hands of a skilled hunter on a good horse.

In preparing for the chase, the hunter stripped to his breechclout and moccasins, and slipped a knife into a sheath at his belt. On his horse he placed a small pad saddle or a piece of buffalo robe secured by a wide band of soft-tanned hide for a cinch. This band could be left loose so the rider could thrust his knees beneath the band during the run to give himself a firmer seat and better control of his weapon. The horse was guided by a thin rawhide thong, often called a war bridle, looped over his lower jaw; the ends were tucked under the rider's belt, leaving both hands free to handle the weapon. The rider directed the horse by knee pressure and a slight shifting of his weight.

The hunters tried to find a small herd feeding in a spot where they could approach from behind a small hill or up a coulee. If this brought them quite close they dashed into sight on a dead run, but if they were still some distance from their quarry they rode slowly and quietly until the first old cow took fright and began to run. If the terrain was favorable for such a maneuver, the men divided and approached from two directions, causing confusion in the herd and a momentary delay in running. On occasion part of the herd would start away from each party of hunters and run into each other, where they would mill around in hopeless disorder while the hunters shot them down.

Once the herd started to run, the fleeter, more agile cows and the younger animals took the lead, with the calves and old bulls bringing up the rear. In the spring and early summer before the calves were old enough to run well, they tired quickly, and dropped in the grass to hide. Then boys too young for the big hunt followed along and practiced their hunting skills on the helpless animals.

The hunters selected the more desirable animals for the kill. From April to September these would be the young bulls or the heifers, but in the fall they chose the fat cows. From midwinter to April the large, middle-aged bulls were in the best condition for camp use. The aged, outcast bulls were never hunted except in times of extreme want.

As he dashed into the herd, each hunter guided his mount toward the animal he wanted to kill. The horse dashed up on the flank of the chosen animal, on the right side for a hunter armed with a bow, on the left for one with a lance.

A buffalo is a large, tough, hardy animal and very hard to kill. Fatally wounded animals have been known to run a mile or more before dropping. The most effective way for the hunter to bring down the animal quickly was to pierce the diaphragm with either an arrow or a lance, collapsing the lungs, or to thrust between the ribs into the lungs or heart, a much more difficult task.

A lance head or an arrow point had little chance of passing the rib barrier, for the ribs are wide and the spaces between them are narrow. The slender lance point and the arrow point, both of chipped flint or similar material, would break if they struck a rib, giving the buffalo only a superficial wound. The lancer would be disarmed, while the bowman would have lost a valuable arrow. Paintings showing the Indians attacking the rib cage are more artistic than accurate.

An Indian hunter knew every organ, bone, muscle, and sinew in the game he hunted. He knew the vulnerable areas, and strove to reach them in the most direct and effective manner. Hence he aimed his blow at the side of the buffalo, just behind the last rib and about a third of the way down from the backbone to the belly. An arrow or lance striking here had only to pierce the hide and a thin muscle layer before penetrating the intestinal cavity. If it ranged forward and downward, it would certainly pierce the liver and probably the diaphragm, while the weapon would be undamaged. If the initial blow seemed ineffective, the hunter would strike again, sometimes needing three or four blows to bring down his prey.

Once the arrow or lance found its mark, there was a real danger that the wounded buffalo would try to gore the horse, so the horse was taught to swerve away at the twang of the bowstring or when the lance was withdrawn. Then at a signal from the rider, the horse moved into position for a second blow or went on to a new victim.

Dashing through a milling mass of buffalo in a cloud of dust at full speed had its dangers for both horse and rider. A wounded buffalo might fall in their path, or one might swerve unexpectedly. A prairie-dog hole, a stone, an old skeleton, or a dry wash could not be seen in the dust and excitement, and any one of them could easily throw the horse. There was little the rider could do to escape death under the churning hooves, although now and again a hunter was able to grab a buffalo and ride it out of the melee before dropping to the ground.

The chase was exciting, packed with action, and soon over. Then the hunters checked their winded mounts and rode slowly back across the plain, now dotted with dead and wounded animals. The wounded might still be staggering along, or they might just be standing with braced feet until they died. These were finished off with another arrow or a lance thrust. Such clean-up work was usually done by the less successful hunters.

A number of women followed the hunters from camp, keeping out of sight until the chase was over, then moving out with their pack horses to the kill. Each was eager to find any animals brought down by her man, identifying the carcasses by the marks on the arrows. A woman could claim the hides and all the choice cuts from these buffalo, but she was expected to share the ordinary cuts and trimmings with any less fortunate person, especially a widow with no close relative in the hunt.

A good hunter with a good horse could kill enough animals to keep several women busy with the meat and hides: there would be enough to feed and clothe twelve to fifteen people. Since the men lived more dangerously than the women, their death rate was much higher and there were many widows. Each year men died in hunting accidents, in war, and in handling unruly horses. Their widows and orphans had to be cared for. In many tribes each good hunter was expected to provide for two or three wives, a widowed mother or aunt, and some children, all in a cooperative group living in two or three tipis. Often each wife had her own tipi.

The first wife approved of the polygamy, for there was always a great deal more work than she could manage, in addition to the burden of producing and raising children. In a cooperative group there was work for all, but few were overworked by Indian standards. Also, the women enjoyed working in groups. Usually the first wife had complete charge of the group, although she might have an older relative to help.

Such a social arrangement had not been possible under the earlier hunting patterns, for one hunter could not provide meat for so many people. In those days there were fewer children, and the older widows might die of want or neglect in hard times. Such tragic situations are found frequently in the old folk tales and legends.

The women had two major tasks in addition to their family duties and camp chores: taking care of the meat and tanning the hides. In the late summer and fall they dried the excess meat, pounded and packed it in buffalo paunches or sections of the large intestine, then poured in melted fat to fill the air spaces. This was the pemmican of the plains, and would keep indefinitely as long as it was kept dry. Or the meat could be left in strips and stored in parfleches. The strips of back fat would keep well if lightly smoked.

None of these methods of preserving meat was new, but now for the first time the tribes had plenty to spare for the winter. They had all the robes they could use, and large tipis for more comfortable living, equipped with inner linings for greater warmth and comfort. All this was made possible by the use of pack horses to move all the reserve food and extra camp gear from place to place.

Strict controls were necessary to prevent any of the village hunters from scaring off the buffalo before a big hunt. In most of the Plains tribes a crier went about the camp announcing the ban on hunting by individuals, and there was one group of young warriors whose duty was to enforce the rule. This method of control was brought to the plains from the eastern woodlands.

A social development made possible through the use of the horse was the setting up of a large midsummer encampment. Here a thousand or more people could gather for several days and be assured of ample food for that period. And with the new leisure, ceremonies became more elaborate, culminating in the sun dance.

With ample leisure time and with horses to carry them to distant places, the men turned more and more to warfare, horse stealing, and raids in faraway lands. These activities became an elaborate game, with complicated rules, in which many ritual honors and economic rewards could be won. It is difficult to determine how far this warrior cult had developed before horses reached the plains, but certainly it became more complex once the warriors had time for such activities. This cult was common throughout the entire plains country, and each tribe counted coups, dressed its warriors in the regalia of the successful fighter, and adopted horse stealing as an honorable pursuit.

The vain, proud warriors, posturing in their finery, lounging in the sun and feasting, never even considered helping the women, who worked long hours each day at heavy tasks. But the women would have been shocked at the offer of help. Those indolent males, resting on the nearby hill, were always alert, watching for game and, more important, for enemy raiders. Any sensible woman preferred safety for herself and her family to being subjected to surprise attacks because her man was helping with family chores.

6

The Southern Plains: Apache and Comanche

In 1541 a small body of Spanish soldiers with a large following of Mexican Indians, all under the command of Francisco Coronado, set out from the Pueblo villages along the Rio Grande to explore the plains country to the east. After the Spanish had crossed the Pecos River they soon found themselves in buffalo country, and from then on, during three months of travel over more than a thousand miles, there was not a single day that they did not see a herd.

As they moved eastward along the Canadian River near the Texas border, they crossed a curious trail. Many small poles had been dragged over the ground, leaving furrows in the dust. The Spanish followed the trail and soon came to a camp of buffalo-hunting Indians with their skin tipis set up for the night, the first such structures the Spanish had ever seen. The furrows had been made by the butts of the tipi poles as they were dragged along by dogs.

The Indians were friendly and showed no fear or surprise at the appearance of a body of mounted men in armor: they had heard reports of the Spanish from the Pueblo Indians along the Pecos. The Spanish were the more surprised. They had never seen Indians like these, and Coronado's scribe, Pedro de Castañeda, recorded the strange ways of these people:

These Indians subsist entirely on cattle, for they neither plant nor harvest maize. With the skins they build their houses; with the skins they clothe and shoe themselves; from the skins they make ropes and also obtain wool. From the sinews they make thread, with which they sew their clothing and likewise their tents. From the bones they shape awls, and the dung they use for firewood, since there is no other fuel in all that land. The bladders serve as jugs and drinking vessels. They sustain themselves on the flesh of the animals, eating it slightly roasted . . . and sometimes uncooked. Taking it in their teeth, they pull with one hand; with the other they hold a large flint knife and cut off mouthfuls, swallowing it half chewed, like birds. They eat raw fat without warming it, and drink the blood just as it comes from the cattle . . . . They have no other food.

They are a gentle people, not cruel, faithful in their friendship, and skilled in the use of signs. They dry their meat in the sun, cutting it into thin slices, and when it is dry they cook it in a pot, which they always manage to have with them. When they put a handful in the pot, the mash soon fills it, since it swells to great size.

When the Indians kill a cow, they clean a large intestine, fill it with blood, and hang it around their necks, to drink when they are thirsty. Cutting open the belly of the animal, they squeeze out the chewed grass and drink the juice, saying it contains the substance of the stomach.

They cut open the cow at the back and pull off the hide at the joints, using a flint the size of a finger, tied to a small stick, doing this as handily as if they used a fine knife. They sharpen the flints on their own teeth, and it is remarkable to see how quickly they do it.

They tan the hides well, dressing skins to take to the pueblos to sell since they go to spend the winter there. For their tents they fasten the poles at the top and spread them apart at the base, and cover them with tanned and greased hides.

They load their dogs like beasts of burden and make light pack saddles for them like ours, cinching them with leather straps. The dogs go about with sores on their backs like pack animals. When the Indians go hunting they load them with provisions, and when they move—for they have no permanent residence anywhere for

[4 9]

they follow the cattle to obtain food—the dogs transport their houses for them. In addition to what they carry on their backs, they transport the poles for the tents, dragging them fastened to their saddles. The load may be from thirty to fifty pounds, depending on the dog.

These seminomadic buffalo hunters were members of the Apache tribe, which at that time consisted of a great many small bands occupying a wide strip of the Great Plains from the Platte River in the north to the Texas Panhandle, and from the foothills of the Rockies eastward about 200 miles into Nebraska and Kansas. The southern bands were usually seminomadic, and they did not change their way of life appreciably in the next ninety years. Here is a report by Fray Alonzo de Benavides on the same bands about 1628:

> By these cattle, then, all of these Vaquero Apaches sustain themselves, for which they go craftily to their watering places, and hide themselves in the trails, painted with red earth, and stained with the mud of that same earth; and stretched in the deep trails which the cattle have made, when they pass they employ the arrows which they carry. And as these are dull cattle, though very savage and swift, when they feel themselves wounded they let themselves fall after a few paces. And afterward the Indians skin them and carry off the hides, the tongues, and tenderloins and sinews to sew with, and to make strings for their bows. The hides they tan in two ways; some leave the hair on them and they remain like plush velvet, and serve as a bed and as a cloak. Others they tan without the hair, and thin them down, of which they make their tents and other things after their usage. And with these hides they trade through all the land and gain their living . . . . These Indians then go forth through the neighboring provinces to trade and traffic with these hides. At which point I cannot refrain from telling one thing, somewhat incredible, however ridiculous. And it is that when these Indians go to trade and traffic, the entire rancherias go, with their wives and children, who live in tents made of these skins of buffalo, very thin and tanned; and the tents they carry loaded on pack trains of dogs, harnessed up with their little pack saddles; and the dogs are medium sized. And they are

accustomed to take 500 dogs in one pack train, one in front of the other, and the people carry their merchandise loaded, which they barter for cotton cloth and for other things which they lack.

The Apaches were the southern prong of the large Athapascan migration. The other Athapascan groups had remained in Alaska and northern Canada and might have pushed the Apaches south, or the Apaches may have moved on of their own accord. They reached the plains country about A.D. 1300 in many small, scattered bands of roving hunters, whose survival depended on securing game almost daily. The bands were usually about twenty people or less, as it would be difficult to kill enough game each day to feed a larger number except in very good hunting country.

Such small bands could have passed through the northern tribes by keeping in the wide open spaces between the scattered villages. There is no tradition among either the Apache or the northern tribes of any important fighting along their line of travel.

On the open plains the Apaches found game animals new to them, particularly the buffalo, and had to adjust their hunting practices to deal with these huge beasts. When they reached the Platte River and began to occupy the land, they could live in larger units, with buffalo supplying the food. Many of them settled in little villages in sheltered spots along streams, where they built warm earth-covered lodges, grew small garden patches of corn, beans, squash, and sunflowers, and made crude pottery. They copied these new skills from people just to the east, who had come across the Mississippi from the Ohio River a short time before.

Some of the Apache bands that continued south into the Texas Panhandle did not settle down, but roamed the high plains following the buffalo herds. They were the people described by the early Spanish travelers.

When Pueblo Indians in the Rio Grande Valley ran away from their Spanish masters, they went to the Apache villages for refuge, sometimes going as far as the Arkansas River to be safe from pursuit. There they found more settled Apaches and taught them improved methods of raising crops, building houses, and making pottery. Both Spanish records of the time and the presence of many distinctively Pueblo pottery pieces show that an appreciable number of Pueblos did join the

Apaches and had a strong influence on their cultural development.

The Pueblos also brought along a few horses and taught the Apaches how to use them. The rapid cultural and economic progress of the Apaches during the latter half of the seventeenth century was cut short and the very existence of the tribe threatened by large-scale attacks from two powerful hostile tribes, one to the west, the other to the east. The Comanches began to move down from the Colorado foothills, while the Osages came across the plains from the Missouri woodlands. Each tribe seemed determined to wipe out the Apaches and take over their land.

The Osages were greatly feared, for they had just begun to secure guns from the French traders, while the Apaches, well to the west, had no chance to buy guns of their own. The Comanches came in large war parties, their raids made more effective once they had secured horses. As the Apaches began to weaken under these two attacks, the Pawnees descended on them from the north. The remnants of the tribe had no hope of escaping destruction except in flight to the south. They fled deep into Texas. The land they vacated was overrun quickly by the victors, with the Comanches claiming about two-thirds of it.

The Comanches were part of the large Uto-Aztecan migration that had come from Asia over a period of several hundred years. They passed through Alaska into Canada and south just to the east of the Rockies. The vanguard of this migration, the Aztecs, reached the Mexican plateau by 1300, while the stragglers, the Shoshoni, spread out from central Alberta southward across Montana, where they split into two prongs, one going across the mountains into southern Idaho, the other staying east of the Rockies and occupying eastern Wyoming. The latter group split again, part of them remaining in Wyoming to become the Wind River Shoshoni, the remainder proceeding southeastward into eastern Colorado and becoming the Comanches, who held the foothills of the Rockies from the northern Colorado line to the Arkansas River.

The Comanches were of average height compared to the Indian population as a whole, but they were much shorter than their neighboring tribes, the Crow, Arapahoe, Cheyenne, Osage, and Kiowa, all of whom were slimmer and had longer legs. The Comanches had powerful bodies mounted on stubby legs, which were a handicap to them on the open plains when they were chased by their long-legged neighbors. They had a hard time holding their own on the plains until they secured horses. Then they found that short legs can be more of an asset than a liability to a rider.

The Comanches began their eastward movement into the plains by attacking the small permanent Apache villages along the streams in southwestern Nebraska and western Kansas. The Apaches were at a great disadvantage in this fighting, for the enemy always knew where to find them and could mount a surprise attack with superior forces against any one Apache village. The hit-and-run raider has always had this obvious advantage against a farming people. The Comanche attacks were more deadly than the usual Indian fights, for they were determined to wipe out each village, killing off all the men, taking captive the women and children, and burning the lodges. Even if the initial attack failed, some of the defenders would be killed and the village could be further weakened by successive raids until it was helpless. And while several Comanche bands could unite for a few days to mount a large-scale attack against a single Apache village, the Apaches could not prepare an adequate defense, for they could not organize and maintain a permanent army to hunt out the raiders and keep them out of the country. This fundamental vulnerability of small permanent settlements against fierce nomads has been demonstrated many times in many different countries.

Modern excavations at the sites of the destroyed Apache villages show that most of them were burned and plundered in the seventeenth century, just when the villagers were making good progress in farming and pottery making. This is also the period when both the Apaches and the Comanches began using horses.

The Comanches probably had secured some horses before the Pueblo Revolt of 1680 and had greatly increased their herds in the next decade from the confiscated Spanish herds. In 1705 Spanish reports from Santa Fe mentioned the Comanches as mounted raiders, and in 1706 they were reported to be stealing horses from the Apaches who lived in northeastern New Mexico, south of Raton Pass.

Once the stubby-legged Comanches had climbed on their horses and learned to ride, they were soon rated with the finest horsemen of the world, the Don Cossacks. Visitors to the Indian camps were struck by the great contrast between a Comanche on foot and the same man on horseback.

George Catlin, on his visit to the tribe in the 1830's, described the Comanches:

In their movements they are heavy and ungraceful; and on their feet one of the most unattractive and slovenly-looking races of Indians I have ever seen . . . . I am ready without hesitation to pronounce the Comanches as the most extraordinary horsemen that I have ever seen and I doubt very much whether any people in the world can surpass them. A Comanche on his feet is out of his element and comparatively almost awkward, but the moment they mount their horses, they seem at once metamorphosed, and surprise the spectator with the ease and grace of their movements.

After the Comanches secured horses to ride, they did almost no walking. A prominent man would order his wife or daughter to fetch his horse so he could ride over to a friend's tipi a hundred yards away. From lack of exercise, Comanche men became fat and lazy, a condition seldom found among hunting tribes.

This constant use of the horse by the Comanche and his great dependence on the animal indicate the profound changes this new servant made in his daily life, but these were changes of degree rather than of kind. The Comanche now lived better, with ample reserves of food and clothing. He had more leisure time and greater security from his enemies. From being a skulker in the foothills, he became a dashing mounted warrior of the plains.

After 1700 the mounted Comanches no longer feared their long-legged enemies of the plains unless they had guns. The tribe moved boldly out from their little foothill retreats, conquering and displacing the Apaches to the east. They strove constantly to enlarge their hunting grounds, partly from arrogance, partly to provide more room for their increased population. Their families were larger, and they were adding hundreds of captive women and children from enemy tribes.

In their expansion attempts, the Comanches had to fight a number of long wars against their neighbors, the Apache, Ute, Pawnee, Osage, Tonkawa, and even the Navaho far to the west across the Rockies. Later they added two new tribes to the list—the Cheyenne and Arapahoe, who moved in from the north. The Comanches seemed to enjoy fighting, and never ceased their attacks until the last of the tribe was penned in on a small reservation by the U.S. Army in 1875.

The Comanches were cruel and relentless toward their enemies, even by Indian standards, and were mean to one another in petty ways. Although they gloried in war and valued war honors above all else, their older men, even the great fighters of former years, were insulted and abused by the young people, with the tacit approval of the whole camp.

The Comanche hated restraint of any kind. He refused to tolerate the camp police customary in other Plains tribes. The only exception was in the communal buffalo hunts, when one man was chosen as leader, for the duration of that hunt only, with the authority to line up the men near the herd and give the signal to charge at the moment he chose. Aside from this one bowing to temporary authority, the tribe relied entirely on social disapproval to restrain its members' social lapses.

These fierce, cruel, headstrong men made up a great fighting force that in many ways was reminiscent of the Mongol horde of Ghengis Khan. They were at their best when fighting on horseback on terrain that permitted them to dash about at full speed, but when they had to dismount to attack the Apaches in the mountains of New Mexico, the Comanches were sometimes badly beaten.

When LaSalle established his short-lived colony on the Texas coast in 1684, the Spanish authorities in Mexico became alarmed. They responded in time by putting in a colony of their own at San Antonio in 1715. Soon the Spanish in the new colony were having trouble with the Apaches who were moving south under the pressure of Comanche attacks. At the same time Jicarilla Apaches, who were being forced westward into New Mexico, petitioned the Spanish at Santa Fe to help them against the Comanches. The Spanish decided they should help, for some of the Jicarillas were baptized Christians.

In 1717, while some of the Comanches were still living part of each year in little farming villages on the upper Arkansas, the Spanish governor amassed a large force of men, disguised them as Indians, and staged a surprise attack on these villages, capturing about 700 men, women, and children. The captives were first taken to Spain, then sent as slaves to Cuba, where they soon died. This was the only real success the Spanish soldiers had against the Comanches in a century of trouble, and it led to a peace agreement between the two sides.

The Apaches in Texas also decided to make peace with the Spanish and to ask them for help. The Spanish agreed to take the Apaches in and settle them at a new mission to be built expressly for them at San Saba, about a hundred miles north of the Spanish settlements. The Apaches were a little slow in becoming Christians, and the mission soon was under heavy attack by the Comanches who had followed the Apaches south. In 1758 the Comanches killed all the mission workers. When the Spanish retaliated by sending an army against them the next summer, the Comanches defeated the soldiers at the Red River and forced them to retreat.

Emboldened by their success, the Comanches visited the San Antonio colony each year to pick up some horses and other plunder. Sometimes they even paraded up and down the streets of the little settlements. Spanish defense against the Indian raids was ineffective, and the Comanche problem still had not been solved when the Spanish finally surrendered the colony in 1821.

During this period, beginning in 1717, the Comanches carried on a war with their kinsmen, the Utes, who lived in the mountains on the northwestern Comanche border. This constant hostility led the Utes to bestow the name Comanche on the aggressors, translating it as "the people who fight us all the time." While the Comanches were never able to mount an effective attack against the Utes in the mountains, they were able to prevent that tribe from moving out into the buffalo country and becoming nomadic hunters. The Utes managed to hunt some buffalo each year, but they were always in danger of an attack, so they killed their meat as quickly as possible and dashed back to safety in the mountains.

The Apache tribes that had retreated to New Mexico under the pressure of Comanche hostility had become fierce mountain people after half a century of hardship. They raided the farms along the Rio Grande each year, and were considered a serious problem by the authorities. In 1786 a new viceroy decided the Spanish should make a new treaty with the Comanches and enlist their help against the Apaches.

The Comanches were pleased, for they wanted to trade with the New Mexico people, especially for guns and ammunition. As part of the treaty the Spanish built them a village on the Arkansas River, but the Comanches never settled there. They did remain on rather friendly terms with the New Mexicans, and turned their attacks against Texas.

By the use of horses, the Comanches, in the course of a century, changed from a weak aggregation of small, scattered bands on a subsistence level in the Colorado foothills to a powerful nomadic people living off the buffalo herds in the plains. This was a voluntary movement on their part, and they never expressed any regret at leaving their old home. By 1800 they claimed a domain that reached from the Arkansas River on the north to central Texas on the south, and from the Rockies eastward about 300 miles. Other tribes composed of small hunting bands existing at subsistence level followed much the same pattern as the Comanches. Among these were the Crow, Wind River Shoshoni, Arapahoe, Assiniboin, and Blackfeet. They too became true nomads, pausing in their travels only to take shelter during the winter months.

George Catlin, visiting a Crow village on the Yellowstone River in the 1830's, observed the difficulties of spending a winter in even the large, improved tipis:

> These lodges are taken down in a few minutes by the squaws . . . and easily transported over the plains . . . to procure and dress their skins . . . and also for the purpose of killing and drying meat; making pemican and preserving the marrow-fat for their winter quarters; which are generally taken up in some heavy-timbered bottom, deeply imbedded within the surrounding bluffs, which break the winds and make their long winter months tolerable. They sometimes erect their skin lodges within the timber and dwell within them during the winter months; but more frequently cut logs and make rude cabins, in which they can live much warmer and better protected from the assaults of their enemies.

Intelligent, able horses were trained especially for the chase. A wounded buffalo might swerve and try to gore the horse, so he was taught to turn away at the twang of a bowstring or when a lance was withdrawn. (Painting by A. J. Miller, The Walters Art Gallery)

Lasting only a short breathless period, the buffalo chase was dangerous but efficient. Hunters preferred short bows or slender lances, which handled well on horseback and were deadly at close range. (Oil on canvas by George Catlin, Smithsonian Institution)

7

Tribes of the Woodland Fringe: Osage and Sioux

THE OSAGES WERE A POWERFUL TRIBE of Siouan stock, living along the edge of the forest from the Arkansas River north to the Missouri, and claiming buffalo hunting grounds to the west in the open plains. They were essentially a farming people, settled in several large, permanent villages, their lodges framed with heavy poles and covered with mats of woven grass and reeds. In later years they sometimes used tanned, smoked hides to patch a lodge covering. A few of the Osage bands had two villages, one for summer use near the cornfields, the other for winter back in the forest where fuel was plentiful.

Corn was the principal crop of the Osages, and supplied about half their food needs. Their supplementary crops were beans, squash, and sunflowers. They caught fish in the rivers, and hunted deer and small game in the woods. Each summer they went out to the plains for buffalo and again in the fall, after the harvest, for winter meat and robes.

The Osages claimed that their ancestors had lived just north of the Ohio River and many years before had moved across into Missouri, where they were identified by Pierre Marquette in 1673. At that time they were firmly established in their villages, which appeared to have been occupied for many years. They were an arrogant, quarrelsome people, with a large number of warriors, and waged almost constant war against several of their neighbors.

Near the end of the seventeenth century the Osages secured horses from the southwest and began using them on the buffalo hunt. Thus they could go farther into the plains in search of the herds and could carry back larger amounts of meat and hides. At about the same time they began to buy guns from the French traders, and with these new weapons they increased their attacks against the Apaches living in the plains to the west.

The noisy new weapons so frightened the Apache warriors that they fled in panic before even a small Osage force armed with five or six guns, leaving their homes and families at the mercy of the enemy, who were not interested in killing people but wanted captives to sell to the French down the Mississippi, who needed slaves for their plantations. As the Osages had no use for the captured lodges, these were plundered and burned, leaving the village a deserted ruin. These attacks from the east were very effective in breaking down Apache resistance, as they coincided with attacks by the Comanches from the west.

The rapid destruction of the Apache villages left a wide area of the plains free from any settlements until the white men came more than a century later to farm the prairie country. In the interval, hunting bands of nomads and seminomads roamed the country unhindered.

The basic pattern of buffalo hunting among the Osages changed very little, but with their horses and their enlarged hunting grounds they had more buffalo, which made for a pleasanter life with less drudgery. Their tipis, weapons, horse trappings, and camping routines were such that a chance traveler meeting them on a hunt would have difficulty in distinguishing them from the true nomads.

Back in their farming villages the Osages still planted their fields in the spring and cared for the crops until the corn had been hoed twice. By then it was tall enough and tough enough that it had little attraction for rabbits and deer. It could be left for a few weeks with little care, although a few villagers probably remained to watch the crops during the summer. Almost the entire population went out on the summer hunt in July and August, returning when the crops were ready for harvesting. After the harvest the people all went hunting again until driven from the plains by the winter storms.

The Osage pattern of development through this period is rather complex, and it is difficult to determine the relative importance of the several factors involved in the changes, but it is evident that the Osages never considered the horse as important in their pattern of living as did many of the other tribes, such as the Comanches and the Cheyennes.

The Osages were in firm possession of farms and permanent villages, and had a substantial supply of basic food in their corn crop. They had little incentive to hunt the buffalo the year around, to follow the herds like true nomads. The Comanches, in contrast, had to become nomads or go hungry much of the time because they were poor farmers on poor land. It was easier for the Comanches to kill surplus meat and tan extra robes to trade for corn than it was to raise their own.

While the Comanches needed large herds of horses and could manage them quite easily, the Osages needed fewer horses and had problems handling those. The Osages had to pasture the animals in the scattered woodlands near their villages, although this meant that the horses got into the crops during the summers and found scant forage among the trees during the winter. It would have been preferable to have pastured the horses on the rich, cured gamma grasses of the plains, but this would have required a strong guard for the herd—and the Osages simply did not possess the organizational and governmental skills to form such a guard at this time.

Because of these two important factors, the farming tradition and the problems of maintaining a horse herd, the Osages retained their basic pattern of living and much of their culture pattern. They added an overlay of plains culture, however, the most prominent addition being the tipi, which was used on the hunts, and the cover of which sometimes served as an emergency patch on a permanent lodge. Elaborate costumes for warriors and showy trappings for the horses were borrowed from their nomadic neighbors. They also indulged in the war game, with its system of honors and counting of coups.

Several other tribes with permanent villages and good corn lands followed the same pattern, among them the Pawnee, Omaha, Kansas, Arikara, and Mandan. Tribes with permanent villages but no farming also followed the pattern when they had a good supply of staple food from the salmon runs. These tribes were found in the Columbia Basin, but visited the Montana plains to hunt buffalo. Among them were the Nez Percé, Yakima, Spokane, Walla Walla, Cayuse, and Coeur d'Alene.

It appears, then, that a tribe with a permanent village and a good food supply could be induced to become buffalo hunters for part of each year but wanted to keep their villages to live in during the winter.

The Sioux to the north were also Woodland Indians. They were forced westward by the settlers until, in the latter half of the nineteenth century, they became the typical Plains Indians in the minds of most Americans. Their spectacular victory over General Custer and their later appearance in the touring Wild West shows helped imprint their image on the American mind. They were a tall, slim, muscular people with strong features, aquiline noses, and small hands and feet.

The ancestors of these Indians had come from Siberia well in advance of the Uto-Aztecans, possibly more than 2,000 years ago. They skirted the Canadian woods on their way to the southeast and settled in the Ohio Valley north of the river, and one small group penetrated to the tidewater of Virginia. They are classed as the Siouan family group, and include several tribes of the woodland fringe—the Iowa, Kansas, Omaha, Osage, Oto, and Ponca—that moved west from the Ohio Valley centuries before the first white explorers reached their country. The northernmost of the Siouan tribes, the Sioux proper, were occupying Minnesota and western Wisconsin when they were first visited by the French in 1673.

At the opening of the eighteenth century the Sioux were people of the woodland fringe, living in substantial rectangular houses constructed with heavy timber frames and covered with slabs of bark. Their villages were usually located in open groves near a lake or a river, and they had both good hunting and good fishing close at hand.

The entire Sioux country had small herds of buffalo on the prairies and meadows scattered among the forests and lakes. Much larger bands roamed just to the west where the country was more open, and the western edge of the Sioux lands bordered on the open plains. Thus the Sioux were well supplied with fish, meat, skins, robes, and furs from their own country.

Unlike their cousins to the south, the Sioux did no farming. About half their food intake was supplied by their staple grain crop, wild rice, which could be had in large quantities just for the harvesting. The women paddled into the rice swamps, bent the stalks over the canoe, and beat out the grain with wooden paddles.

To increase their crop, the women planted wild rice in any patch of shallow water where the plant did not grow naturally, and in several localities they made a practice of tying up the heads of the maturing rice in bundles of several stalks each and wrapping the heads with strips of hide or bark to keep the birds from pecking out the grain.

This staple grain crop, which needed attention only in late summer, left the Sioux freer for summer hunting than were the corn growers, and they did not have to go so far from their villages to find buffalo. Instead of packing up the whole village and trudging fifty or a hundred miles to the plains, they could live at home and just send the hunters out for a few days at a time. Hence it took quite a bit of pressure to induce them to move out onto the plains as true nomads.

The Sioux were a warlike people. They fought with their neighbors on all sides, but especially with the Crees to the north and the Chippewas to the east. After French traders reached those two tribes about 1670 and supplied them with guns, they used their new weapons in a strong attempt to drive the Sioux from their homes.

Stubbornly and reluctantly the Sioux gave ground, and as early as 1700 the large Teton band had been pushed west into the open plains, where they held a strip of the Dakotas about a hundred miles wide. Their westward movement was checked there by the powerful Arikara, Mandan, and Hidatsa living in large farming villages along the Missouri River.

About 1750 the Teton Sioux secured their first horses. Then their life on the plains became easier and richer, and other Sioux bands, the Oglala and Hunkpapa, partly attracted by the Teton success and partly pushed by their enemies, also moved out to the plains. There probably was an increase in population among the Sioux at this time, adding to the pressure for westward expansion. By 1800 about half the tribe had become true nomads, following the buffalo herds the entire year. They had reached the Missouri in two places, ready for further expansion to the west when the opportunity offered.

The Sioux remaining in the woodland villages also secured horses and used them on summer hunts, but they still lived in their permanent houses, harvesting wild rice, until forcibly ejected from the lake country by the advancing farming frontier in the 1860's.

It is evident from this division of the Sioux, lasting over half a century, that the ownership of horses and easy access to the buffalo herds were not enough to lure a settled people with a dependable grain supply to abandon their homes and become wanderers on the open plains. Instead, they spent the summer in traveling, living in tipis and following the buffalo, but when the first snows blew in from the north they were happy to return to their snug houses and ample supply of firewood.

The Siouan corn growers to the south had much the same pattern of living, keeping their winter homes and hunting in the summer. Although many people consider them as Plains tribes, they remained only seminomadic. This group included the Iowa, Kansas, Omaha, Osage, Oto, and Ponca. Their neighbors, the Pawnees and Wichitas of the Caddoan family, were also corn growers and followed the same pattern.

The Cheyennes were closely related to the Sioux and followed a similar pattern. When the Cheyennes were driven from their farming villages along the Iowa-Wisconsin border, they secured horses and turned to buffalo hunting for a living. In less than fifty years they had become true nomads, ranging throughout the western part of the Platte River drainage upstream from the junction of the North and South Platte forks in Nebraska.

8

The Blackfeet

THE PROFILE OF A PLAINS INDIAN is fittingly placed on the obverse side of the "buffalo" nickel, the two being emblematic of life on the Great Plains before the coming of the white settlers. The Indian, Blackfoot chief Two Guns White Calf, with his strong face and aquiline nose, is to millions of Americans the typical Indian of the plains. The stately Blackfeet can still be seen in war bonnets and buckskin in the parades and ceremonies at Glacier National Park each summer. Here Blackfoot place names dot the land and Blackfoot traditions and legends abound.

This popular concept uniting the Blackfeet and the buffalo is based on a solid historical foundation, for 150 years ago the tribe claimed a large tract of the finest buffalo range in the west. At that time the Blackfeet were a proud, powerful, warlike people vigorously engaged in a program of aggression and conquest to find living space for their increasing population.

Initially the Blackfeet were a small, weak people, the tag end of a large migration of Algonquin-speaking people moving from Siberia to the woods of northern Canada and on to the southeast. The Blackfeet reached the Mackenzie River country about 500 B.C. and later were pushed across the river into the deep woods by a new migration, the Uto-Aztecans. When the last of these, the Shoshoni, had passed on to central Alberta, the Blackfeet returned to the west bank of the Mackenzie and followed closely behind.

In the northern woods the Blackfeet had lived entirely on game.

This had forced them to break up into small family groups wandering widely in their hunting and finding only a bare subsistence, with periods of want a common thing and starvation always a threat. When they moved south to the valley of the North Saskatchewan River, they found more open country, with conifers still growing on the hills and ridges but groves of aspen and thickets of willow along the lakes and rivers, and many open stretches of good pasture. In these glades small bands of buffalo ranged, a more abundant meat supply than these hunters had ever known in the deep woods. All they needed to secure plenty of meat was to devise some fairly safe, effective way of killing the animals.

At first the Blackfeet found their surest and safest hunting during the winter blizzards. Then the buffalo sought shelter in the patches of timber, where a large band of hunters, approaching downwind yelling and waving their robes, could sometimes stampede the herd, driving it in a blinding rush into the open and possibly into deep drifts on the lee slopes, or onto a lake, its surface swept bare by arctic gusts. In either case the huge beasts were helpless for a time and easy prey to the hunters' spears and arrows.

In the summer it was possible at times to find a small band of buffalo that could be surrounded by a ring of people and could be kept milling in a tight bunch while the hunters dashed up and shot a few before the herd could run for safety, scattering their tormentors, perhaps trampling a few in the rush.

Both these methods had defects. Too often the buffalo refused to be at the right place at the right time, and in a herd small enough to handle. Luck was a big factor in placing a herd upwind of drifts or an ice-covered lake. In the surround the herd might break through the line of hunters at the first sign of danger, and once they started running, they could not be turned. In searching for a surer, safer method of killing more buffalo, the Blackfeet developed a corral or pound for entrapping them. This was called a piskin, and the basic idea of it was probably used long before the hunters came to the plains.

Early Europeans who came to the Blackfoot country were impressed with the piskin. Here is an eyewitness account of one:

It is a circle fenced round with trees laid one upon another, at the foot of a hill about 7 feet high and a hundred yards in circumference; the entrance on the hill-side where the animals can easily go over, but when in cannot return; from this entrance small sticks are laid on each side like a fence, in form of an angle extending from the pound; beyond these to about 1½ mile distant buffalo dung or old roots are laid in heaps, in the same direction as the fence. These are to frighten the beasts from deviating from either side.

This piskin was built in the mouth of a small draw so that the buffalo approaching it would find a natural pathway leading down the slope to the opening. The logs forming the fence were lashed to large posts set in the ground on the outside. Sharpened stakes rested on the bottom log, their butts braced against the ground outside, their points projecting inside at about the height of a buffalo's ribs. These stakes helped prevent the trapped herd from jamming against the fence and pushing it over.

Even with such a clever trap it required some luck to get the buffalo herd into position above the corral. Once it was in position, all the village turned out and crept into place behind the piles of roots along the wings. Then a line of men approached the herd upwind to start the animals running in the right direction.

Many things could go wrong, any one of which could send the quarry dashing off in the wrong direction. At times the village went on short rations for two or three weeks as attempt after attempt failed. But in time some more animals were corraled and everyone feasted again.

According to Blackfoot tradition, the first piskin was built after one of the men accidentally found out that he could "call" the buffalo to follow him. One hot summer day he was on a grassy ridge where the flies were bad, with the buffalo feeding a few hundred yards away. When the man began flapping his robe to drive off the flies, a few of the buffalo cows began walking toward him. He ducked down and ran to the next ridge and flapped his robe again. Soon the cows came running toward him, followed by the rest of the herd. He barely escaped being crushed under the hooves of the rushing animals as he crouched behind a small boulder for protection.

When he told his friends about this, they decided to build a piskin for him to fill with buffalo. When the corral was ready, he went out and called in a herd, while the rest of the people helped along the wings. The drive was so successful that this type of hunting became the common practice of the village, and soon spread throughout the tribe. This is an interesting tradition, but it is more probable that the process evolved slowly, with much trial and error.

Eventually the tribe came to regard buffalo calling as an art, and only a few gifted persons who had received the right visions following a period of fasting and prayer dared to class themselves as buffalo callers. Some of them worked on foot, wearing a light robe and imitating the antics of a buffalo calf. In later times the callers rode, using a large buffalo robe to cover both horse and rider, with the rider being the "hump" of the imitation.

After a kill, the whole area soon became a stinking place as the offal and blood decayed. The dogs helped clean up the mess, and in winter snow soon covered the place, making it suitable for another drive, but in the summer the buffalo could smell the place of a kill for a mile or so, until the sun and rains and wind had time to purify it.

To build a large corral and to supply the large number of people to man the wings and later take care of the meat, several small hunting groups had to combine their efforts. Their mutual interdependence and related success welded them into permanent bands of twenty to forty families, with one hunter and four or five dependents being the usual number to a family. Such a band required more cooperation, more social control, and a leader to make decisions. This adjustment to the larger group and its restrictions was agreed on by the people when they found it gave them more security from their enemies as well as more food.

With an increased meat supply, families raised more children and the small bands grew larger. From a weak, scattered people the Blackfeet grew into three large related tribes, the Piegans, Bloods, and the Blackfeet proper, all friendly toward one another. They moved farther out onto the plains in search of more buffalo, and fought with other tribes for the new hunting grounds.

Out on the open plains there were few places where enough timber could be found for constructing good piskins. The new surroundings called for new hunting methods, and the Blackfeet adopted a method that had been used on the plains for several thousand years: they found sheer cliffs at the edge of a grassy plateau and drove the buffalo over. Such places are commonly called buffalo jumps in the west, but the Blackfeet called them piskins although there was no corral at the place.

Grassy plains stretch from the Front Range of the Rockies far to the east, their gently rolling surface underlaid by soft horizontal rock strata that form rimrock cliffs where the streams from the mountains have cut valleys across the plains. At the foot of a rimrock cliff the soft ground slopes steeply to the valley floor. Although the sheer face of the cliff may be no more than twenty feet high, a buffalo plunging down from the plain above would land on his front legs and sink to his knees in the soft soil. The momentum of his body would then tip him forward in a somersault, breaking his legs and leaving him helpless.

At a good buffalo jump the kill could be quite large, a hundred or more animals in one drive, but about fifty furnished a better kill, for the meat and hides could be saved with less waste when the carcasses were not heaped too high. The effectiveness of a good buffalo jump can be seen on the south slope of the Sun River Valley west of Great Falls, Montana. Here bones and debris cover five acres to a depth of several feet, the animal residue being estimated at 25,000 tons. This jump was used for hundreds of years before the Blackfeet moved so far south.

The Sun River jump was one of the best. To the south several thousand acres of good pasture lie just beyond the rimrock, and slope gently toward the rim. A wide, shallow draw seemingly offers a safe passageway to the valley below. The draw gradually narrows and becomes deeper as it approaches the rim. The usual breeze here in the summer is from the southwest, which enabled the hunters to approach downwind and start the herd moving down the draw.

At the end of a successful drive the herd dashed over the cliff in a brown flood and ended in a mass of dead and crippled beasts at the foot of the slope. Then the people climbed down from their places along the wings of the drive and moved their camp to the bank of the Sun River just north of the kill. This was a hectic time, for the meat had to be stripped from the carcasses at once and put on the drying racks in thin slices before it could spoil. Any meat not cut off the bodies by nightfall would have spoiled before morning.

At dusk the tired, happy people rested around the cooking fires, feasting on tidbits after the tons of meat were sliced and spread out for the dry air to suck out the moisture, aided by the blazing sun during the day. Just one good drive, although it worked the people to the point of exhaustion, could supply each family with fresh meat for several days, a large reserve of dried meat, and one or two skins to tan. As soon as the meat was dried, the camp moved away, the offal was left to the scavengers and the wind and sun, and in two or three months the buffalo jump could be used again. If the drive was made using fire, as happened at times, no other drive was possible at that place until the grass grew up the next summer.

While more animals would be killed at a good buffalo jump than with the piskin and, from the nature of its surroundings, the buffalo jump could be used more frequently, it required a large number of people to stage the drive and handle the meat. As the bands increased in size by natural growth, with a good buffalo jump and some other hunting the men could still secure enough meat for everyone, but in the larger community it was necessary to make more rules of conduct and appoint authorities to enforce them. The most important rule, probably borrowed from the Sioux, prohibited any individual hunting when a big drive was being planned. An organized group of young warriors served as the police to enforce this rule.

As the Blackfeet prospered on the plains they tried to push southward against the Shoshoni, who resisted successfully for many years. During the eighteenth century the line of separation between the two tribes was the south bank of the Red Deer Fork of the Saskatchewan River. Here about 1730 the Shoshoni rode out boldly on their newly acquired horses, expecting to overwhelm the Blackfeet with this new weapon, but the Blackfeet soon had new weapons of their own: guns secured from the Crees, who were buying them from the French traders. In a few more years the Blackfeet had horses too, supplied by the Flatheads, who held the foothills at the eastern entrance to Marias Pass. For a time there was a stalemate between the two hostile forces. The Shoshoni had many more horses, but they had no place to buy guns and so were forced on the defensive.

As the Blackfeet became more numerous, their strength in fighting men increased and they organized them more effectively. They continued to send out a large war party under some popular leader at the end of the big sun-dance ceremony each summer. In 1781 Blackfoot scouts found a large Shoshoni village on the south bank of the Bow River. The place was strangely quiet, with no sign of life, not even a stray dog. At first the scouts feared a trap, but they finally ventured into the tipis and found them full of dead people. The entire village had been wiped out by smallpox. By the time the Blackfeet had despoiled the camp they were infected with the dread disease and unknowingly carried it back to their own villages.

Possibly two-thirds of the Blackfeet died in the next few weeks. The frightened remnants concluded that the disease had been sent to them as a punishment for their war against the Shoshoni. They sent envoys south to find the Shoshoni and propose a peace settlement, but the whole Shoshoni country south to the Marias River was deserted. The few Shoshoni who survived the plague had retreated far to the southwest, beyond the mountains.

With the Shoshoni menace removed, the Blackfeet attacked the Kutenai, who at that time held the upper basin of the Bow River as far south as Waterton Lakes. In a series of fierce attacks the outnumbered and outgunned Kutenai were forced west across the continental divide into the upper Columbia country. Then the Blackfeet turned against the Flatheads and pushed them back through Marias Pass.

As the Blackfeet moved south into new plains country, they killed more and more buffalo by the chase, but they continued to use the piskin, for the wise old men of the tribe said it was not right to let the ancient sacred customs die.

The Blackfeet continued to drive to the south, seemingly determined to take all the old Shoshoni lands. By 1811 Blackfoot camps were common along the Sun River, and the tribe claimed the land up the Missouri to Three Forks and beyond. In time this southward push to dominate the upper Missouri drainage at length brought the tribe into fierce conflict with the American fur traders pushing westward, up the Missouri, up the Yellowstone, and into the upper Snake River country from the south.

Thousands of years ago, long before bows and arrows, horses, and guns were introduced into North America, Indians lit fires and drove stampeding buffalo off cliffs, or jumps, such as the one shown in this diorama. (Montana Historical Society)

9

Buffalo East of the Mississippi

IN THE SUMMER OF 1612 Samuel Argoll was exploring along the western side of Chesapeake Bay. There he found a river and sailed up it as far as his ship could go, "and then marching into the countrie, I found a great store of cattle as big as kine, of which the Indians that were my guides killed a couple, which we found to be very good and wholesome meate, and very easy to be killed, in regard they are heavy, slow, and not so wild as other beasts in the wildernesse."

These shaggy beasts in lowland Virginia were the extreme eastern fringe of the wandering herds that had pushed across the Mississippi River when the grasslands of the Great Plains became crowded. The buffalo first crossed the Mississippi in significant numbers about A.D. 1000 and gradually worked their way east until they reached the Atlantic coast about the end of the sixteenth century.

This eastward movement was but part of the spread of the buffalo during that period. Other herds were moving northward to the Canadian forests and into the mountain valleys and passes of Montana and Wyoming. The movement to the east through the Ohio Valley was in a country of open hardwood forests interspersed with small meadows. The buffalo avoided brushy country and dense evergreen forests, such as those in northern Wisconsin and much of Michigan, where they could find no pasture.

As the herds built up in numbers along the west bank of the Mississippi, some of the animals found easy crossings near the Falls of St. Anthony at low water in late summer or on the ice in winter. Once across the river they had all of southern Wisconsin, Illinois, Indiana, Ohio, and western Pennsylvania open to them.

After the herds were well established in southern Ohio, some of them managed to cross the Ohio River, either by swimming or on the ice, and filled the Kentucky lowlands and the western valleys of West Virginia. They continued south to the Tennessee River and worked their way east along its northern bank, up the Great Valley until they could go east again through the water gap into Virginia, the Carolinas, and northeastern Georgia. One small herd even wandered across Georgia to its extreme southwestern corner. Other herds coming from Kentucky used the Cumberland Gap as a passage to the east. The buffalo had just begun to get settled in the new country when the northern fringe of the advancing herd was reported by Argoll.

There are several indications that the buffalo were newcomers to the Atlantic seaboard. The herds were small, widely scattered, and the total number much less than the pasture could easily support; nor had they reached any major barrier to their onward movement. If the herds had completely stocked the pastures of Virginia, the pressure of their numbers would have pushed bands northward into Maryland, eastern Pennsylvania, Delaware, and New Jersey, all suitable areas. They would have gone southward into all of Georgia, and probably into northern Florida. Capacity herds in Tennessee would have stocked Alabama and Mississippi.

The hunting and killing of buffalo in Virginia east of the mountains received little attention in the old accounts, giving the impression that the animal was not considered an important resource by the early settlers. In 1701 a new colony of Huguenots on the James River captured some buffalo calves and attempted to domesticate them, but the calves were too stubborn and unruly. In 1729 Colonel William Byrd, when surveying the Virginia-Carolina boundary, reported sighting buffalo about 150 miles inland from the ocean.

Near Roanoke, Virginia, was a large salt lick where buffalo were common until about the middle of the eighteenth century. In 1750

Thomas Walker visited the place and reported, "This lick has been one of the best places for game in these parts and would have been of much greater advantage to the inhabitants than it has been if the hunters had not killed the buffalo for diversion."

Several early references mention buffalo in the northwestern counties of Virginia. These would be on the western drainage on streams flowing into the Ohio, in modern West Virginia. Scattered herds of buffalo were found in both South Carolina and Georgia from the Piedmont to the coast. George Oglethorpe, first governor of Georgia, reported in 1733 that buffalo were among the wild animals native to the colony. Up country, in 1739, an account mentioned "Killing buffaloes . . . of which there is a very great plenty, and they are very good eating. Though they are a very heavy beast they will outrun a horse and quite tire him." And that same year, in another part of Georgia, "We seeing several herds of sixty or upwards in a herd." But by 1770 all the buffalo in Georgia had been killed.

Buffalo were hunted for many years in the Piedmont region of South Carolina, and a herd of 300 was reported about 1770, but the last of the animals were killed off by 1775. The presence of fairly large herds, for the Atlantic seaboard, in both Georgia and South Carolina suggests that the animals had come in appreciable numbers through eastern Tennessee into these states, with the southern edge of the occupation only a short distance south of the Savannah River, although that one small stray herd was found 250 miles to the southwest in the remote corner of Georgia in 1698. This pattern shows that these southern buffalo did not go around the southern flank of the Appalachians in Georgia, but came down from the north. There is no good evidence for any buffalo trails crossing the Appalachians except up the Great Valley in eastern Tennessee and through the Cumberland Gap from southeastern Kentucky.

As the early pioneers worked their way south and west in Virginia, they crossed the mountains through the Cumberland Gap into Kentucky or proceeded down the valley into Tennessee, along the trails the buffalo had followed on their way east. In both states they found much larger herds than they had ever seen east of the mountains. Daniel Boone reported vast herds in 1764 on the upper Cumberland, and an early traveler named Ramsay found "an immense number of buffalo and other wild game. The country was crowded with them. Their bellowings sounded from the hills and forests." This report was from what is now the city of Nashville. Many large salt licks, each visited by buffalo herds, were reported all along the Cumberland Valley.

When the first settlers to Kentucky had passed the Cumberland Gap, they continued northwest and finally emerged in the lowlands. Here they were surprised to find a great open space of grasslands, 6,000 square miles, which they called the Kentucky barrens, thinking at first that the soil was too poor to grow timber.

In a short time they found that the soil was very good indeed and that the original forests there had been cleared by the Shawnee Indians, who each year crossed the Ohio River to hunt big game, particularly buffalo and elk. They burned off the dried grass each fall, and in the process burned some of the adjacent woods to make larger pastures for their game animals.

Although the soil in the barrens proved to be excellent for farming, the settlers put their farms along the woodland fringe, where the soil was a little poorer and encumbered with large trees that had to be cleared before crops could be planted. It was easier to carve out little cornfields from the open timber than it was to transport enough logs into the barrens to build houses, barns, fences, and to supply firewood. This dependence of the pioneers on nearby timber continued until they had better means of transportation.

The Kentucky barrens furnished much better buffalo range than did the Cumberland Valley to the south, which in turn was superior to the Piedmont east of the mountains. With the better pastures, the herds of buffalo in Kentucky were larger and more numerous than those to the south or east. Early visitors from the east frequently expressed surprise at the large number of animals in one place, usually at a salt lick. While a herd of sixty had been considered large among the scattered pines of the Piedmont, and in Kentucky a herd numbering from 300 to 600 animals would be called vast, out on the Great Plains it would require a herd of several thousand to rate such adjectives.

Colonel George Croghan, who visited the central part of Kentucky in 1765, noted, "In our way we passed through a fine timbered clear wood; we came into a large road which the buffaloes have beaten, spacious enough for two wagons to go abreast, and leading straight into the lick."

Captain Harry Gordon visited the same place the next year.

We encamped opposite the great Lick, and the next day I went with a party of Indians and batteaumen to view this much talked of place. The beaten roads from all quarters to it easily conducted us, as they resemble those to an inland village where cattle go to and from a large common. The extent of the muddy part of the lick is ¾ of an acre. This mud being of salt quality is greedily licked by buffalo, elk and deer, who come from distant parts in great numbers for this purpose.

Daniel Boone reported of the Red River country in 1770: "The buffaloes were more frequent than I have ever seen cattle in the settlements, browsing on the leaves of the cane, or cropping the herbage of those extensive plains, fearless because ignorant of man. Sometimes we saw hundreds in a drove, and the numbers about the salt spring were amazing."

Simon Kenton, an early settler in Kentucky, estimated that he had seen about 1,500 animals in one herd near this lick.

The large number of buffalo and their lack of fear led to senseless slaughter. In May 1775, a traveler named Henderson wrote this entry in his diary:

We found it very difficult at first to stop great waste in killing meat. Some would kill three, four, five, or half a dozen buffaloes, and not take half a horse load from them all. . . . Our game was driven off . . . [until] fifteen or twenty miles was as short a distance a good hunter thought of getting meat, and sometimes they were obliged to go thirty miles, though by chance once or twice a week a buffalo was killed within five or six miles.

In addition to attacks by the hunters, the buffalo suffered in winter when snow turned to cold rain then froze, making a crust of ice on the snow, which prevented them from feeding. Simon Kenton reported a very severe winter in 1779–80, "when from the middle of November to the last of February all Kentucky was shrouded in snow and ice . . . and even buffalo would come so close to the settlements that they could be shot from the cabin doors."

A large portion of the Kentucky herd survived even this, for Kenton reported sizable numbers at the forks of Licking River in 1782, and John Filson, a writer visiting Kentucky, reported in 1784: "I have heard a hunter assert that he saw above one thousand buffaloes at Blue Licks at once; so numerous were they before the settlers wantonly sported away their lives. The amazing herds of buffalo which resort hither, by their size and numbers, fill the traveler with amazement and terror."

When the Kentucky settlements were new and the settlers few, they had plenty of wild meat for their tables. Some of the older settlers thought the supply of game had a bad effect on the farmers, for they put in less time and effort on their crops when they had plenty of food from hunting. The game, including the buffalo, was killed off in about thirty years, the last buffalo on record in the state being killed in 1800.

On the northern side of the Ohio River the whole Ohio Valley had long been occupied by Indians living in farming villages and growing corn as their chief crop. These Indians spent much of their time heaping up huge earthworks of various shapes over their dead and thus earned themselves the title Mound Builders.

Their whole culture complex of raising large quantities of corn and building great mounds changed rapidly about the time the first buffalo herds came in from the west, leading some scholars to suggest that the presence of the buffalo in appreciable numbers was the prime factor in the change. The herds overran the cornfields, eating the young plants in early summer and trampling down the stalks at any season, drastically cutting the yield and imperiling the food supply. The Kentucky pioneers had this same problem with buffalo in their corn until the herds had been killed.

The Mound Builders did not need to go hungry when their corn was damaged; they killed the buffalo. The suggestion is that the tribes shifted much of their attention to hunting as more rewarding, for it gave them more desirable food.

Another important factor in the change was a series of attacks from tribes that invaded the Ohio country from the northwest. The Mound Builders finally gave up the struggle. The survivors took to their canoes and escaped down the Mississippi to less dangerous lands. One such tribe was the Mosopelea, which left the Ohio Valley about the middle of the seventeenth century and moved south to the Yazoo Valley in Mississippi.

For at least two centuries, 1600–1800, the valley was in constant turmoil as tribe after tribe came in and fought for land. Whole tribes were destroyed by merciless enemies, leaving waste lands to be occupied by newcomers from the north. In all this fighting in the seventeenth century, the Iroquois were the chief aggressors. From their point of vantage in upper New York State they secured guns from the Dutch traders along the Hudson River, and used the new weapons with deadly effect against the tribes to the west. First they wiped out the large Erie tribe along the south shore of Lake Erie, then extended their power ever westward, levying tribute on each conquered tribe in turn until their war parties reached the Mississippi, and even the Illinois had to bow to their demands. The Iroquois sent one large war party west of the Mississippi to attack the Pawnees. In time the Iroquois' many campaigns wore them down. After 1700 they lacked the manpower to dominate the western lands and withdrew into their own borders.

New tribes came into the Ohio Valley on the heels of the Iroquois withdrawal. The Shawnees, driven from central Tennessee, moved northward in several scattered groups, which then combined to dominate much of Ohio until Mad Anthony Wayne defeated them soundly in 1793–95. The Shawnees then moved west into Indiana, only to be crushed in 1811 by General William Henry Harrison.

Other tribes moved south from Michigan and Wisconsin. A few had come in even before the Iroquois conquest, the chief of these being the Illinois. They were followed later by the Sauk, Fox, Ottawa, Huron, Miami, Potawatomi, and Kickapoo, each anxious to settle on the good corn land. All this movement of the many tribes and their constant struggles with one another made the Ohio Valley undesirable and unsafe for white farmers until the campaigns of Wayne and Harrison opened up the whole country to the Mississippi.

The buffalo bands from the Alleghenies to the Mississippi were all destroyed during this hectic period, most being killed by Indian hunters. When the white settlers finally crossed the mountains, they found only a few herds, small and widely scattered, in the mountain valleys of Pennsylvania and West Virginia. The whites slaughtered these in short order, and the United States was without a buffalo herd until President Jefferson bought Louisiana, and with it the Great Plains with buffalo numbering many millions.

The remnants of the Indian tribes from the Ohio country moved west ahead of the farming frontier, crossing the Mississippi into Iowa, southeastern Missouri, and eastern Kansas. In their new homes the buffalo were more plentiful than in the old, and some of these Indians continued as buffalo hunters for another half century.

10

The Golden Age of the Plains Indians

LIEUTENANT LAWRENCE KIP, at the Walla Walla Council in 1855, reported:

We saw them approaching on horseback in one long line. They were almost entirely naked, gaudily painted and decorated with their wild trappings. Their plumes fluttered about them, while below, skins and trinkets and all kinds of fantastic embellishments flaunted in the sunshine. Trained from early childhood to almost live upon horseback, they sat upon their fine animals as if they were centaurs. Their horses, too, were arrayed in the most glaring finery. They were painted with such colors as formed the greatest contrast, the white being smeared with crimson in fantastic figures, and the dark colored streaked with white clay. Beads and fringes of gaudy colors were hanging from the bridles, while the plumes of eagle feathers interwoven with the mane and tail, fluttered as the breeze swept over them, and completed their wild, fantastic appearance.

When about a mile distant they halted, and half a dozen chiefs rode forward . . . . Then on came the rest of the wild horsemen in single file, clashing their shields, singing and beating their drums as they marched past us. Then they formed a circle and dashed around us, while our little group stood there, the center of their wild evolutions. They would gallop up as if about to make a charge, then wheel round and round, sounding their loud whoops . . . .

The above describes a large delegation to a treaty council. The following by Francis Parkman describes a parade in an Indian camp:

Suddenly the wild yell of the war-whoop came pealing from the hills. A crowd of horsemen appeared, rushing down their sides, and riding at full speed toward the village, each warrior's long hair flying behind him in the wind like a ship's streamer. As they approached the confused throng assumed a regular order, and entering two by two, they circled the area at a full gallop, each warrior singing his war song as he rode. Some of their dresses were superb. They wore crests of feathers, and close tunics of antelope skins, fringed with scalp-locks of their enemies; many of their shields, too, fluttered with the war eagle's feathers. All had bows and arrows at their backs; some carried long lances. A few were armed with guns. The White Shield, their partisan, rode in gorgeous attire at their head, mounted on a black-and-white horse . . . .

The warriors rode three times around the village; and as each noted champion passed, the old women would scream out his name, to honor his bravery, and excite the emulation of the younger warriors . . . .

Although the two parades were staged by two quite different tribes, the Nez Percé and the Oglala Sioux, a thousand miles apart, the similarity of the pageantry is striking. Both parades are good examples of the highly stylized, elaborate plains culture that came to full flower early in the nineteenth century. For six decades the nomadic tribes basked in its effulgence, while the seminomads on the fringe of the plains carefully copied much of its color.

This gorgeous hybrid culture owed its firm economic base to the vast herds of buffalo, which supplied an abundance of food, robes, and hides for comfort, and a large amount of leisure time that could be used to expand and enrich the whole culture pattern.

But this culture could not flower until pollinated by contributions from the encroaching Europeans. The mobility of the tribes and their ability to harvest buffalo at almost any time of the year depended on the horse, supplied by the Spanish colonies. While this contribution came late in the seventeenth century, it had not spread to all the Plains tribes until a century later. But the horse alone would have been of little immediate use to the Indians; they also had to borrow its gear, trappings, and methods of management from Europeans. The whole economic structure of the Plains tribes was further strengthened by other items from the European traders—steel knives, needles, cloth, and guns.

Several cultural elements common to the many diverse peoples throughout the plains were supplied by tribes from the woodland fringe, who in turn may have learned them from others in the Ohio Valley. Most spectacular of these, and with the widest distribution, were the grand ceremonies with religious overtones that white men combined under the title sun dance. Another common practice was the elaborate war game with its complicated rules and scoring system.

Important political ideas also came from the woodland tribes, the most important being the pattern for the dog soldiers, or camp police, so necessary when nomads from several bands assembled in a large group for ceremonies or for hunting.

At the opening of the nineteenth century most of the woodland fringe from Canada to central Arkansas was held by the several tribes of the Siouan family, with a total population of about 63,000 people. Of these, 27,000 were true nomads by this time, living on the open plains throughout the year. These included the Teton and Hunkpapa Sioux, Crow, and Assiniboin, who ranged throughout Dakota and eastern Montana, and spilled over into Wyoming to the south and Manitoba to the north.

In addition to the Siouan seminomads of the woodland fringe, several other tribes of seminomads held most of the Missouri Valley for hundreds of miles, living in large villages with permanent lodges and growing large fields of corn. These were the Hidatsa, Mandan, Iowa, Oto, and Omaha. When the sun-dance ceremony was brought to the plains by the Sioux, it soon spread to all these related people, then to tribes to the west, north, and south. The Blackfeet had it quite early, while it did not reach the Comanches, the last of the nomadic tribes to adopt it, until about 1875.

The basic concept of the sun dance, the seeking of spiritual help through dancing, fasting, and self-torture, was very old, and each tribe staging a sun dance followed a common pattern, but there was considerable diversity in the accompanying activities.

In early summer, when the buffalo bulls were fat again, the scattered bands of a tribe would assemble at a location where there was good water, plenty of pasture, and some timber. A tall, slim tree with a fork near the top was chosen for the center pole of the ceremonial sun lodge, and was cut down by some special person, such as a noted warrior or a chaste woman. Once the tree fell, it was attacked by all the warriors as though it were a fallen enemy, each man striking it with a weapon as the branches were broken off. Then the pole was carried to the lodge site, and a bundle of brush and a buffalo hide were lashed to the fork before the pole was raised. The lodge was then constructed with rafters extending from the center pole to posts marking the outer wall. Near the base of the pole a cleared space decorated with buffalo skulls was used as an altar.

Each man volunteering for the sun dance had a skewer thrust through the skin and muscle of each breast, with thongs from the skewers fastened high on the center pole. The dancer then leaned back, keeping the thong taut, his dance step consisting of raising himself on his toes and settling down again until he fainted or the skewers tore loose. This self-torture was the central part of an elaborate ceremony lasting several days. The skulls, thongs, buffalo hide, and the feathers of the war eagle were the only animal parts used in the ceremony, although the bundle of brush in the fork of the center pole symbolized an eagle's nest.

In the northern plains a special dance was developed to call the buffalo herds to the hunting grounds near the villages. The Mandan dance was the most elaborate of these, requiring three days for the complete ceremony. The old men of the tribe sat in a group in the middle of the dancing place and were offered honors while many hunters disguised as buffalo circled around·and were pursued by other hunters. Each disguised hunter wore on his head a mask made by tanning an entire buffalo head, keeping the horns and hair intact. About fifteen hunters danced at a time. George Catlin, who visited the Mandans in the 1830's, described the scene:

When one becomes fatigued of the exercise, he signifies it by bending quite forward, and sinking his body towards the ground; when another draws a bow upon him and hits him with a blunt arrow, and he falls like a buffalo—is seized by the bystanders, who drag him out of the ring by the heels, brandishing their knives about him; and having gone through the motions of skinning and cutting him up, they let him off, and his place is at once supplied by another, who dances into the ring with his mask on; and by this taking of places, the scene is easily kept up night and day, until the desired effect has been produced, that of "making the buffalo come."

The Hidatsa, living just to the north and west of the Mandans, had a similar dance, held in a large ceremonial lodge. Six old men were chosen to represent buffalo bulls; they carried sticks ornamented with bells obtained from white traders and hooves from buffalo calves, sang special songs, and imitated the bellowing of the bulls. Dishes of boiled corn and beans were passed around, and each tasted the food. Then empty dishes were passed around, and each man pretended to taste the buffalo meat that would be served on these dishes if the magic dance brought a herd within range of the hunters.

Among the Blackfeet, the person initiating the mystic rites to attract buffalo had to own a "buffalo stone," a small brown stone three or four inches long naturally shaped like a buffalo. A few of these were found over the years in the gravel beds of streams in the Blackfoot country and were treasured family heirlooms.

The owner of a buffalo stone invited a number of hunters who were believed to be especially favored by the Sun to come to his lodge for the rites, which did not include dancing by a large group; following a successful hunt the hunters did sing and dance in thankfulness for the help the Sun had given them. A successful buffalo caller was always sought to join the group in the lodge for the preliminary rites.

During the larger part of each year the Plains tribes wandered in small bands, each going its separate way, although two or more bands might join forces at any time for visiting or a big hunt. When a band was by itself, the people usually behaved quite well, needing no more than social pressure from their relatives and friends to keep their conduct at a satisfactory level. But when the bands gathered in the early summer for the sun dance or for a great communal buffalo hunt, it was sometimes difficult to keep order among the 2,000 or 3,000 people in the camp. The most serious problem was the supervising of the hunters lest a few go out at the wrong time and stampede the buffalo herd into distant pastures before the communal hunt could be staged. One man, a respected chief, was put in charge of all the camp, and he made the hunting rules from day to day. These were announced each day to the whole camp, and were enforced by a designated body of young men, in some tribes called the dog soldiers.

The pattern for this type of control, like the pattern for the sun dance, had been developed by some of the woodland tribes long before they moved out onto the plains, and was used for various situations. Once in the open country such restrictions were needed less often than when the tribe lived in the large communal houses. In some tribes the dog soldiers were used only for special circumstances in the hunting of the buffalo, but in other tribes they had several functions.

An early account of the hunting control was recorded by Louis Hennepin, who was camping at the time near the upper Mississippi River. The year was 1680.

> Fifteen or sixteen savages came into the middle of the place where they were, with their great clubs in their hands. The first thing they did was to overset the cabin of those that had invited us. Then they took away all their victuals and what bears oil they could find in the bladders, or elsewhere, with which they rubbed themselves all over from head to foot . . . . We knew not what these savages were at first, but it appear'd they were some of those that we had left above the Falls of St. Anthony. One of them, who called himself my uncle, told me that those who had given us victuals, had done basely to go and forestal the others in the chase; and that according to the laws and customs of their country, 'twas lawful for them to plunder them, since they had been the cause that the Bulls were all run away, before the nation could get together, which was a great injury to the publick; for when they are all met, they make a great slaughter amongst the Bulls; for they surround them on every side, that 'tis impossible for them to escape.

David Thompson, a trader among the Blackfeet for the Hudson's Bay Company in the 1790's, found that they had much the same kind of camp police:

> The same evening a Chief walked through the camp informing them that as the bisons were too far off for the hunting party they

had given orders to the Soldiers to allow no person to hunt until further notice. Such an order is sure to find some tents ill provided. While we were there, hunting was forbidden on this account. Two tents which had gambled away their things, even to dried provisions, had to steal a march on the Soldiers under pretense of looking after their horses; but finding they did not return were watched. In the evening of the second day they approached the camp, with their horses loaded with meat which the Soldiers seized, and the owners quickly gave up; the former distributed the meat to the tents that had many women and children, and left nothing to the owners; but those that had received the meat, in the night sent them a portion of it. Not a murmur was heard, every one said they had acted right.

These men received very light punishment, even for the Blackfeet. Another hunter under like circumstances had his bow and arrows broken, his saddle broken, his whip and rope cut into small bits, and his clothing torn.

The camp police sometimes punished people who disturbed the peace of the camp. Meriwether Lewis witnessed camp discipline in an Arikara village on the Missouri in 1804:

> While on shore today we witnessed a quarrel between two squaws, which appeared to be growing every moment more bois-terous, when a man came forward, at whose approach everyone seemed terrified and ran. He took the squaws and without any ceremony whipped them severely. On inquiring into the nature of such summary justice we learnt that this man was an officer well known to this and many other tribes. His duty is to keep the peace, and the whole interior police of the village is confided to two or three of these officers, who are named by the chief and re-main in power for some days . . . his power is supreme, and in the suppression of any riot or disturbance no resistance to him is suf-fered . . . their distinguishing mark is a collection of two or three raven skins fixed to the girdle behind the back in such a way that the tails stick out horizontally from the body. On his head, too, is a raven skin split into two parts and tied so as to let the beak project from the forehead.

Among the Sioux and several other tribes, police duties devolved on one of the young men's societies, numbering perhaps thirty. Among the Crows, each spring the chief would appoint one of the societies to act as police until the tribe separated into small bands in the fall, emphasizing that they were needed only when several bands camped together. The Mandans, living in large permanent villages, needed their police the whole year.

Among the smaller, poorer tribes punishment was usually more severe and the destruction of property belonging to the culprit greater, although the poor tribe could ill afford such an economic loss. Evidently these Indians did not consider it sufficient punishment to confiscate the property and give it to poorer families, especially to widows with children, but instead indulged in what to us is a shocking waste.

In the seventeenth century, when Indians began to ride horses, mounted hunters could drive buffalo from a cliff. Sometimes much of the meat spoiled before the Indians could process it. (Painting by A. J. Miller, The Walters Art Gallery)

Hunters take the hump rib from a slaughtered buffalo. Ingenious Indians could use buffalo parts to supply almost all their needs, but much offal was left behind when a large kill made meat plentiful. (Painting by A. J. Miller, The Walters Art Gallery)

11

Explorers and Mountain Men

IN 1803 THOMAS JEFFERSON at one stroke of the pen took title to 30 million buffalo and all their grazing land, with a few million elk, deer, and antelope thrown in for good measure. Thus overnight the United States went from possessing a few hundred scattered buffalo in the remote corners of the Ohio drainage to ownership of four-fifths of the world's herds. It was the largest single purchase of livestock in history.

President Jefferson's main objective in negotiating the Louisiana Purchase was to acquire the port of New Orleans and with it free passage down the Mississippi River to the Gulf of Mexico for American goods, especially farm products, from the Ohio Valley. He gladly took the Great Plains with the buffalo herds as part of the bargain when Napoleon offered them at a bargain rate.

For many years Jefferson had been interested in the great unexplored region stretching to the Pacific coast. Even while the land was still in the possession of Spain he had made several attempts to interest private individuals to cross the Great Plains and the Rocky Mountains. As soon as the treaty had been signed and the land firmly under the American flag, the President wasted no time in sending out two parties of explorers.

The lesser-known exploration was headed by Zebulon K. Pike, who was sent up the Mississippi to find its source. Pike finished this assignment so quickly that he was sent out again, across the plains to the Rockies in Colorado. The more famous exploration, commanded by

Meriwether Lewis and William Clark, was ordered to go up the Missouri River to its head, then cross the Rocky Mountains and find a way to the Pacific coast. All their route beyond the crest of the Rockies would be outside the United States in a region claimed by Spain, Great Britain, France, and Russia at various times.

In 1803 the United States had within its borders more farmland than even the rapidly growing population could settle in forty years, so there was little interest among the pioneer farmers for any movement across the Mississippi into the wild country infested with wild Indians and vast herds of buffalo. But the adventurous ones, the traders and trappers, flocked in to explore and exploit the new land. Lewis and Clark, returning from the Oregon coast in the fall of 1806, met boat-loads of eager men some 1,500 miles up the Missouri from St. Louis, all of them pressing on to the wild country, with a special interest in furs. When they found that the Missouri region provided a rather scant supply of the standard furs, many of them turned their attention to buffalo robes and such by-products as fat and dried and smoked meats.

Until the coming of the railroads, the only good approach to the buffalo country was through St. Louis and on up the Missouri. In this newly acquired country, the great river was the main highway for travelers and all the products of the region on their way to market. Travelers and traders from the east came down the Ohio or up the Mississippi to St. Louis, where they had to regroup and change boats. This route up the Big Muddy offered the only practicable passage from the banks of the Mississippi through the forest belt to the Great Plains between the Falls of St. Anthony, at the head of navigation on the north, and the Red River in Louisiana. Any substantial shipments of trade goods to the western Indian tribes, and the return bales of buffalo robes, had to be carried on the Missouri.

The fur traders scanned Lewis and Clark's detailed reports of avail-able furs and hides from the Indian tribes along the Missouri. All the tribes visited by the explorers from St. Louis to the Mandan villages were seminomadic, raising crops of corn and beans along the streams and hunting buffalo in season. For many years the French had traded for furs along the river, chiefly beaver, raccoon, and wolf, but these were of poorer quality than those found in the northern woods. They had also brought in tanned buffalo robes in small numbers.

Lewis and Clark found large herds of buffalo all along their route from the mouth of the Platte to the headwaters of the Missouri, although at times the herds might be several miles back from the river's edge. Buffalo meat was the staple for the party during this stage of the journey, supplemented with deer and antelope. The journals contain their hunting experiences with the buffalo, this one in December 1804 near the Mandan villages in Dakota:

> The Big White Grand Chief of the first village came and informed us that a large drove of buffalow was near and his people was waiting for us to join them in the chase. Capt. Lewis took 15 men & went out and joined the Indians, who were at the time he got up, killing the buffalow on horseback with arrows which they done with great dexterity. His party killed ten buffalow, five of which we got to the fort by the assistance of a horse in addition to what the men packed on their backs. One cow was killed on the ice after drawing her out of a vacancy in the ice in which she had fallen, and butchered her at the fort. Those we did not get in was taken by the Indians under a custom which is established amongst them i.e. any person seeing a buffalow lying without an arrow sticking in him, or some peculiar mark takes possession, many times a hunter who kills many buffalow in a chase only gets part of one.

In the spring the Indians throughout the buffalo country burned off the old grass in places where they had not used a fire drive in the previous autumn. On March 6, 1805, "A cloudy morning & smokey all day from the burning of the plains, which was set on fire by the Minetarries for an early crop of grass, as an inducement for the buffalow to feed on." Until the new grass attracted the herds, the Indians hauled in the animals drowned in the river during the winter:

> The ice has stopped running owing to some obstickle above . . . but few Indians visit us today. They are now attending on the river bank to catch the floating buffalow.
> The obstickle broke away above & the ice came down in great quantities. . . . I observed extraordinary dexterity of the Indians in jumping from one cake of ice to another, for the purpose of catching the buffalow as they float down many of the cakes of ice when they pass over are not two feet square. The plains are on fire in view of the fort on both sides of the river. It is said to be

common for the Indians to burn the plains near their village each spring.

As the explorers traveled up the Missouri, camping at night on the bank, they found that a stray buffalo bull could be a real danger:

Last night we were alarmed by a new sort of enemy. A buffaloe swam over from the opposite side and to the spot where lay one of our canoes, over which he clambered to the shore; then taking fright, he ran full speed up the bank toward our fires, and passed within eighteen inches from the heads of some of the men, before the sentinel could make him change his course; still more alarmed, he ran down between four fires and within a few inches of the heads of a second row of men, and would have broken into our lodge if the barking of the dog had not stopped him. He suddenly turned to the right and was out of sight in a moment, leaving us all in confusion.

As they passed through the Missouri River "breaks" near the mouth of the Judith River they saw a large buffalo jump. The herd had been chased across the level ground above a rimrock cliff.

Today we passed on the starboard side the remains of a vast many mangled carcasses of buffalow which had been driven over a precipice of 120 feet by the Indians and perished; the water appeared to have washed away a part of this immense pile of slaughter and still there remained the fragments of at least a hundred carcasses they created a most horrible stench . . . for this purpose one of the most active and fleet young men is selected and disguised in a robe of buffaloe skin, having also the skin of the buffaloe's head with the years and horns fastened on his head in the form of a cap . . . the part of the decoy I am informed is extremely dangerous, if they are not very fleet runners the buffaloe tread them underfoot and crush them to death, and sometimes drive them over the precipice also where they perish in common with the buffaloe.

When a buffalo cow in good condition was killed, the strips of back fat helped make a special dish, called white pudding:

. . . from the cow I killed we saved the necessary materials for making what our cook Charbono calls boudin (Powdingue) blanc

. . . this white pudding we all esteem as one of the greatest del[ic]acies of the forrest . . . . About 6 feet of the large gut of the buffaloe is the first mo[r]sel the cook makes love to, this he holds fast at one end with the right hand, while with the fore-finger and thumb of the left hand he gently compresses it and discharges what he says *is not good to eat* . . . the mustle lying under the shoulder blade next to the back, and the fillets are next saught, these are needed up fine with a good portion of the kidney suet; to this composition is then added pepper and salt and a small quantity of flour. [The intestine is then tied at one end, turned inside out and stuffed with the mixture. The other end is tied.] It is then baptised in the Missouri with two dips and a flirt and bobbed into the kettle; from whence, after it be well boiled, it is taken and fryed with bears oil until it becomes brown . . . .

Twice in the following weeks Lewis lamented that the party was reaching the limits of the buffalo range and would have no more white pudding.

Lewis found that the Teton band of the Sioux held two small stretches of the west bank of the Missouri, one at the mouth of White River, the other at the mouth of Cheyenne River. The Tetons claimed the hunting grounds up both these rivers to their heads. They lived in tipis the year around, and planted no gardens of any kind, trading with the farming villages for any corn and beans they needed. They were much too far from the wild-rice country of the other Sioux bands either to harvest rice or buy it. Lewis disliked the Tetons from the first, finding them difficult to deal with. In his notes he stated that they were the vilest miscreants of the savage race, and he predicted that they would cause trouble in the future until subdued by force. How-ever, he had no serious trouble with them.

On the entire trip from St. Louis to the Pacific coast and back, the party had real trouble with only one tribe, the nomadic Blackfeet. On the return trip in July 1806, Lewis with three companions went north from the Sun River in central Montana to the Marias River to learn if that stream headed north or west. He hoped that Marias Pass, men-tioned by some of the Indians, might prove to be a shorter and better way to the west than the one he had just traveled.

After sighting Marias Pass, a deep notch in the continental divide, Lewis moved down the Marias River toward the Missouri. Along the way he met a party of eight Blackfeet who seemed friendly at first, but the next morning they tried to steal his guns and horses. In the resulting struggle two of the Blackfeet were killed. The rest retreated hastily, leaving behind most of their gear and a few of their horses.

The returning explorers met some fur traders moving up the Missouri from St. Louis, who assured them that their brush with the Blackfeet was of minor importance, for all the other tribes had been friendly, or at the most, indifferent to the explorers. The traders then continued upriver to their winter trading places, and returned to St. Louis with large packs of good furs. This stimulated the interest of other groups in the upper Missouri.

One of the new groups was led by Manuel Lisa, an important figure in the Missouri fur trade for many years. In the spring of 1807 he left St. Louis with a keelboat-load of trade goods, hoping to reach the rich fur country in the Montana mountains ahead of all competition. At the mouth of the Platte River he had a stroke of luck. Down the river came a dugout canoe, its lone occupant John Colter, who had been with Lewis and Clark. Lisa immediately signed Colter on as his guide and followed him up the Missouri, then up the Yellowstone to the mouth of the Bighorn River, in Crow country. Here Lisa built his trading post and sent out his trappers.

Colter took a single companion, John Potts, and set out up the Yellowstone along the path followed by the buffalo herds, the same trail Colter had traveled eastward with William Clark a year earlier. They crossed through Bozeman Pass to the Gallatin Fork, then went down to Three Forks and began trapping in the river bottoms there.

On a crisp summer morning about the end of July, with a morning fog on the river, Colter and Potts were in a canoe lifting their beaver traps when they heard the trampling of many hooves. They hoped for a harmless herd of buffalo, but when the fog drifted away they saw a party of about 200 Blackfeet on the river bank, motioning to them to come ashore. Potts, instead of surrendering his gun peaceably, shot and killed one of the Indians, and immediately died under a shower of arrows.

The angry Blackfeet decided to have some sport in killing Colter. They stripped him and turned him loose on a broad, sandy plain covered with short grass full of prickly pear, giving him about a hundred yards' head start before they took after him, yelling at the top of their lungs. For six miles Colter outran all but one of the pursuers, a big man who gained steadily. On the bank of the Madison River, at the other edge of the plain, Colter turned at bay and managed to kill his pursuer with his own spear, taking the broken spear and a shred of blanket as his rightful loot. Then he dived under a large mass of driftwood lodged along the river and lay there until nightfall. With his feet full of prickly pear needles, naked, and his only weapon a broken spear, Colter retraced his steps 250 miles to Lisa's post, reaching there somewhat underweight and completely tanned by the summer sun, but ready for more trapping in a few days.

The Bighorn post built by Lisa furnished the Crows an outlet for their buffalo robes, acknowledged by both Indian and white to be the finest produced anywhere in the west. Although the furs never produced much profit at Bighorn, a steady supply of fine robes moved down the river each year to the St. Louis market until the last of the buffalo herds had been slaughtered in the Crow country seventy-five years later.

When Manuel Lisa returned to St. Louis he helped organize the Missouri Fur Company, which was entrusted to return a Mandan chief safely to his home after a visit to Washington, D.C., with Lewis and Clark. After some serious trouble with the Arikara villages, Lisa finally took the chief home and continued upriver in 1809 to put in a new post at Three Forks to exploit the fine beaver country in the upper Missouri drainage. The spot seemed ideal, in a pleasant valley with adequate timber for buildings and firewood, and plenty of pasture for the many buffalo nearby.

But by 1810 the Blackfeet had developed a deep enmity toward all American fur men and, having driven the Shoshoni back into Idaho, were claiming the Three Forks country. They considered themselves disgraced that Lewis had killed two Blackfeet and had escaped without punishment. When Colter and Potts killed two more, and Colter escaped, the blood debt grew. Then, early in the spring of 1810, a Blackfoot war party went on a big raid into Crow country along the Yellowstone, only to suffer a serious defeat when they were intercepted by a large number of Crows armed with their new guns purchased from Lisa's post. The Blackfeet hated anyone who would help arm their enemies.

As soon as the Blackfeet learned that Lisa was building a new post at Three Forks, about a mile from where Colter had hid in the driftwood, they gathered about 200 warriors and kept the post under constant harassment. Trappers were killed or wounded, traps and furs were stolen, hunters were attacked, the horse herd was always in danger, until Andrew Henry, in charge of the post, decided to abandon the place while he still had some men able to work.

Henry packed up his stock of goods, destroyed the post, and retreated up the Madison River and across Reynolds Pass to the headwaters of the Snake, which is called Henry's Fork to this day. Here he spent the winter, but found the snows deep, the hunting poor, and his men suffering from cold and hunger, but with a great deal of hard work they managed to secure forty packs of beaver, which Henry brought down the Missouri in 1811. These troubles with the Blackfeet blocked the American fur men from trading with the tribe for buffalo robes for twenty years, a rather serious situation, for the Blackfeet had the biggest supply of robes handy to good river transportation.

That same year, 1811, Wilson Price Hunt and his men, on their way overland to help set up Oregon fur posts for John Jacob Astor, blazed a new path through the buffalo country to the Rockies. Hunt decided he would not follow up the Missouri as Lewis and Clark had done, braving the hostile Blackfeet for about 300 miles. Instead he bought horses from the Arikaras and started out to the west overland, passing just to the north of the Black Hills and crossing the middle of the great rampart of the Bighorn Range. He found the traveling easy and the buffalo plentiful, but no good beaver country until he reached the mountains. He went on west, with many trials and tribulations, and finally reached the mouth of the Columbia and the new fur post, Astoria.

The next new route across the buffalo country was opened up by Robert Stuart, one of Hunt's men. He was sent back from Astoria with five men to carry messages to Astor in New York. He had trouble with both the route and a shortage of food until he reached the headwaters of the Platte River in southern Wyoming. Along the Green River just west of the continental divide they found a few buffalo:

> To our great joy we discovered three buffalo bulls, and after considerable trouble, we, about 2 P.M., killed one (an old run down one), which soon made us determine on camping. So ravenous were our appetites, that we ate part of the animal raw; then cut up most of what was eatable and carried it to a brook at some little distance, where we encamped, being hungry enough to

relish a hearty meal. We sat up the greater part of the night eating and barbecuing meat; I was very much alarmed at the ravenous manner in which all ate, but happily none felt any serious effects therefrom—probably in consequence of my not allowing them to eat freely before they had supped a quantity of broth.

Once the party had reached the eastern slope of the divide, the traveling was much easier and they were in good buffalo country. "We killed three buffalo cows this morning, which are the first of these animals we have been able to lay our paws on, the hump meat is by far the most delicious I have ever tasted."

Once Stuart reached the North Platte, he followed that stream down to the Missouri, but found it too shallow for canoes. Later flat-bottomed boats were used to go down the Platte on the spring flood.

Hunt's westward journey showed that it was practicable to carry trade goods across the plains by pack train, and Stuart found a good trail for the trains along the Platte River to the heart of the Wyoming mountains. Both parties found plenty of buffalo east of the mountains, and neither had trouble with the Indians. Hunt's experience with the Cheyennes indicated that the nomadic tribes of the plains, ranging well to the west of the Missouri, would welcome traders in their own lands, instead of having to depend on other tribes to act as middlemen.

12

The Santa Fe Trail

SANTA FE, QUEEN OF THE SOUTHWEST, and for two centuries the northern outpost of the Spanish empire in North America, was also the only gateway to the southern plains for a century and a half of that period. The viceroy in Mexico and the governors at Santa Fe kept a watchful, jealous eye on the French trading and exploring activities in the Mississippi basin, and especially for any movement from the Illinois country that might look like encroachment on the Great Plains, which Spain looked on as her own.

In 1720, when the Spanish learned that French traders were visiting tribes in the Missouri country, they sent a detachment of soldiers to the Platte River to investigate. This force was surprised by an Indian war party with a few Frenchmen accompanying it, and was driven back to Santa Fe without accomplishing anything.

Twenty years later two Mallett brothers, Pierre and Paul, brought a supply of trade goods out from Illinois to the Great Plains and set up a small trading post on the Arkansas River near the Rocky Mountains. The Spanish governor had them arrested and their goods seized for what he called an invasion of Spanish lands, but the traders appealed their case, claiming they were operating within the boundaries of French Louisiana. It took years for the case to pass through the Spanish court system, until finally a high court at Havana ruled that the traders had been seized in French territory and that they must be released and their goods restored.

Before other French traders could take advantage of this ruling, the

Treaty of Paris in 1763 changed the whole situation. The French surrendered the eastern half of Louisiana to Great Britain, and ceded all their holdings west of the Mississippi to Spain in payment of an old debt, thus giving Spain almost all of the buffalo of North America in addition to a great deal of land.

Twenty-three years later the governor at Santa Fe signed a treaty with the Comanche tribe, which removed the most serious threat to peaceful travel by outsiders across the southern plains and opened up the possibility that Santa Fe might secure a shorter, better route to the outside world. Since the founding of the colony, the only route had been south into Mexico over 2,000 miles of mountains and deserts. A trade route to St. Louis would be only half as long, and over much more favorable terrain. It could also serve as a trade route to the buffalo hunters on the southern Great Plains.

As a first step in establishing the route, the governor sent a party of three men across to St. Louis to open communications with the Spanish officials there. The three were captured by the Kansas Indians, but were released to French traders on the Missouri. Then troubles at the Spanish court and more wars in Europe prevented any further activities along the trail for several years. Before the officials at Santa Fe could resume the matter, St. Louis had been turned over to the Americans, and the first traders had begun to open the route to Santa Fe. As soon as the United States took possession of St. Louis in 1804, Batiste LaLond went west through the Pawnee villages and on up the Platte Valley to the Rockies, then south to Santa Fe. He settled there instead of returning to St. Louis.

Surprise and excitement gripped the Pawnee villages two years later. The Spanish, to offset the American activities out of St. Louis, sent an expedition to march through the buffalo country and visit some of the important Indian tribes there. They marched into the Pawnee country, a column of 600 Spanish soldiers, colors flying in the breeze and weapons gleaming in the sun, 600 baggage mules, and 1,200 spare horses, all under the command of Don Facundo Malgares. He had orders to hold a grand council with the Pawnees and to impress on them the wealth and might of Spain and the desirability of friendly relations with the Spanish.

This expedition had resulted directly from Spanish uneasiness over the purchase of French Louisiana by the United States. For forty years while the whole southern plains country was claimed by Spain there had been little incentive to establish a definite boundary between New Mexico and Louisiana, but with the Americans encroaching onto the plains, such a line was needed. Spanish interest in the boundary waned as a new Napoleonic War engulfed the country, and the matter went unsettled until Spain and the United States signed the treaty of 1819, one clause of which established the exact boundary.

The Pawnees were duly impressed by Don Malgares and his army. They held the council meeting and professed friendship toward the Spanish. Don Malgare then marched back into the southwest, banners flying as he made his way through the vast buffalo herds on his way to New Mexico.

A few days later an American detachment came up the Kansas River to the same Pawnee villages. Lieutenant Zebulon K. Pike had finished his exploration of the upper Mississippi rather quickly and was now on his way west to the Colorado Rockies. Part of his task was to determine the possibilities of navigation on the Kansas, Arkansas, and Red rivers. He had a party of twenty-three whites and fifty-one Indians in a number of small boats, all his men being equipped for work rather than for show, so both in splendor and in numbers he made a poor showing in comparison with the resplendent Don Malgares. The contrast between the Spanish and American forces gave the Pawnees the conviction, which was an accurate one at that time, that Spain was the wealthier and more powerful nation.

Pike soon discovered that he could not go up the Kansas River by boat, so he bought horses from the Pawnees and proceeded overland, his men riding and his camp equipment and supplies carried by pack train, a common method of travel in the buffalo country for years to come. His men ate fresh buffalo meat as they moved west, and reached the Rockies without undue hardship. Pike was captured in the mountains by a Spanish patrol from Santa Fe. He was taken to Mexico, then later sent home by ship.

Pike's arrest seems to have deterred the traders from St. Louis for a time from attempting to open trade with Santa Fe. Then in 1812 twelve traders made the crossing with a pack train of goods, only to have everything confiscated and themselves imprisoned. In 1814 a party of trappers crossed the Rockies to the Spanish settlement at Taos and were well received. They sought permission from the governor at Santa Fe to trap in the colony, but he could not legally grant it without approval from Mexico City. When the trappers returned two years later, they found a new governor, who ordered them out of the country and had them arrested and imprisoned when their departure was delayed by a storm.

The severity of the Spanish officials is better understood when we realize that they were acting strictly according to Spanish law and that it was their duty to keep the Americans out. They had some border troubles too, from attacks by hostile Indians accompanied by American trappers. A war party of Pawnees was intercepted and defeated on the northwestern border of New Mexico in 1819, and an American with the band was captured.

The American traders wanted the governors to ignore the laws so that they could make more profit. They were all pleased, then, when Mexico became independent of Spain in 1821 and many of the restrictive laws were repealed. The new government welcomed American traders to Santa Fe and Taos. In a short time trading parties were on their way, not only for profit, but also to secure the release of friends and relatives imprisoned earlier by the Spanish. They were successful in both instances.

The resulting travel was through the very heart of the southern plains buffalo country, where the herds at times were so huge that the travelers estimated them in the millions. The assured presence of buffalo at several points along the trail enabled the travelers to plan with some certainty; they knew they would have fresh buffalo meat for a good deal of the journey and did not need to stock up heavily on food reserves from the settlements. The extra space could be used for more goods to be sold at a profit.

The first successful trading expedition to Santa Fe was organized in 1821 by William Becknell of Missouri. He took seventy men and a pack train of goods out that year, returning the next spring with a substantial profit. Several other groups were then organized, some of them strictly for trade, others for some trapping in the mountains before going on to Taos, which over the next thirty years attracted a large number of the mountain men.

Becknell decided after surveying the trail on his first trip that wagons could be used to advantage on the route, so in the spring of 1822 he tried the experiment with twenty-one men and three loaded wagons. He had very little trouble on the way. The first 500 miles was across the gently rolling plains. Josiah Gregg stated later, "The route, indeed, appears to have presented fewer obstacles than an ordinary road of equal length in the United States."

Although the surface of the trail offered little difficulty, any breakdown of a wagon along the way could cause serious trouble, for there was no timber near the roadside to provide a new axle or new reach. To ensure against a delay from a broken axle, many of the wagon drivers cut suitable hardwood logs at Council Grove, 150 miles west of Independence, Missouri, the last good timber along the route. A log was lashed to the underside of each wagon against the time of need. Some of the logs went unused, and were hauled to Santa Fe and back again, to make the trip another year.

The wagon trains started in the spring as soon as the new grass would nourish the teams. At this time the small streams were full from the spring rains, and draws that normally were dry most of the year had a little water or a boggy stretch in the bottom. Here a wagon might stick in the mud and block the trail. When camping near a stream, the teamsters always tried to get across in the evening, for their teams would pull more willingly even at the end of a long day than they would when cold and stiff in the early morning. Josiah Gregg described the method used in crossing:

> Early the next morning we reached the Little Arkansas which is only a small creek with a current but five or six yards wide. Its steep banks and miry bed annoyed us exceedingly in crossing. It is the practice upon the prairies on all such occasions for several men to go in advance with axes, spades and mattocks, and by digging the banks and creating temporary bridges, to have all in readiness by the time the wagons arrive. A bridge over a quagmire is made in a few minutes, by cross laying it with brush (willows are best but even long grass is often employed as a substitute) and covering it with earth across which a hundred wagons will often pass in safety.

Beyond the Arkansas River crossing, lack of streams was the real problem. For much of the year this stretch of the trail is a real desert with water hard to find. When William Becknell opened the trail from the Arkansas across to the Cimarron, he had this experience, reported by Gregg:

Frequently led astray by the deceptive glimmer of the mirage, or false ponds, as those treacherous oases of the desert are called, and not suspecting they had already arrived near the banks of the Cimarron, they resolved to retrace their steps to the Arkansas. But they were no longer equal to the task, and would undoubtably have perished in those arid regions had not a buffalo, fresh from the river's side, and with a stomach distended with water, been discovered by some of the party . . . . The hapless intruder was immediately dispatched, and an invigorating draught poured from its stomach.

Although the wagon trains depended on the buffalo for most of their food, this is the most dramatic use of a buffalo in the personal experiences along the trail. Buffalo herds were common in most of the area throughout the year, but in the spring were found much nearer the settlements than at any other time. The eastern edge of the plains is at a much lower altitude, giving it an earlier spring, and the tall prairie grass there grows faster than the gamma grass of the high plains. This early spring growth sometimes brought the herds as far east as Council Grove.

Other game was plentiful too, particularly deer and antelope, but in the opinion of the plainsmen, nothing could take the place of good buffalo meat. The sighting of the first herd was an event, which Gregg described:

Our eyes were greeted with the sight of a herd amounting to nearly a hundred head of buffalo, quietly grazing in the distance before us. Half our company had probably never seen a buffalo before and the excitement that the first sight of these "prairie beeves" occasioned among a party of novices beggars all description. Every horseman was off in a scamper, and some of the wagoners, leaving their teams to take care of themselves, seized their guns and joined the race afoot. Here went one with his rifle or yager, there another with his double-barrelled shotgun, a third with his holster pistols, a Mexican perhaps with his lance, another with his bow and arrows, and a number joined without any arms whatever, merely for the pleasures of the chase.

Whenever the train had a chance to make a good kill, the extra meat was sliced thin and dried for future use. Sometimes this reserve food supply was neglected, or used too freely, and a few days of travel without sighting any buffalo would reduce the men to cornmeal and old bacon. Sometimes the train met Indian hunters who offered to trade their goods for the dried meat.

Near the New Mexico border, Gregg reported, they sometimes met a different kind of hunting band:

> Every year ciboleros [buffalo hunters] form large parties and go from the New Mexican settlements to the buffalo plains. Some are provided with mules and asses, others with carts and oxen. They hunt, like wild Indians, chiefly on horseback, and with bow and arrow or lance. They cur   eir meat in the Indian fashion, slicing it thin and suspending . in the sun. During the curing operation they often follow the Indian practice of beating or kneading the slices with their feet, which is supposed to speed up the drying.

The meat never spoiled in the pure, dry air if the animal heat was allowed to escape quickly. Seemingly there were no harmful bacteria on the high plains, and there were no blow flies or horse flies on the southern plains in the early years.

When Josiah Gregg first crossed the plains, he was with a large wagon train of a hundred vehicles and more than 200 men, plus a small family party of Spanish who were returning from exile now that Mexico was free from Spain. The train was a conglomeration of many small groups with no common bond except that they were all going to Santa Fe and wanted company across the plains, for there was danger of an Indian attack on a small party.

For security and police purposes, the train was divided into four columns of twenty-five wagons each, and each train was under an elected leader. Each column marched and camped as a unit. For camp guard at night each of the 200 men was assigned to one of the eight watches, and had to stand one watch every other night even though he might be injured or sick, unless he was too weak to get out of his bedroll.

Travel on the Santa Fe Trail grew rapidly, the trains following one another in close order. In the twenty-one-year period 1822–43, about 3,150 men and 1,563 wagons passed through the Indian country. In addition, several small parties without wagons went through each year. Out of this large number only seven people are listed as having been killed by Indian attacks. While an all-out assault by a large war party would probably have met with success against some of the trains, and the plunder would have been fabulous to the red men, they did not care to try for even that much loot if it meant losing a few of their number.

The large, well-organized trains, with a hundred or more armed men on guard, appeared a formidable force, with a guard detachment on each side, in front, and at the rear during the march. In camp the wagons were put in a circle, and when danger threatened, the horses, mules, and oxen were held within the wagon circle at night, or picketed under heavy guard close by.

In spite of their appearance, the trains were not always so formidable as they looked, as this extract from Gregg shows:

> In accordance with the habitual carelessness of caravan traders, a great portion of the men were unprepared for the emergency. Scores of guns were empty, and as many more had been wetted by recent showers and would not go off. Here was one calling for balls—another for powder—a third for flints. Exclamations such as, "I've broke my ramrod," "I've spilt my caps," "I've rammed down a ball without powder," "My gun is choked, give me yours," while a timorous greenhorn would perhaps cry out, "Here, take my gun, you can out-shoot me."

Luckily this time the Indians were friendly, so no harm came from the confusion and lack of preparedness.

In addition to the treaty that the Spanish made with the Comanches in 1786, the New Mexicans tried to make peace with other tribes of buffalo hunters. They sent a party of twenty-five men to Council Bluffs, Iowa, in 1824. There the United States Indian agent helped them hold a council, which resulted in an agreement that Pawnee war parties would not interfere with traders on the trail. The next year United States commissioners met with the Osages at Council Grove, Kansas, and secured from them a similar agreement covering the eastern part of the trail.

Even with these tribes peaceful, the trains were in danger of raids from bands living much farther away. In 1826 a poorly armed band of twelve men on the Cimarron lost their entire herd, 500 head, to marauding Arapahoes. Two years later when two men from a train were killed away from camp, the whites in retaliation shot four or five friendly Indians as they approached the train. Friends of the slain struck back by stealing 1,000 horses from the train. Gregg mentions war parties of Sioux, Gros Ventre, and Blackfeet along the trail, the two latter groups coming from southern Canada.

In 1829 Senator Thomas Benton of Missouri secured an army escort for the traders to the Arkansas crossing, the boundary with Mexico, composed of three companies of infantrymen and one of riflemen commanded by Major Bennett Rily. The train was met at the river crossing by a Mexican force and escorted the rest of the way to Santa Fe. These troops, commanded by Colonel Antonio Vizcarra, were attacked at the Cimarron by a war party of Gros Ventres and lost a captain and three privates while killing several of the Indians.

The Santa Fe trade was of more importance to the United States than even the large profits indicate. The returning traders brought jacks, jennies, and mules for the southern plantations. Of equal importance were the large supplies of gold and silver coin. Until the California gold rush in 1849, the country was in woeful want of hard money for ordinary business and for deficit payments to foreign countries. Hence when one caravan brought back $180,000 in coin, it stimulated trade in the entire Mississippi basin.

Comanche women dry meat and dress robes. Adze-like tools were used to make skins uniformly thin, brains or a mixture of brains and liver to make them soft. (Oil on canvas by George Catlin, Smithsonian Institution)

Loading pack horses and dogs alike, a Pawnee tribe migrates. Many semi-nomadic tribes roamed buffalo lands from spring until fall, settling in some protected spot to wait out harsh winters. (Painting by A. J. Miller, The Walters Art Gallery)

13

Blackfeet and the Upper Missouri Fur Trade

IN 1812, WITH THE BRITISH NAVY blockading the mouth of the Mississippi and British agents stirring up the Indian tribes all along the northern frontier, the western fur trade was thoroughly disrupted. Piles of furs accumulated at St. Louis, and prices there dropped when the dealers could not move their stocks to the European markets. Buffalo robes were unsalable and the Indian tribes along the Missouri suffered, for they had nothing to substitute for robes in trading for the white man's goods.

The United States government appointed Manuel Lisa as Indian sub-agent on the upper Missouri in a move to weaken British influence in Dakota and Minnesota. Lisa proved to be a capable man who had the confidence of most of the tribes. He consolidated his wartime activities at a new post at Council Bluffs. His efforts dissuaded many of the tribes from sending war parties against American settlements, while he helped organize raids against northern tribes who were favoring the British.

Just as the western fur trade was recovering from the war, Manuel Lisa died and his holdings in the Missouri Fur Company were taken over by Joshua Pilcher, who then tried to develop more trade on the Yellowstone and Missouri rivers in Montana. By the spring of 1822 he had built a new post at the mouth of the Bighorn and had about 300 men working in the area. His trappers made good catches, but they had to beat off several Indian attacks. The most severe blow came when a party of twenty-nine men, with fifty packs of beaver from Three Forks, were ambushed on the Yellowstone by a large party of Blackfeet, losing seven men killed, five wounded, and thirty-five packs of beaver. Other losses about this time to the Arikaras on top of this disaster ended the Missouri Fur Company.

The Rocky Mountain Fur Company, organized by William Ashley, took its place. Ashley's second in command, Andrew Henry, continued to have bad luck. On his way up the Missouri, he lost a keelboat and its entire cargo of trade goods in the river, and later had fifty horses stolen by the Assiniboins. He spent the winter at the mouth of the Yellowstone, planning to go up the Missouri in the spring and build a post at the mouth of the Marias River. His party was attacked by Blackfeet and lost four men before they could even pick a building site, so they retreated to the mouth of the Yellowstone.

Ashley came up the river with a new supply of goods, planning to buy horses at the Arikara villages to send upriver to Henry. The Arikaras were hostile that summer and tried to wipe Ashley out with a treacherous attack, and he was forced to retreat down the Missouri to reorganize his men. A messenger carried news of Ashley's troubles to Henry, who packed his furs and came down the river, running the Arikara danger. A call for help to the army post farther downriver quickly brought a relief column under Colonel Henry Leavenworth, but he failed to punish the Arikaras, asking them for a peace treaty instead.

Following this fiasco, Henry went back to the Bighorn post and sent a successful trapping party southwest through Wyoming into the Green River country. This success inspired Ashley to turn all his attention to the Wyoming mountains. There he started the famous Green River rendezvous, where trappers and Indians gathered each year to trade their furs for new supplies and trade goods. William Sublette, Ashley's successor in the mountains, knew of the successful use of wagons on the Santa Fe Trail and decided he might be able to use them up the Platte River to the rendezvous. He took ten loaded wagons west in 1830 with little trouble and returned with them in the fall with his furs, thus opening the eastern half of the Oregon Trail to wheeled traffic. By 1830 the buffalo country had been sliced through by two wagon roads from the Missouri to the mountains, the harbingers of great changes on the plains in the next half century.

While Ashley and his Rocky Mountain Fur Company were developing the Wyoming country after the Blackfeet had blocked them from Montana, the American Fur Company was working its way up the Missouri. They were fortunate in hiring Kenneth McKenzie, formerly employed by the Northwest Company of Canada, who lost his job when that company merged with the Hudson's Bay Company in 1821. By 1828 McKenzie was in command of the Upper Missouri Outfit, an important section of the American Fur Company, and began his trade expansion on the upper river by building Fort Union at the mouth of the Yellowstone, to be followed by another post upriver in the Blackfoot country if he could just convince the tribe they would profit from a post.

McKenzie was fortunate in finding an old trapper, Jacob Berger, who had worked for the Hudson's Bay Company in the Blackfoot country and knew their language. Berger went up the Missouri with a small party to visit a Blackfoot camp on the Marias. There he was recognized and warmly welcomed. He persuaded forty of the Blackfeet to go with him to Fort Union to talk with McKenzie, who managed to convince them that they would benefit greatly from a post on their own lands. The Blackfeet offered no strong objections to a trading post, but insisted that the whites do no trapping of any kind in the area. Once this point was settled the Blackfeet were quite friendly.

This was the first of several posts built near the mouth of the Marias in the next twenty years under a variety of names and at a number of locations along a seven-mile stretch of river. It had a successful trading season, but when the trader went down the river with his furs in the spring, none of his men were willing to stay as caretakers and the Indians soon burned the deserted buildings. The next year the post was rebuilt six miles farther up the river, then moved and renamed Fort McKenzie until in 1847 it received a permanent site and a permanent name, Fort Benton.

McKenzie also rebuilt the Bighorn post, this time as Fort Cass, and thus controlled all the fur trade of the upper Missouri and the Yellowstone. He advised the company to get a river steamboat to bring the supplies up and the furs down the river. The company then ordered the steamboat *Yellowstone* built on contract. The boat made its first run to Fort Union in 1832, with the western artist George Catlin as one of its passengers. Catlin recorded the life at the post, in sketches and in his journal. In this extract he describes a buffalo hunt: ▲

I mentioned the other day that M'Kenzie's table from day to day groans under the weight of buffalo tongues and beavers' tails, and other luxuries of this western land. He has within his fort a spacious ice-house, in which he preserves his meat fresh for any length of time required; and sometimes, when his larder runs low, he starts out, rallying five or six of his best hunters (not to hunt but to "go out for meat"). He leads the party mounted on his best buffalo horse (i.e. the horse amongst his whole group which is best trained to run the buffalo) trailing a light and short gun in his hand, such a one as he can easily reload whilst his horse is at full speed . . . .

They had five or six men, each with a cart, follow to bring in the meat. Then they rode out west of the post and climbed out of the river bottom to the open plain.

There in full view of us was a fine herd of some four or five hundred buffaloes, perfectly at rest . . . . Some were grazing, and others were lying down sleeping; we advanced within a mile or so of them in full view. Mons. Chardon "tossed the feather" (a custom always observed to try the course of the wind), and we commenced "stripping" as it is termed (i.e. every man strips himself and his horse of everything extraneous and unnecessary appendages of dress, etc., that might be an encumbrance in running). Hats are laid off, and coats—and bullet pouches; sleeves are rolled up, a handkerchief is tied lightly around the head, and another around the waist—cartridges are prepared and placed in the waistcoat pocket, or half a dozen bullets "throwed into the mouth," all of which takes some ten or fifteen minutes, and is not, in appearance and effect, unlike a council of war. Our leader lays the whole plan of the chase, and preliminaries all fixed, guns charged and ramrods in our hands, we mount and start for the onset. The horses are all trained for this business and seem to enter into it with as much enthusiasm, and with as restless a spirit as the riders themselves. While stripping and mounting, they exhibit the most restless impatience, and when "approaching" (which is all of us abreast, upon a slow walk and in a straight line toward the herd until they discover us and run) they all seem to have caught the spirit of the chase, for the laziest nag amongst them prances with an elasticity in his step, champing his bit—his ears erect, his eyes strained out of his head, and fixed on the game before him, whilst he trembles under the saddle of his rider. In this way we carefully and silently marched until within forty or fifty yards, when the herd discovering us, wheeled and laid their course in a mass. At this instant we started (and all must start for no one could check his steed at that moment of excitement) and away all sailed, and over the prairie flew, in a cloud of dust, which was raised by their trampling hoofs. M'Kenzie was foremost in the throng; and soon dashed amidst the dust and was out of sight—he was after the fastest and fattest. I had discovered a huge bull whose shoulders towered above the whole band, and I picked my way through the crowd to get alongside of him. I went not for "meat," but for a trophy. I wanted his head and horns. I dashed along through the thundering mass as they swept over the plain, scarcely able to tell whether I was on a buffalo's back or my horse—hit, and hooked, and jostled about, till at length I found myself alongside of my game, when I gave him a shot as I passed him. I saw guns flash in several directions about me, but I heard them not. Amidst the trampling throng Mons. Chardon had wounded a stately bull, and at this moment was passing him again with his piece leveled for another shot; they both at full speed, and also within reach of the muzzle of my gun, when the bull instantly turned and receiving the horse upon his horns, and the ground received poor Chardon, who made a frog's leap of some twenty feet or more over the bull's back and almost under my horse's heels. I wheeled as soon as possible and rode back where lay poor Chardon, gasping to start his breath again and within a few paces of him his huge victim, with his heels high in the air and the horse lying across him . . . . In a few moments he arose, picked up his gun, took his horse by the bit; which then opened its eyes . . . sprang to his feet, shook off the dirt, and here we were, all upon our legs again, save the bull . . . .

I rode back with M'Kenzie, who pointed out five cows which he had killed, all of them selected as the fattest and slickest of the herd. This astonishing feat was all performed at full speed, within the distance of one mile, and every one shot through the heart . . . .

In the short space of time required for a horse under full whip to run the distance of one mile he had discharged his gun five times, and loaded it four times—selected his animals, and killed at every shot. [Note: McKenzie was using a muzzle loader, charged with powder and ball, and a percussion cap.]

Such is the mode by which white men live in this country—and such is one of their delightful amusements—at the hazard of every bone in one's body, to feel the fine and often thrilling exhilaration of the chase for a moment, and then as often upbraid and blame himself for his folly and imprudence.

On another chase Catlin was thrown from his horse and had the stock of his gun broken in the fall. His horse ran away too, and had to be chased on foot for a distance, but Catlin escaped with only a few bruises. The successful hunt described here secured enough meat to fill five carts and load several pack horses, possibly two tons in all. The bulls and the trimmings from the cows were left for the wolves.

Kenneth McKenzie, with a gift for securing able, well-trained men, was able by exercising considerable tact, patience, and firmness to keep the Blackfeet reasonably peaceful for the next decade or so, to the benefit of the American Fur Company's trade. He even managed a short truce between the Blackfeet and the Assiniboins, the latter promising to stay east of the mouth of the Milk River and to do their trading at Fort Union. This truce lasted a year and ended abruptly when the Assiniboins made a dawn attack against a Blackfoot camp under the walls of the upriver post.

Although the Blackfeet suspended hostilities around the trading post, they were fighting with nearly everybody in sight, especially those to the south and west. When they went to war during this period, particularly against the Shoshoni, they wanted to gain more than just the honors from coups: they wanted to exterminate the enemy and take over his land—a war of conquest. This pattern comes out strongly in a study of their conduct as they advanced on the upper Missouri country, from Three Forks to the continental divide. This beautiful basin, a complex of wide, grassy valleys completely surrounded by mountain ranges, was well watered and stocked with large herds of buffalo. To seize and hold this country the Blackfeet were ready to fight against all opposition.

Although the Blackfeet had sent many war parties into this country as early as 1807, and small Piegan bands had sometimes gone up the

Missouri to Three Forks to spend the summer during the 1820's, the Shoshoni and the Columbia Basin tribes still hunted there, and disputed possession with the hostile Blackfeet. And although the Blackfeet had destroyed Lisa's post in 1810 and had roughly handled Pilcher's men in 1822, the pesky mountain men still came in from the south to trap the beaver. These included parties led by Jim Bridger, Kit Carson, Tom Fitzpatrick, and William Sublette, who often joined with the Flatheads and Nez Percé to fight off large-scale Blackfoot attacks.

Tension built up in the disputed valleys until the Blackfeet decided to join with the Gros Ventres to kill off or drive out all the interlopers on their claimed land. The spark that set off the prolonged fighting, and that made the Gros Ventres willing allies, was one of the classics of the western fur trade, the fight at Pierre's Hole in Idaho in 1832. Several villages of Gros Ventres had been south into Colorado to visit their kinsmen, the Arapahoes, and one Gros Ventre party, trying to avoid the Crow country, went west into the Snake River country. Just inside the Idaho border they collided with a body of mountain men gathering for the rendezvous. After some heavy fighting, the Gros Ventres slipped away, eastward across the rugged mountains, only to be discovered by the Crows and wiped out.

By the middle of October 1832 the Blackfeet and Gros Ventres were ready to start trouble. They ambushed Henry Vanderburgh, an American Fur Company agent, near Alder Gulch, later famous for its gold. Then they went around shooting up camps, stealing horses, and wiping out strays from parties under Bridger, Carson, Nathaniel Wyeth, Captain Benjamin de Bonneville, Andrew Drips, and Sublette. In between these activities they picked a fight with any Shoshoni or Flathead camp they could find.

One camp of Shoshoni and Bannocks, on Big Lost River, proved to be larger and tougher than the Blackfeet had expected. When the raiders retreated before superior forces and took shelter in a willow thicket, a fire chased them out to be slaughtered. Forty of the Blackfoot fighting men, and five women along to do the cooking and mend the moccasins, lost their scalps.

And so it went all through the winter and well into the spring, with the Blackfeet winning a few, losing a few, and causing plenty of trouble all around. Once they managed to surround and wipe out a hunting party of forty Flatheads, but suffered severe losses at the hands of those skilled fighters. Finally, with their ammunition running low, the Blackfeet and Gros Ventres went back to Sun River country and down to Fort McKenzie to replenish their supplies. Although they continued to fight in the upper Missouri country for the next four years, their attacks were never again so strong or so well sustained.

During this same period, 1820–37, the Blackfeet were busy in other fields. They fought against the Crows every year, with the fighting zone anywhere between the Missouri and Yellowstone rivers, with an occasional Crow raid as far west as the Sun River. Although the two tribes were bitter enemies for about a hundred years, they had occasional truces for trading purposes, for the Crow women tanned the finest buffalo robes in all the plains and the Crow warriors made the best war bonnets.

Adventurous war parties traveled far to the south, reaching New Mexico on at least one occasion, and being reported along the Cimarron in Texas in the 1820's. This seems to mark the high point of Blackfoot expansion. After their fights in the 1830's they gave up such travels.

The Blackfeet justified their attempts to keep the trappers from the Montana mountains by claiming they wanted to do all that trapping themselves, yet they were indifferent trappers, reluctant to work in the cold water to take beaver, and they did not properly care for pelts they did secure. Their yearly catch of furs could pay for only a small portion of the goods they wanted to buy at the trading post.

The Hudson's Bay Company, with trading posts in the Blackfoot country in Alberta, had never been interested in taking buffalo robes in trade. They were bulky and heavy, and worth very little by the pound compared to other furs. Transporting the robes from Alberta to the coast by canoe ate up all the profit. But the American Fur Company, from its Fort McKenzie post on the Missouri, could send its furs down the river by boat, with no portages, and could afford to buy any quantity of buffalo robes the Indians chose to bring them. The Blackfeet, in order to pay for their increased wants, soon had their women tanning thousands of extra robes each year.

Good buffalo robes were made from the hides of young cows killed in the late autumn when the new winter coat was short and thick, like plush. The fresh skins were pegged flesh side up to dry, then each one was carefully chipped with an adze-like tool until it was uniformly thin. A highly skilled Crow woman could produce a robe with the skin nearly as thin as cloth. The Blackfeet were less skillful, but their robes were of acceptable quality. The thin chips of dried skin from this process were saved and boiled for breakfast food.

The chipped skin was rubbed with brains, or a mixture of brains and liver, making it permanently soft and pliable if it did not get wet. Then the skin was carefully trimmed to remove the tags and the peg holes around the edge and was ready for use. Special skins might have some art work on the smooth, white surface, or a skin might be smoked to keep it soft and pliable even after wetting.

The finished robe weighed about ten pounds, and with reasonable care would last ten years or more. The amount of back-breaking toil involved in preparing a robe was tremendous, yet each Piegan or Blood woman was expected to prepare eight or ten each year for the trader, in addition to several for her family.

The robes were rolled up tightly in bundles of ten for transporting. The cheapest downriver freight was by a mackinaw boat with a crew of four men. This was a flat-bottomed craft with both ends pointed, about twelve feet wide by forty feet long. It was built by the workmen at the post from boards whipsawed from timber cut in the river bottom. A large sweep at each end of the boat, each sweep handled by two men, served to steer the craft, and the river current provided the motive power to carry it downstream. A mackinaw boat could carry 3,000 buffalo robes at a cost of about $2 a day, or $600 at the most for the whole voyage, 20 cents a robe. At the end of the voyage the boat was sold cheaply or was broken up for lumber.

When robes could be hauled at a profit from Fort McKenzie, 2,400 miles upstream from St. Louis, it is obvious that all the other trading posts along the Missouri could also profit from buying robes. Lewis and Clark listed about fifteen tribes that were trading robes by 1804, and some of them were also supplying buffalo tallow. The Yankton, Brulé, and Teton Sioux and the Cheyenne and Kiowa also traded dressed and smoked skins.

Buffalo fat, often called grease, oil, or tallow, found a ready market at St. Louis. In the days before petroleum wells and kerosene lamps, each family needed a large amount of tallow for candles, and a great deal more for soap, in addition to any used in cooking. Fat for candles and soap did not have to be handled too carefully or be kept as clean as cooking fats. Even its flavor was unimportant. Hence no one worried about a lack of sanitation among the Indian tribes that prepared the buffalo fat.

Along the Missouri much of the tallow was brought down the river by dugout canoes. First the canoe was emptied, cleaned, and dried. Then it was filled to the brim with melted tallow, which soon cooled and hardened, and the top covered tightly. The canoe was then towed down the river. It could not leak, nor could the cargo spill or spoil even if the rig overturned in a rapid.

The Missouri traffic in robes and dressed skins became much more important when beaver fur went out of fashion in European court circles in the 1830's, much of this fur being replaced in the manufacture of hats with silk from China. A marked increase in robes handled at St. Louis closely followed the slump in beaver handled in that market. In 1840 the American Fur Company alone shipped 67,000 buffalo robes to market, and by 1848 this number had grown to 110,000. For a few years in the 1840's the market was glutted by the enormous increase in this commodity.

In addition to the traffic in buffalo tallow, there was active trading in buffalo tongues on the Missouri. These were brined and shipped in kegs and made quite an addition to the yearly trade. In 1848 the St. Louis market reported the receipt of 25,000 tongues. Tongues were easy to harvest, and the easiest part of the buffalo to ship for food. Old buffalo bulls, which were of very little value for anything else, provided large tongues that pickled readily.

Even with the increased trade in robes, and some increase in the number of Indians hunting on the plains, the accelerated rate of killing had little effect on the size of the herds. They were forced into a smaller range year by year, but the steep decline toward total destruction did not become very noticeable until after the Civil War.

14

The Great Killer

THE SAD EXPERIENCE of the Plains tribes with the white man's diseases proved again that primitive man has little resistance to the contagions of civilization. Measles, scarlet fever, tuberculosis, and venereal diseases all took their toll of the red men, but the deadliest killer of all was smallpox. Much in the same manner as this dread plague wiped out the armies of Montezuma and paved the way for the Spanish conquest of Mexico City, it cut down the flower of the Plains warriors all along the Missouri, opening an easier path for the westward thrust of the American frontier.

Methods of smallpox vaccination developed in urban centers were not available to the Indian tribes of the upper Missouri in the 1830's, and it is doubtful that the Indians would have willingly submitted to such practices. When the Indians did come down with the disease, there was no way to give them adequate care in their tipis. Camps were normally kept clean by moving them to new locations every few days, but when smallpox struck, they had to remain in one place and soon became filthy pest holes. The white man's practice of placing the victim in isolation to live or die, and thus protect his fellows from the contagion if possible, was repugnant to the Indians.

In the summer of 1837 an especially virulent strain of smallpox came by the steamer *St. Peter* up the Missouri from St. Louis with the annual supply of trade goods for the upriver posts. It is possible that the disease was carried in some of the bales of clothing and blankets aboard; by the

[118]

time Fort Pierre was reached, people on the boat were sick with the pox. The American Fur Company, instead of delaying the boat until the victims had recovered and the boat could be fumigated, sent it on upstream, hoping to keep the Indians away from the sick. The traders feared that any long delay in the arrival of the steamer would annoy the crowds of Indians waiting at each post for their annual trading spree, and would lead to a serious loss of trade and profits.

Although the Indians at each stop were warned of the danger, they refused to believe the traders, thinking it a trick of some kind. They resorted to all sorts of stratagems to break the quarantine, sneaking on board the boat or slipping into the forbidden sections of the post, determined that they would not be put off in their attempts to trade; nor would they stay away from places they had been accustomed to visit.

At the Mandan villages one chief managed to slip aboard and reach the sick bay, where he stole a blanket from a smallpox patient lying helpless on his cot. The chief then hurried ashore and hid his loot. He refused to surrender the blanket, even in exchange for a new one. Soon the germs from the stolen blanket spread throughout the Mandan villages, and proved to be exceptionally deadly, killing many of the victims within a few hours after the first symptoms were noticed.

Panic seized the villages. The people hastily threw their dead off the nearest bluff, and many committed suicide when they thought they might be getting the pox. By the end of the summer only a few old men and some young boys, thirty in all, were left alive in the whole Mandan tribe. Across the Missouri an Arikara village also suffered great losses, as did the Hidatsa camps to the northwest.

Up the river at Fort Union two of the company men broke out with the pox, then thirty of the Indian women at the post. Although the trader locked the gates and warned the Assiniboins to keep well away from the walls, he found them stubbornly determined to trade, hanging around as close to the walls as they could get, until they too caught the disease, with fatal results for about half the tribe.

At Fort Union the supplies for Fort McKenzie were loaded on a keelboat, which also carried a few passengers. Three of these, including one Blackfoot, broke out with the pox. In an effort to keep the pox from spreading to the large bands of Piegans and Bloods that had come in for the annual trade, the boat was tied up at the mouth of the Judith River, about forty miles downstream from Fort McKenzie, so that the invalids could recover before reaching the post. When the Indians heard that the boat was being held downriver, they threatened to go and capture it if it did not come up at once. Then when the boat did arrive, the Indian customers insisted on starting trade immediately.

They secured their new goods and started back toward the hunting grounds before the pox struck. Then the epidemic started in all the camps at once and the people died in large numbers. In some camps only two or three people were left alive, often the old ones who had survived the pox of 1781.

The Crows, more sensible than the other tribes, fled from the fur post and the Yellowstone Valley at the first news of the scourge. They retreated to the mountain fastnesses high on the Wind River until October. When they did come in to trade late in the fall some of them caught the pox, but it was less deadly to them. The strain might have lost some of its virulence, or the cold weather might have given the victims a better chance to fight off the sickness. Certainly in winter their camps would be more sanitary.

At the height of the plague the Assiniboins, instead of fleeing to distant hunting grounds, stayed near Fort Union and traded every robe they could lay hands on, even those they should have kept for their own use during the coming winter. They explained that so long as they were going to die soon, they would not need the robes and might as well have what fun they could.

While most of the river tribes blamed the traders for the plague, refusing any responsibility on themselves for breaking the quarantines, the Blackfeet concluded that the pox had been sent to them as a punishment for their warlike ways, their plan to attack Fort McKenzie the coming winter, and their many far-ranging war parties, which had kept the region in a state of war for twenty years. Partly as a result of this conviction of guilt, and partly because they had lost so many of their fighting men to the pox, they abruptly ceased their aggressive attempts to take hunting grounds from other tribes. They fought no more wars of conquest and were content to withdraw from some of the fringe territory they had occupied in recent years. They gave up all claim to the Missouri Valley above the Gates of the Mountains, and even Sun Valley became a place to visit in the summer instead of a winter camping ground. Their winter camps were never put south of the Marias again, but kept near the Canadian border, about where they had been in 1807.

The withdrawal might not have been entirely voluntary. The Flatheads and Nez Percé and their allies from the Columbia Basin had escaped the plague and could now muster as many fighting men on the buffalo grounds of central Montana as could the Blackfeet. They were well armed too, buying guns from their trader friends. After 1837 the western tribes frequently came across to the Sun River to hunt, going on east another hundred miles into Judith Basin if the herds had moved away.

In Dakota the smallpox left a wide stretch of open land on both sides of the Missouri from Fort Pierre about 250 miles upstream, in country formerly claimed by the Arikara, Mandan, and Hidatsa. At the same time the Sioux in Minnesota came under heavy pressure from the advancing settlers. Year by year the Sioux reluctantly gave up some of their forest land with its fishing lakes and wild rice, and moved farther west into the buffalo country. Thus the plague was an important factor in forcing the reluctant Sioux to change from their seminomadic state into true nomads as they were able to acquire large, new buffalo ranges in Dakota to compensate for their losses in Minnesota. By 1850 they had established some claim to the Black Hills and the Powder River country.

After a buffalo run, carcasses scatter the plains. By 1884, five years after this photograph was taken, Congress had noticed that buffalo were diminishing, but no laws were made to protect the herds until 1905. (Montana Historical Society, photo by L. A. Huffman)

15

Buffalo and the Canadian Fur Traders

NORTH OF THE CANADIAN BORDER buffalo ranged from the Red River Valley in the east to the front range of the Rocky Mountains in the west, and northward until stopped by the dense coniferous forests. Canadian fur traders could approach this buffalo range from two directions, either by a series of portages from Lake Superior across to Red River, or up the swift Nelson River from Hudson Bay. Geographically the best route was up the Missouri, but that led through American territory.

Late in the seventeenth century French traders had mapped out the Grand Portage, actually a series of portages, from Lake Superior to the Red River Valley, which was a broad, flat bed of an ancient lake overgrown with grass and filled with buffalo. From the western end of the Grand Portage the French could go down the Red River into Lake Winnipeg, then west up the Saskatchewan to the Rockies. The valley of the Saskatchewan marked the approximate northern limit of the large buffalo herds, although some woods buffalo ranged farther north in the foothills. North of the Saskatchewan the forests were dense and filled with swamps and lakes. Here was excellent trapping, and this district produced furs of the finest quality. The furs from the entire

Saskatchewan–Red River drainage could be transported by water to the western end of the Grand Portage.

About the time the French began to collect furs around Lake Winnipeg, English traders formed the Hudson's Bay Company to exploit all the Hudson Bay region, including the rivers and streams emptying into the bay. They could have gone by boat and canoe up the broad, swift Nelson River to Lake Winnipeg and had all the upper country open to them if it had not been for the hostile French. For about a century the Hudson's Bay Company was content to build posts on the shores of the bay and let Indian tribes from the back country bring in the furs.

During this hundred years the French traders fought the English as their mother countries warred in Europe. When the series of European conflicts was finally resolved by the Treaty of Paris in 1763, Great Britain had secured all of Canada and the French were no longer a menace, but there was still strong rivalry between the French traders, now British subjects, working west out of Montreal, and the Hudson's Bay Company men.

About 1790 a number of Scots moved into Montreal and took over the management of much of the fur trade centered in that city. They were an intelligent, ambitious group, and when they began to divert the Saskatchewan trade to their posts, the Hudson's Bay men responded with countermeasures that in time led to open conflict. The resulting scandals reached the ears of Parliament and threatened to bring drastic action from that august body. To avoid such a catastrophe the two groups hastily compromised their differences and joined forces in 1821. The Scots gave up their Northwest Company name in return for good jobs and a share in the profits under the broad charter of the Hudson's Bay Company.

Largely as a matter of geography, the fur trade along the Saskatchewan differed in some important respects from that on the Missouri. On the Canadian side of the border the Indian tribes had no crops of any kind, and consequently no permanent farming villages where trading posts could be located to advantage. In addition, the Canadian traders lacked cheap water transportation to the world markets, although they did have adequate river travel from one post to another. While the Americans could float their furs downstream all the way to St. Louis in mackinaw boats, keelboats, and steamboats, the Canadians had to take their cargoes of furs to market in small boats and canoes, whether they went down the Nelson River to tidewater or across the Grand Portage to Lake Superior, and each route involved portages, over which the bales of fur had to be carried on the backs of men, a slow, expensive operation.

This lack of cheap transportation prevented the Canadian traders from buying the bulky buffalo robes, which were worth so little per pound. This is underscored by reports of fur shipments from the Red River district in the heart of the buffalo country. For the year 1803–04, with 105 packs of furs, 90 pounds to a pack, or a total weight of 9,450 pounds, only 18 buffalo robes were included. These were probably of some special kind, such as the rare "silk" robes. The following year, with 144 packs of furs and a weight of 12,960 pounds, there were 40 robes. This is in marked contrast with the thousands shipped along the Missouri.

The Canadian Indians were forced to do a great deal of trapping of small fur bearers to pay for all the trade goods they wanted to buy at the posts. This activity in turn kept them widely scattered in small groups in the woods during the winter, and prevented several of the tribes from becoming nomads following the buffalo on the plains the year around, although they did follow the herds in the summer and fall, putting up thousands of bags of pemmican and thousands of kegs of tallow each year for the fur posts.

The fur posts were scattered all over the area so to be accessible to the many Indian bands. A few of the posts were along the Red River and its principal tributary, the Assiniboin, while the rest were along the Saskatchewan all the way west to the Rockies. Boats and canoes brought the bales of trade goods up the rivers each spring to the posts, and returned with the packs of furs for market. These boats and canoes required a great many more men to transport goods than was required for an equal tonnage of freight on the Missouri.

Posts were located in or near the buffalo range, on a bank some thirty feet above stream level, and near a grove of timber that would supply both building logs and firewood. The people at the post had to live off the country, and also had to secure provisions for the boatmen on the river. At times too they had to feed some of the Indian bands coming in to trade. The amount of game and fish required to meet these needs reached imposing totals. Here is a list of the provisions consumed at Alexander Henry's Pembina River post from September 1, 1807, to

June 1, 1808, by 17 men, 10 women, 14 children, and 45 dogs: buffalo, 112 cows killed between September 1 and February 1, 45,000 lbs.; 35 bulls (probably killed in the spring), 18,000 lbs. (This was all usable meat, no bones, weighed at the post.) In addition there were 3 red deer, 5 bears, 4 beavers, 3 swans, 12 geese, 36 ducks, 1,150 fish, taken in nets, 775 sturgeon weighing from 50 to 150 pounds each, 410 pounds of buffalo tallow, 140 pounds of dried meat, and 325 bushels of potatoes and vegetables, the last two items from the post garden.

While the sturgeon totaled in weight about as much as the buffalo, most of the fish were given to visiting Indians. The people at the post, men, women, and children, each averaged about five pounds of buffalo meat a day for 270 days, plus some other foods, and the forty-five sled dogs ate mostly fish, but were given some of the meat—possibly a total of 20,000 pounds of food for the period.

No pemmican was mentioned in the list of food eaten at the post. This concentrated food was reserved for the boat crews or for real emergencies, and was never eaten when other food was available.

While the Indian hunters usually made a good deal of pemmican each year for their own use, some of the fur traders preferred to buy dried meat and buffalo grease separately and mix their own. At Pembina this was done early in April to have it ready for the boat brigades in the summer. Alexander Henry learned that if the pemmican was well made and carefully packed in good containers of rawhide it would keep indefinitely, even under adverse conditions: "We are now obliged to eat pemmican. I had a few bags remaining from last spring which had been lying all summer in a heap covered with a leathern tent, and had never been stirred or turned, in a damp warehouse. I was apprehensive it was spoiled . . . but was surprised to find every bag excellent . . . . I am confident that my method of mixing and preparing it is good." Henry mentioned that he used fifty pounds of dried meat to forty pounds of grease. Some of the men at his post made soap from buffalo grease.

In Alberta one of the posts had an efficient way of refrigerating buffalo meat, which enabled the hunters to kill enough buffalo in the fall when the animals were in prime condition and have this top-quality meat to eat in the spring, when some posts had to resort to killing bulls in rather poor condition. Paul Kane, a wandering artist, described the meat storage pit:

This is made by digging a square hole, capable of containing 700 or 800 buffalo carcasses. As soon as the ice in the river is of sufficient thickness, it is cut into square blocks of uniform size with saws; with these blocks the floor of the pit is regularly paved, and the blocks cemented together by pouring water between them and allowing it to freeze solid. In like manner, the walls are solidly built up to the surface of the ground. The head and feet of the buffalo, when killed are cut off, and the carcase, without being skinned, is divided into quarters, and piled in layers in the pit as brought in, until it is filled up, when the whole is covered with a thick coating of straw, which is again protected from the sun and rain by a shed. In this manner the meat keeps perfectly good through the whole summer, and eats much better than freshly killed meat, being more tender and better flavored.

Although Alexander Henry did not describe his meat storage at the Pembina post, it probably was constructed on a similar pattern, but he kept his meat only to June 1. After that the bulls around his post were in good condition again. At his post the meat for immediate use was divided into twenty standard pieces as it was carved from the carcass: two hump pieces, two strips of back fat, two shoulders, two upper shoulders, two fillets, two thighs, two sides, one belly, one rump, one brisket, one backbone, one neck, and one heart. The tongue was usually kept by the hunter, or was bought separately. The hunter could also keep the tripe, liver, kidneys, and sweetbreads if he chose.

At Pembina each winter a number of buffalo were killed almost at the gates of the post, usually when a herd moved by in a snowstorm seeking shelter in the woods to the north. Here are a few extracts from Henry's diary:

On the 22d (Dec.) the plains were covered with buffalo in every direction. I went hunting on foot with one of my men; we killed three cows. My people killed three bulls within 100 yards of the stockades, which served for our dogs.

Jan. 14th. At daybreak I was awakened by the bellowing of buffaloes . . . . On my right the plains were black, and appeared as if in motion, S. to N. . . . Our dogs were confined within the fort, which allowed the buffalo to pass within a few paces.

Jan. 15th. The plains were still covered with buffalo moving slowly northward.

Similar entries can be found each winter until about 1810, when the herds changed their pattern and wintered farther to the west.

The Red River Valley is the bed of an ancient lake, flat and treeless, with rich alluvial soil, a truly astounding place to a person raised in the barren Scottish Highlands. When Thomas Douglas, the earl of Selkirk, heard of these thousands of acres lying ready for the plow, he decided that here he would establish a colony for the many poor Scots being evicted from their Highland crofts to make way for bigger sheep runs. For ten shillings he bought the whole valley from the Hudson's Bay Company, which held the land under its charter from Charles II.

Recruiting the Scots was an easy task, but getting them out to their new land was quite another matter. Lord Selkirk brought the first contingent from Scotland to Hudson Bay, then up the Nelson River and across Lake Winnipeg, taking most of a year for the trip. He finally had the men on the land by the summer of 1812. The second contingent had a more difficult time on account of the war in Europe, and severe sickness and unnecessary hardships along the way. These Scots farmers were hardy people and willing workers, but they suffered from a lack of tools and supplies, and did not have a working knowledge of the soils and climate of this new land.

Their troubles were intensified by the enmity of the Northwest Company, which disputed the claim of the Hudson's Bay Company to the Red River Valley. Over the next few years the Northwesters shot down twenty-one of the Scots and burned some of their homes. But the Scots held on, barely surviving at times, their crops twice entirely destroyed by locusts, and their new homes swept away in a great flood. To save themselves from starvation the Scots turned to the buffalo herds for food, and with some help from the Indians many of them became skilled hunters, able to bring large supplies of dried meat, grease, and pemmican to the settlements from the herds, which now pastured far to the southwest.

The new colony received unexpected and unwelcome reinforcements from the west and north: métis. Most of them half white, half Indian, the métis were the children produced by the Northwest Company men and their Indian wives. These unfortunate people were considered a nuisance around a trading post, for they expected all the prestige and social status of their white fathers and all the privileges of spoiled Indian children. They could not settle down with their mothers' tribes because they were unwilling to conform to tribal customs, and many of the second-generation métis had métis mothers with no tribal ties. A small group of métis from the Red River Valley gathered near the new Scots settlement and the fur post at Pembina. Soon other métis came to visit them, some of them from posts several hundred miles away. They liked the place, settled, and eventually made up about half the total population.

At first the Hudson's Bay Company encouraged the métis to concentrate in one place, and offered land to those interested in settling down and learning farming, but the call of the roving life on the open plains was too strong. The métis seemed to have buffalo hunting in their blood, so they and their children and their grandchildren followed the buffalo, but not their great-grandchildren, for by that time the buffalo herds had disappeared.

Once the Hudson's Bay Company resolved its differences with the Northwest Company by absorbing it, the officers were able to make plans for the development of the Red River settlements. They wanted some industry that could use local raw materials to manufacture goods for sale in Europe at a profit. With thousands of buffalo hides going to waste each year, and tons of buffalo wool to be had for the gathering, they decided to form the Buffalo Wool Company, to weave high-grade cloth for the European upper class and to tan all the extra buffalo hides into leather.

The basic idea was sound, but gross mismanagement depleted the entire working capital in a year or so, with very few tanned hides and very few yards of woolen cloth for the market. Neither of these could be sold at a profit when produced by such wasteful methods. The cloth was warm and durable, but it could not be sold at a premium, for it was woven from dark-brown wool and could not be dyed in the fashionable shades. The project did benefit the colony, even in failure, for it brought in a supply of ready cash in wages for the settlers.

One of the Red River métis saw an opportunity for a nice profit. He went south to the Mississippi Valley near Fort Snelling and bought a herd of 300 cattle from the American settlers there. He was able to bring the animals safely to the settlement and sell them at a good profit, and in this way provided the breeding stock for both dairy and beef herds, which throve on the rich grass.

The Hudson's Bay Company then built a large new post, Fort Gary, at the mouth of the Assiniboin River, as a center for the fur trade for the whole region and as a supply depot to furnish food for all the boat crews. The post manager offered to buy a large quantity of dried meat each year, plus all the buffalo grease and tallow the hunters could furnish. This boon led to the organization of the Red River hunt, composed mostly of métis, but with a sprinkling of Scots and others. For sixty years this unique, colorful pageant roamed the western plains each summer, an important economic enterprise hidden under gaudy trappings.

The distinctive badge of the Red River hunt was the Red River cart, something of a curiosity in its own right, a small, light rig designed to be drawn by a single horse or ox. It was made entirely of local products, wood and rawhide, and was light enough to float across a stream. The basic pattern for the cart came from rural France to Montreal, and was brought west by the French Canadians. The first contemporary record of the carts was made by Alexander Henry at Pembina, September 1, 1801: "I also sent off Langlois with four men and five small carts, each drawn by one horse, loaded with three packs of goods and baggage." He described the wheels as one solid piece, sawed off the ends of trees, with a diameter of three feet. Two years later Henry estimated that one cart could haul as much as five pack horses could carry, about 800 to 1,000 pounds.

A few years later, when the métis had become more skillful at building carts, they made spoked wheels, much larger in diameter but about the same weight. The larger wheels could roll over small bumps more easily, an important advantage on the trackless plains. The wheels, solid or spoked, were fitted to an axle made from the trunk of a poplar tree, and were run without grease, for grease would pick up the fine dust so plentiful on the plains in dry weather. This mixture of dust and grease would bind the wheels to the axle, causing rapid wear and considerable friction. The ungreased wheels rubbing on the dry axles produced a terrific screech, like a thousand fingernails being scratched across a thousand windowpanes. When several hundred carts started along the trail in a body, no one needed to go ahead to announce their coming.

So closely did the Crees associate the métis with the carts that their name for the métis in sign language signified half-man, half-cart.

Alexander Ross described the métis: ". . . they possess many good qualities; while enjoying a sort of licentious freedom, they are generous, warm-hearted, and brave, and left to themselves, quiet and orderly. They are, unhappily, as unsteady as the wind in all their habits, fickle in their dispositions, credulous in their faith, and clannish in their affections."

For the big summer hunt each man liked to take two carts to bring back his meat and grease. He also needed a horse or an ox to pull each cart, a buffalo horse, a gun, many rounds of ammunition, camp gear, and a small supply of food for the trip out to the buffalo. The rest of the summer he expected to live well on meat. A provident man might own all or most of these needed items, many had about half of them, and at the bottom of the scale were the shiftless, lazy ones who owned nothing at all, yet had to go on the hunt or starve. These people went through the settlement begging, borrowing, going heavily into debt, and promising double prices in order to get the needed credit. The higher prices bothered these lazy borrowers not at all, for they seldom paid back more than a part of the debt before asking for more credit from the same person.

About the middle of May the hunters began their preparations for the start on June 15. At that time most of the carts started out promptly, with a few stragglers racing madly to catch up. The caravan made an imposing sight, with several hundred carts in the line and a large herd of stock, the buffalo horses, and the spare draft animals being driven alongside the trail. On a large hunt the men and women totaled the number of carts, with about half that many dogs, a third that many buffalo horses, and a fourth that many children. Most of the children were left in the settlement with relatives. About a third of the hunters had no buffalo horses. They were too poor to own one and too shiftless to be trusted with a borrowed one. They expected to secure their meat by begging from the good hunters, or gleaning from the carcasses abandoned after a big kill.

Once the buffalo were sighted, the hunters rode out in a body and killed as many as possible the first day, even though they could not save the meat from more than half of them. After a successful hunt the camp spent most of the next day drying the meat, then went hunting again. If only small herds were sighted, only a few of the hunters went out each time, but such smaller hunts might be made each day while the buffalo were near. In three weeks of good hunting, a rare occurrence, enough meat could be secured to fill all the carts, but most of the time the carts went back partly empty.

In 1840 the hunt went well, and the 1,210 carts returned, each loaded to capacity, with a total of about 1,008,000 pounds of dried meat and grease, pemmican, and tallow. This was the equivalent of about 4 million pounds of fresh meat, or 7,000 buffalo. Alexander Ross, who was with this hunt, estimated that as much meat was wasted as was used.

Of this imposing stock of meat and grease, Fort Gary took 150,000 pounds, most of it in payment for goods charged out to the hunters for the trip. Another large portion went to pay the people in the settlements who had extended credit in the form of horses, oxen, and carts. The remainder was soon devoured in a series of feasts for all the friends and relatives of the hunters, who sat idle as long as there was a bite left. Then they had to rustle around and prepare for the fall hunt if they expected to have any meat for the winter.

Improvident families returning from the fall hunt often were entirely out of meat in a few days, and had to start out at once for the hunting grounds, 250 miles away by 1840, in hopes of killing enough buffalo to carry them through the winter. If the herds shifted their range, as they often did, or if a severe blizzard blew in, the little bands might lose several of their number. One winter thirty-three died before rescuers could find their snowbound camp.

In spite of all the hardships and privations of this life, the métis would try no other. To them the freedom and excitement more than compensated for the dangers and sufferings. Perhaps the dangers were an important part of the charm. Each succeeding generation of métis raised its children in the same pattern and in the same environment, so the number of dedicated hunters grew year by year until they presented a serious problem to the community and to the government, a problem that became very serious as the buffalo herds dwindled and moved farther and farther away. The more restless of the métis moved on west following the retreating herds and for a few years lived near the Montana border in the Cypress Hills, with one camp in central Montana in the Judith Basin, but they all had to leave when the last of the buffalo were killed in 1883.

After Canada gained dominion status in 1867, the métis made strong demands for equality with the whites. They were led by the fiery Louis Riel, a métis who had failed in his studies to become a priest. They demanded equality of citizenship, with education for their children and training for them in the crafts and professions. They resented being barred from equal rights because they had some Indian blood, and being refused any of the treaty payments and land settlements given to the Indians on account of their white blood.

With no more buffalo herds to follow, the métis squatted on lands along the South Saskatchewan River, laying out their claims in long, narrow strips, each with a small river frontage, as the farms were laid out along the St. Lawrence River. When the government surveyors arrived to lay out the permanent boundaries, they insisted on the standard gridiron type of land plots, to the dismay of the métis, already disturbed by the end of the buffalo hunting.

Early in 1885 the métis began organizing for resistance and invited Louis Riel to come back from his exile in Montana, where he had fled for safety after some earlier trouble. Riel set up a provisional government at Batoche and seized government stores at Duck Lake, killing twelve Northwest Mounted Police in the process. The Canadian government brought in an army from eastern Canada and overwhelmed a force of 500 métis and 500 Indian allies on May 12, 1885. Louis Riel was captured and after a stormy trial was found guilty and hanged on November 16, 1885, thus achieving martyrdom in the eyes of many French Canadians.

16

The Oregon and California Trails

FROM THE EASTERN SLOPE of South Pass, Wyoming, the little streams drain off into the Sweetwater River, then into the Platte, and eventually into the Missouri, hundreds of miles to the east. The gentle slope of the streams, their broad valleys, and their rather direct easterly courses combine to make this an inviting way for the traveler. The Platte River, with its strong flow of water from the mountains, gliding down a broad valley with no canyons, falls, or even bad rapids along its course, seemingly should be a good route for water-borne traffic, comparable to the Missouri. But the Platte carries such a volume of sand from its upper reaches that its bed consists of a multitude of sand bars, over which the water flows in trickles, sometimes four miles from bank to bank, but only an inch or two deep.

During the spring floods, it was sometimes possible to take boats of shallow draft down the river, but no one would attempt to go up the Platte in either a boat or a canoe. Even for boats riding on the spring flood, sand bars could be quite a problem. Robert Stuart, on his way from Astoria to St. Louis, had this experience with dugout canoes on the North Platte in March 1813:

Breakfasting at an early hour we embarked but on descending a few hundred yards found the water so low that Mr. McClellan and myself went by land hoping thereby that the Canadians would be able to proceed. The other canoe being small went on tolerably; but it was with very considerable labour in wading and dragging that ours got down eight miles by the middle of the afternoon . . . . To the Fork we went on well, but immediately below the river became much wider and so shallow that it was with great exertion we reached another Pen on the left bank, seven miles below our last station . . . being very doubtful whether we can in any reasonable time proceed by water, it was agreed we should try it once more on foot . . . the river running . . . so shallow as makes us happy at having abandoned our canoes for its bed is for the most part upwards of a mile wide and the sand bars so numerous and flat it would require more water than we have any right to expect to make it fit our purposes.

In some years flat-bottomed boats could get down the river on the spring flood, but it was hard going:

We started in a Mackinaw boat which had been made at the foot of the mountains . . . thirty-six feet long and eight feet wide. We had several hundred buffalo robes on board and four hundred buffalo tongues . . . . The water was very shallow and we proceeded with great difficulty, getting on sand bars every few minutes. We were obliged to push the boat most of the way for three hundred miles which took us forty-nine days.

This is the most successful voyage on the Platte for which a good account is given.

Even when the river was in full flood, the problems were there. John Charles Frémont, an officer in the United States Topographical Corps, recorded a party's misadventures on the river in late April 1842.

Sixty days since they had left the mouth of Laramie's Fork, some three hundred miles above, in barges laden with the furs . . . . They started with the annual flood, and drawing but nine inches of water, hoped to make a speedy voyage . . . but after a lapse of forty days, found themselves 130 miles from their point of departure. They came down rapidly as far as Scott's Bluffs, where their difficulties began. Sometimes . . . they toiled from morning until night, making only two or three miles in as many days. Sometimes they would enter an arm of the river, where there appeared a fine channel, and after descending prosperously for eight or ten miles, would come suddenly upon dry sands, and be compelled to return, dragging their boat for days against the rapid current . . . finding the Platte growing every day more shallow they discharged their cargoes . . . and leaving a few men to guard them, attempted to continue their voyage, laden with some light furs and their personal baggage. After fifteen or twenty days more struggling in the sands, during which they made but 140 miles, they sunk their barges . . . and commenced their journey on foot to St. Louis.

At times a boat caught on a sand bar might have other problems. This is from Francis Parkman in 1846:

Fifty times a day the boats had been aground; indeed, those who navigate the Platte invariably spend half their time upon the sand bars. Two of the boats . . . got hopelessly involved in some shallows, not very far from the Pawnee villages, and were soon surrounded by a swarm of the inhabitants. They carried off everything they thought valuable, including most of the robes, and amused themselves by tying up the men left on guard, and soundly whipping them with sticks.

Even this kind of boating was possible only in the spring and early summer. The large amount of furs brought east each year from the rendezvous usually came across South Pass and down the Platte Valley in August, and no attempt was made to use boats at that season of low water. The furs came by pack train and wagon all the way from the rendezvous to Westport on the Missouri.

While the Platte River presented obstacles to boatmen, pack trains and wagon trains found the broad, sandy valley a good highway that needed no grading or bridges. Even though the river carried a large flow of water, it was so wide wagons could ford it at several places, although they had to keep moving to avoid sticking in the sand.

Heading for California in 1849 to prospect for gold, J. Goldsborough Bruff noted in his journal:

My New York friends got all their train over without an accident, except one wagon, which sank so in the sand that they had to leave it for the day. It was about fifty yards from shore, and about 400 below the landing and the camp, and contained a sick man. It looked queer to see a man wading down the stream, waist deep in the rapid river, with a pot of coffee in one hand and a plate of bread and meat in the other, going to the wagon, to the relief of his comrade.

The next morning a team of twelve mules dragged the wagon out.

The river was turbid with a heavy load of sediment, but the water was drinkable and the low banks posed no problem to the draft animals going down to drink. In this respect the Platte route differed greatly from the Santa Fe Trail, with its miles of desert between water holes for most of the year.

The Platte River attracted the wagon trains, for it led directly to South Pass, where the wagons could cross the continental divide with little difficulty. Then they crossed the Green River country into the upper Snake Valley and on to Oregon. The Platte was the boundary between lands claimed by the hunting tribes, so travelers along its banks did not have to cross any of the tribal hunting grounds. However, they were in the path of raiding parties using the north-south trails.

Minor Indian troubles developed along the eastern end of the Oregon Trail, from the Kansas River crossing for about 250 miles northwest to the Platte near Fort Kearney. This stretch was divided about equally between the Kaws and the Pawnees, and both tribes made it a practice to rob lone travelers or small groups. The Kaws in 1839 drove the buffalo away from the main trail to keep the travelers from doing their own hunting and force them to purchase meat from the Indians.

The Pawnees, to the northeast, were more numerous and more troublesome than the Kaws, but they seldom killed any travelers. They stole horses and cattle, and robbed small groups. Neither tribe paid much attention to the fur traders passing with their outfits, going to the mountains in May and returning in late summer. The fur men were on their guard and understood Indians quite well, and were let alone.

But in 1839 a new kind of wagon train started west along the trail, the first to take families in covered wagons to new homes on the Pacific coast. With women and children in the wagons and milk cows ranging alongside, this train was obviously different, and the people acted differently. They were more careless about guarding their stock, showed an unfamiliarity with the problems and dangers of the trail, and could be intimidated quite easily by a show of force.

Indian tribes on the plains regarded all strangers as possible enemies, and had no scruples about stealing from them. Hence any Indian visiting a wagon train or camp felt free to appropriate any unguarded article that caught his fancy. Stealing horses from a stranger was a long-established custom, almost an obligation, and once the Indians started eating cattle, these animals were added to the list of desirable items. Thus, in taking advantage of passing strangers on tribal lands, the Indians were not displaying actual hostility, although now and again they might kill a stray or two.

Usually the Indian objective in a raid on a wagon train was to secure as many horses and cattle as possible without losing any warriors. Parkman recorded this account of a raid as told to him a week later:

> They had . . . encamped by the side of the Platte, and their oxen were scattered over the meadow, while the horses were feeding a little farther off. Suddenly the ridges were alive with a swarm of mounted Indians, at least six hundred in number, who came pouring with a yell down toward the camp . . . suddenly wheeling, they swept toward the band of horses, and in five minutes disappeared with their prey . . . .

The 600 warriors was a hasty estimate by excited people.

Roving bands of warriors made it their practice to stop small parties of two or three men and take any of their belongings that looked interesting, usually the horses first, and people who resisted might get killed, as in this case which Parkman cited: "Two men, at a distance from the rest, were seized by the Pawnees, but, lashing their horses, they broke away and fled. At this the Pawnees raised the yell and shot at them, transfixing the hindmost through the back with several arrows."

Through this period Pawnee war parties along the trail were usually estimated at 200 men, possibly because the later travelers had heard that number from earlier reports. Some travelers suggested that the tribe kept a force of that size near the trail most of the season to plunder the weak and to levy toll in the form of tobacco, food, or a beef animal, in payment for permission to pass. One traveler, Joseph Williams, reported that "about two hundred Indians . . . had robbed four men of all they had, stripped them naked, and left them on the open prairies to perish."

The following incident was recorded in the Bruff journals:

Met Mr. Hughes with a wagon and five men . . . . He said that two days ago a little above the old Pawnee Village he was attacked by a war party of 500 Cheyennes, who robbed him of all his provisions. I sold him 30 pounds of flour, 20 of bacon, and six of sugar. He stated that they came down on him, when he halted, closed his wagons, and stood his men to their arms. Perceiving this, the chief with three or four other Indians rode over, with a white flag tied to a rifle, and he went out to meet them. The chief spoke Spanish, and said it was folly . . . to attempt repelling the Indians by force, and he might just as well give up his provisions and save their lives— This he had to do—as the Indians rode up and pillaged his wagons— After which they threw down some beadwork, moccasins, sashes, etc.—telling Mr. Hughes that there was pay for the provisions they had taken.

These Indians were well behaved. They offered no violence or insult, and were under no obligation, by the Indian code, to offer any payment whatever. They also, with an overpowering force, could have wiped out the whites and taken everything, but they might have lost a man or two, a price the chief dared not pay if he valued his reputation as a war leader. Here is another incident that occurred in the same area:

The Pawnees commenced gathering around us, they seemed to rise from the earth on both sides as far as the eye can distinguish them. I divided my mounted men in two parties, one as an advance guard and the other as a rear guard . . . . If the Pawnees had made a demonstration, we would most assuredly have *made* some ponies. But Alas, the great warriors, arabs and terror of the plains, turned out to be a sadly reduced, starving, contemptible race. They begged me for bread, opened their dingy robes, and exhibited their prominent ribs and breast-bones. As they were actually starving, famine might drive them to rob and break up some small party, maybe family, in the rear, and we had plenty; so I ordered a halt, gave the Indians about a peck of hard bread, half a middling of bacon, and a hat full of tobacco. They spread a skin on the plain, by the roadside on which was placed the bread, etc, some of my boys threw in bells and other trinkets . . . .

These two incidents from the Bruff journals could be matched many times over from other journals and diaries of the trail, except for minor details. They illustrate the difference in treatment accorded to a well-guarded train and one too small to be out in the Indian country. Indian begging, especially by individuals and small family groups, was quite common along the trail just beyond the Kansas River crossing. Here one party doled out dimes, as they did not expect to need such small coins again. Often the Indians led up to their begging by first making a small present. This incident happened on the North Platte:

> I found at my tent two young warriors, one of whom presented me with a piece of buffalo meat, which like all Indian gifts cost me in presents double its value. He commenced by begging for bread, meat, and whiskey . . . . He very soon left, but not without getting a little whiskey, which he cooly put into the tripe of a buffalo which he had killed that day . . . . What the taste of it could have been by the time he drank it will not be very difficult to imagine.

Other instances of Indian conduct along the trail before 1851 indicate that the Indians had little malice toward the whites, and allowed many small parties to pass unmolested. The Mormon handcart migration, composed of small groups of young men with their supplies and camp gear in small handcarts, attracted some attention, but no enmity. These men, too poor in the Indian's eyes to afford horses to ride, or even an ox to pull the cart, were not worth plundering.

Then there was the odd solitary traveler on the North Platte. Madison Berryman Moorman wrote in his journal on July 3: "We passed also a fat-faced, simple looking, good natured and recently imported German, who started from St. Jo afoot—driving a cow, packed with his little budget. He was moving on finely and said he used the milk of the cow night and morning. He looked stout enough to stand the trip. . . ."

Once the wagons started rolling along the trail in large numbers, some of the Kaw Indians put in small toll bridges on the creeks near their villages. These streams were tributaries of the Big Blue River. Moorman wrote that "across one of the creeks were two bridges, such as they were, belonging to two Indian youths who were dressed very gaudily . . . . One asked five cents, and the other, ten. The one who asked ten cents would point out the defects in the other's bridge, the rival would speak of the difference in price. We decided on the best bridge and over we went."

Although these streams were rather small, it was worth a dime a wagon to use a bridge during the spring rains. Another entry was made by Moorman in his journal:

> We made an early start and made but one mile in an hour and a half; one of those difficult and muddy little creeks crossing our road, at which Patterson and Henkle's wagon turned over making a smash of the bows and throwing many of the contents into the water . . . . Two other streams were crossed by fastening a rope to the aft of the wagon and holding it back off the heels of the mules . . . . To ascend the opposite bank, teams were doubled, and the rope . . . was tied to the end of the wagon tongue and all hands laid hold with might and main . . . to draw it up, the bank being so slippery as to make it difficult for the mules to keep their feet.

The early wagon trains, before 1849, depended on securing plenty of fresh buffalo meat along the trail as far as South Pass, but they dried very little meat, depending on their bacon for a reserve. There was always great excitement when the first buffalo were sighted, an excitement shared by the horses and cattle. Loose stock often had a great urge to run off with the buffalo, never to be seen again. Occasionally one would be recaptured later, by lucky accident. Alexander Henry, out hunting near Pembina, had such luck one day. He found a black horse that had been lost a month earlier and had been feeding with the buffalo ever since.

Kit Carson was once thrown by his horse during a buffalo hunt. The horse managed to scramble to its feet and run away before Carson could catch his breath. A comrade pursued the horse and was about to shoot it in order to rescue the fine Spanish bridle, but was able to catch the runaway instead.

Mules also tried to escape. John Frémont reported that "one of our mules took a freak into his head, and joined a neighboring band of buffalo today. As we were not in condition to lose horses, I sent several of the men in pursuit . . . but we did not see him again."

At times, Frémont wrote, the buffalo reversed the procedure: "There were seven or eight buffaloes seen coming up with our oxen . . . they seemed to form an attachment for each other."

One day Frémont and his men stopped to cut some meat from a buffalo they had killed after quite a chase. "We neglected to secure our horses, thinking it an unnecessary precaution in their fatigued condition; but our mule took it into his head to start, and away he went, followed at full speed by the pack horse. . . . They were recovered and brought back, after a chase of a mile."

In Kansas a caravan forced to march until midnight found the buffalo along the trail a problem. Obadiah Oakley, bound for Oregon in 1839, recorded this incident:

> At night their progress was greatly retarded by the herds of buffalo which lined the road and covered the plain. They were as thick as sheep were ever seen in a field, and moved not until the caravan was within ten feet of them. They would then rise and flee at random, greatly affrighted, and snorting and bellowing to the equal alarm of the horses and mules.

If the herds were moving at night instead of resting, they could be a serious problem to any camp in their path. While this account by Frémont comes from Dakota, well to the north of the Oregon Trail, it illustrates the problem:

> Toward nightfall we found near the shore good water and made there our camp on open ground. Nothing disturbed our rest for several hours, when we were aroused by a confused, heavy trampling and the usual grunting sounds which announce the buffalo. We had barely time to get our animals close in, and to throw on dry wood and stir up the fire, before the herd was upon us. They were coming in to the lake for water, and the near ones being crowded forward by those in the rear and disregarding us, they were nigh going directly over us. By shouting and firing our pieces, we succeeded in getting them to make a little space, in which they kept us as they crowded down to the lake. The brackish, salty water is what these animals like, and to turn the course of such a herd from water at night would be impossible.

At times along the Platte, women with the wagons shouted and waved their aprons to keep the buffalo away from their cooking fires while their men folk were out on the hills dashing madly over the rough country hoping to get a shot at one of the animals. Men new to the plains were heedless and reckless in the heat of the chase. One train captain, Bruff, had this comment on the hunting his men did:

The casualties of buffalo hunting are very common. Men charg'd by wounded bulls, unhorsed, and many badly hurt—the horses generally running off with the band of buffaloes, for the Indians to pick up hereafter. Lots of rifles and pistols lost, as well as horses; and many a poor fellow, after a hard day's hunt, on an empty stomach, unhorsed some distance from camp, has a long and tiresome walk, after night, to his own, or the nearest camp he can make.

Each year the wagon trains moved up the Platte Valley, hemmed in between the low bluffs and the river. For a month or more they plodded along from Fort Kearney to Fort Laramie, and each year their numbers grew. The trail became rutted, the remains of campfires marked the middle of large bare patches of ground where the hungry draft animals had cropped the grasses to their roots. The buffalo herds moved away to the south, leaving the river valley empty for most of May and June. The herds that did come down to the river for water during that period were usually stampeded by the mad rush of excited men anxious to kill them.

As the wagons rolled along the valley floor, bands of warriors—Pawnee, Sioux, Cheyenne, and Arapaho—watched from the hills, or approached to demand food and tobacco or to steal any stock carelessly guarded. The Indians did not seem to be deeply disturbed by the invasion, perhaps because none of the whites tried to settle along the trail.

Then came the spring of 1849, and the Indians recoiled aghast at the mad rush of wild-eyed gold seekers bound for California. For several weeks the trail was filled from one end of the valley to the other with an almost unbroken line of canvas-topped wagons during the day, while hundreds of campfires dotted the river bank each night. From the east they came, in a seemingly endless flood—40,000 people, 50,000 draft animals, 12,000 wagons, mixed with a few individuals or small groups leading pack animals.

The vanguard of the marching columns started from the west bank of the Missouri in early May, as soon as the new grass had sprouted on the prairies, and the last stragglers brought up the rear at Fort Laramie in early July. The swarming horde left the valley one vast waste of rutted trails, littered camp sites, broken wagons, discarded goods, and carcasses of oxen and horses fallen by the wayside. Fortunately for the draft animals, the rains were abundant that year, making for very good pasture, but even so, hardly a blade of grass was left from the river to the crest of the hills. Draft animals from some of the later trains were herded as much as eight miles from the trail, there to feed and rest for a few days, building strength against the rugged terrain and scanty pasture ahead.

Buffalo and antelope fled from the valley. In other summers the herds had moved just beyond the crest of the hills, but this summer the hunters often had to ride twenty miles or more to the south in search of fresh meat. No longer could the travelers depend on the herds for a freshly killed animal every day or so on the 400 miles of trail along the Platte. Once in a while a small herd did wander into the valley in search of water, but left hastily when the hunters swarmed out in pursuit. Even after the last of the wagons had passed and the trail lay open under the summer sun, the wide, barren strip had little appeal for grazing animals.

The summer of 1850 brought even greater crowds along the trail to California, and the scanty rainfall that year made the pasture problem more acute. Although this summer marked the peak of the gold rush to California, a succession of rich gold and silver strikes throughout the northwest and in Colorado and Nevada brought treasure hunters in large numbers for the next fifteen years. Farmers eager for new lands and hoping to raise food for the new mining towns, and many other settlers looking for adventure or a new life in the west, swelled the ranks.

Stage and freight lines were established to carry people and supplies to the boom towns. With these vehicles moving both west and east, the trail was busy until late October. Year by year the Platte Valley became a place for buffalo to avoid at all seasons.

Friction between the Indians along the trail and the intruding whites increased greatly with the increased travel, and demands were made that the army send troops to protect the travelers. At the same time Indian problems in several other areas were demanding attention from federal officials.

Until 1849 all Indian affairs had been handled by the army through the Bureau of Indian Affairs in the Department of War. It was decided to replace the military control with civilian officials under the new Department of the Interior, in hopes that these new men could take a broader, long-range view of the problem.

The major source of trouble for travelers in the buffalo country was the roving war parties of various tribes going forth to raid their enemies. The Indians were out for glory and loot, and any depredations they might commit on the hunting grounds of another tribe should, by Indian logic, be charged against that tribe, whose duty it was to police its own lands. Hence Indians who would be peaceful and friendly toward whites visiting the tribal villages felt free to raid the same whites later on when they had passed onto lands claimed by another tribe. Even in lands claimed by no tribe, disgruntled warriors returning from an unsuccessful raid might plunder a small train rather than go home empty-handed.

The Indian Bureau decided to ask each tribe to delineate the boundaries of its tribal lands, then promise to stay within those boundaries. If the Indians agreed, this would put a stop to the roving war parties, and would reveal large areas of land claimed by no tribe, open to all travel at no risk. As far as possible, trails would be routed through the unclaimed spaces. When a route had to cross tribal land, a yearly payment could be made for the use of the trail and for the land necessary to establish a few army posts along the way.

To implement this plan, the old fur trader and mountain man Thomas ("Broken Hand") Fitzpatrick was sent to Fort Laramie in 1851. There he held a great council with all the buffalo hunters of the northern plains from Canada to the Arkansas River and west to the continental divide in Wyoming and Montana. The Indians came in by the thousands —Sioux and Cheyenne, Crow, Arapahoe and Gros Ventre, Wind River Shoshoni, and even remnants of the once powerful Arikara.

The Crows objected when the Sioux claimed the Powder River country, which had been Crow hunting grounds for a century or more until the Sioux moved west in force a decade earlier. For the rest, the boundaries were rather easily set, with Fitzpatrick attempting no objections or adjustments. At the end of the council all the tribes had concluded treaties. So successful was this council that several others were held throughout the west, and similar treaties were negotiated with most of the western tribes.

Treaties signed at Fort Laramie made traveling much safer for the white men in the lands of the Sioux, northern Cheyenne, and northern Arapahoe. The peaceful interlude lasted about eight years, and may be illustrated by a brief account of an elaborate hunting expedition conducted by an Irish nobleman, Sir St. George Gore, who spent three years on the plains with buffalo as his chief quarry while some of his companions made scientific observations on the fauna and flora.

In the spring of 1854 Gore assembled a large party at Fort Leavenworth, well equipped for a lengthy stay away from the settlements. He had about seventy-five rifles of many sizes and kinds, most of them made to order, and twelve shotguns for birds and small game. He took along about fifty good riding horses for running buffalo, and a large pack of greyhounds and staghounds to chase wolves, coyotes, and antelope. Seventy-four horses, mules, and oxen hauled the twenty-one carts and six large wagons with the supplies and gear, and three milk cows trailed along to provide the milk and butter.

After a leisurely trip up the Platte River, Gore spent the fall hunting on the slopes of the Colorado Rockies, returning to Fort Laramie for the winter. Here he met Jim Bridger and hired him to be his chief guide. In the spring Bridger led the party north to Powder River and on down to the Yellowstone. A fort for the coming winter was built on the Tongue River, but Gore and Bridger preferred to live a few miles away near the Yellowstone where grass for the horses was very good and the hunting excellent. They went out nearly every day with their horses and dogs and killed a great deal of game of many kinds.

Some fuss was made by the Indians that the white men were wasting a great deal of meat by killing so many animals for trophies. Gore's total of 2,000 buffalo is imposing, but this covered a period of three years, and his party of fifty, with their large pack of hunting dogs, could eat the meat from several hundred animals in that time. It is probable that the Gore party had a higher rate of usage for their game than most sportsmen in the west, and about as good as any band of Indians over a like period.

Summer and winter, Gore hunted nearly every day and brought in plenty of game, although his daily hunting schedule was something of a scandal to an old mountain man who liked to be out at the crack of dawn and have the day's work taken care of by dark. Gore slept until midmorning, then ate a leisurely breakfast about eleven or twelve o'clock. Rested and fed, he started out about midday, and it might be long after dark before he got back to camp with his trophies.

In his snug tent at night Gore would often read to Bridger from Shakespeare or Baron Münchhausen. Jim allowed that the obese Falstaff drank too much beer and that he would have done much better by taking the same amount of alcohol in whisky. Jim did not believe everything the baron wrote, although he did say that some of his own exploits with the Blackfeet might seem as wild if put into a book.

Gore spent three years in the Indian country, more than a year of it in the Powder River area, which was such a trouble spot during the next two decades, and reported no trouble from any of the tribes he met, a record for which Jim Bridger deserves much of the credit, but at least some part of the peaceful conditions of this period, 1854–57, resulted directly from the council at Fort Laramie.

Michel Pablo surveys his buffalo rounded up for shipment to Canada. In 1900 more than 80 percent of the buffalo in the United States could be traced to the herd Pablo and Charles Allard had bought and raised. (Montana Historical Society, photo by N. A. Forsyth)

When the U.S. refused to buy the Pablo herd, he shipped it for sale to the Canadian government. Driving and loading the buffalo was a wild and woolly affair, but this stubborn bull finally met his end. (Montana Historical Society, photo by N. A. Forsyth)

17

Comanche Wars for the Southern Buffalo Range

"THE COMANCHE MEN ARE SHORT AND STOUT . . . on foot they are slow and awkward, but on horseback graceful."

"The men are about medium stature, with bright, copper-colored complexions and intelligent countenances, in many instances with aquiline noses, thin lips, black eyes and hair, with but little beard."

"The appearance of a Comanche fully equipped on horseback, with his lance and quiver and shield by his side is beautifully classic."

The women usually wore "a gown or slip that reaches from the chin quite down to the ankles, made of deer or elkskins," and, by one soldier's estimate, were good looking. The men were generally bare except for moccasins, leggings, and breechclout, and were "fine looking."

These are independent observations, cited by Rupert N. Richardson, of three of the men who accompanied Colonel G. M. Dodge and his dragoons on a visit to a large Comanche village near the Arkansas River in the summer of 1834. They found the Comanches peaceful and friendly, feasting on the fat of the land, for the buffalo were in prime condition and so numerous along the river that at times they were a nuisance, even a danger. George Catlin recorded the following:

> In one of these spirited scenes when the regiment were on the march, and the Indians with their bows and arrows were closely

plying a band of affrighted animals, they made a bolt through the line of dragoons, and a complete break, through which the whole herd passed, upsetting horses and riders in the most amusing manner, and receiving such shots as came from those guns and pistols that were aimed, and not fired into the empty air.

On another occasion,

> . . . the poor beasts seem completely bewildered, running here and there, and as often as otherwise come singly advancing to the horsemen, as if to join them, and are easily shot down. In the turmoil and confusion, when their assailants have been pushing them forward, they have galloped through our encampment, jumping over fires, upsetting pots and kettles, driving horses from their fastenings and throwing the whole cantonment into the greatest consternation and alarm.

But even in this fine buffalo country the herds would wander off from their accustomed ranges and be gone for weeks at a time, and the Comanche hunters would return to camp empty-handed. Even after two centuries of following the herds for their living the Indians were unable to predict their movements according to any regular pattern. With the buffalo absent, the hunters chased and killed horses from the many wild herds all about and thus kept the camp supplied with fresh meat until the buffalo reappeared. Only in times of real distress did the Comanches kill and eat any of their own stock.

Far to the south in Texas the Comanche bands were much less friendly and less prosperous than these along the Arkansas. A Texan who showed no appreciation for any Indians, and who seemed to have a special apathy for Comanches, visited a southern village:

> . . . we found the village of the principal chief to be filled with naked, half-starved savages; and one of the very lowest of the human species. They appeared to be but one removed from the brute creation . . . . They were badly armed—not having more than six or eight guns in the village, and were but indifferent marksmen . . . . They have about five hundred horses and mules, some of very good quality . . . . The women are destitute of even the semblance of virtue, and the men as corrupt as the females are degraded.

This village was in poorer hunting country and bordered by unfriendly white settlers. These two accounts give some indication of the wide expanse of the Comanche lands, the varying quality of their hunting grounds, and the diversity to be found in widely separated bands of one tribe. In fringe areas with scanty buffalo herds, the conduct of a Comanche band toward a body of white visitors might depend on the extent of the whites' competition for the buffalo.

Once the Comanche tribe had become firmly established on the plains, it had the continuing problem of protecting its new hunting grounds against enemy attacks and intrusions from all sides, for there were no natural barriers to block raiders and the possession of good buffalo country was essential to the very existence of the tribe.

A secondary problem for the tribe, especially in the nineteenth century, was that of securing guns, ammunition, and an adequate supply of trade goods from a reliable source. This problem of trade with the outside world was complicated by the shortage of commercial furs in Comanche lands. While the tribe could produce a large supply of buffalo robes and dressed skins each year, only a small number could be marketed; but the traders gladly paid with their goods for Comanche horses. Comanche attempts to protect their buffalo lands and secure trade goods strongly influenced their relationships with all their neighbors, and help explain their seemingly inconsistent pattern of behavior toward whites in various places around the tribal domain.

The Comanche trade meant very little to the Texas settlements to the southeast, for the settlers had no use for Comanche horses when they were raising a surplus of their own, and they were understandably reluctant to sell guns and ammunition to their enemy. Over a long period the Comanches had been making occasional raids on these settlements, lifting a scalp here and there, picking up a captive woman or child, and running off stock. When the Anglo-Americans moved into Texas in large numbers at the invitation of the Mexican government, they settled along the outer edge of the settlements, encroaching on Comanche lands, and thus bore the brunt of the Comanche attacks.

After Texas secured its independence in 1836, both the Texans and the Comanches knew that they would profit greatly from a permanent peace on the border, but the many attempts at securing a formal treaty always failed. The Texans insisted that the Comanches stay far from the settlements, behind a boundary along the western and northern limits of the pioneer advance. The Comanches demanded a boundary farther to the south and east, which would permit them to continue hunting on some of their best buffalo country along the Colorado River, and they wanted the Texas officials to give a binding promise that no Texan would cross the boundary without Comanche permission. But the officials would make no such promise. They wanted the boundary to work just one way, against the Indians, and they were both unwilling and unable to halt the westward push of their people.

The border problem was complicated further when the smallpox scourge of 1837 finally reached the Comanche country. In May 1838 the Indians wiped out a trading party of fifteen suspected of deliberately introducing the disease into one of their villages. Later that year all peaceful communications were broken off for several months when the Texans treacherously attacked sixty-five Comanche delegates attending a meeting on a specific invitation. Thirty-five of the Comanches were killed, and the rest were taken prisoner. A retaliatory raid by a large Comanche force proved costly to both sides. Later a force of Texans made a surprise attack on a small Comanche village, killing or capturing every person. All captured Comanches were sold as slaves.

In this fighting on the Texas border and other places the Comanches showed great ability as raiders fighting in small groups, but they were rather ineffective in a large war party. They lacked the discipline, training, and organization to win a pitched battle against a force of trained soldiers. It is probable that the unwillingness of the Comanche individual to accept firm control, even from a war leader, was the key factor. Hence a large Comanche war party acted like a disorganized mob, and they were further handicapped by a shortage of good guns.

Along the northeastern border the Comanches lost a wide strip of their buffalo grounds to the better-organized and better-armed Osages and their allies, the Wichitas. As the federal government continued to move Indian tribes from the southeastern states into Indian Territory, the Osages welcomed the newcomers as allies in taking over more of the plains country and in beating back the Comanches. On the north, just across the Arkansas River, the Comanches were driven back by a large force of Cheyennes and Arapahoes in a bloody battle in 1838.

With such aggressive enemies encroaching on Comanche lands on three sides, the tribe had little time, energy, or inclination to attack the wagon trains on the Santa Fe Trail. Also, they wanted to remain friendly with the traders so they could buy goods from them each year.

In 1840, after the Texas border had erupted into more fighting, the Comanches met with the Cheyennes and Arapahoes near Bent's Fort on the Arkansas and negotiated a lasting treaty with them, with the Arkansas marking the boundary line between the hunting grounds of the two groups. Then in 1843 they even agreed on a treaty with the Osages, and a brisk trade sprang up between the two tribes. The Comanches brought in large herds of horses stolen on the Texas frontier, more horses and some mules from the Mexicans, and a few captives from both groups. In return the Osages gave them guns, ammunition, and trade goods, all at a very high price. The Indian agent for the Osages reported in 1847 that his tribe had bought 1,500 mules from the Comanches that summer.

When the United States acquired Texas in 1845, the Comanche problem came as part of the package. The army built a string of posts along the Texas frontier to restrict the movements of the tribe, especially to keep them from raiding the farms. This caused some hardship for one band that had customarily hunted buffalo along the Colorado Valley during those seasons when the herds wandered so far south. This band was promised that it could still hunt in the area around San Saba but must first receive permission from the commander of the nearest army post. This permission was always refused.

In the summer of 1848 smallpox again took a heavy toll in the Comanche villages. Then in 1849 cholera spread from the gold seekers along the Platte until it reached the tribes along the Oregon Trail. They in turn took it south to a large summer encampment on the Arkansas, where bands from many tribes had gathered to erect a large medicine lodge, among them a number of Comanches, who took the cholera back to their villages. With these two killers attacking in successive years, the Comanches lost about half their total population. In their weakened condition they were more amenable to proposals from the Indian Bureau officials.

In 1853 officials came to Fort Atkinson, Kansas, to propose a treaty along the same lines as that signed by the northern tribes at Fort Laramie in 1851. In return for a yearly annuity of $18,000 in trade goods for ten years, the chiefs agreed to stay within the boundaries of the tribal lands and to allow free passage of travelers along the Santa Fe Trail. But the Indians considered the treaty goods as presents from their friends, the officials, and still expected presents of sugar and coffee from the wagon trains. Also, they considered the treaty a strictly local one, for the northern border only, and not including either the Texans or Mexicans and their territories.

The Comanches felt rich with all their free treaty goods. They would no longer pay the Osages excessive prices, especially after those sharp traders tried to convince the Comanches that the free goods were injurious. Trade relations were broken off, and the two tribes drifted back into sporadic warfare.

To make up for the loss of the Comanche horses they had been buying each year, the Osages turned to border raids on the Texans, taking along their allies, the Wichitas. Then some enterprising Texans who lived along the border entered the game, rustling horses from their neighbors and trading them off in Indian Territory to the north. The Comanches were often given all the credit for these raids.

The Comanches earned their greatest notoriety in their fierce, large-scale raids against the settlements of northern Mexico. As early as 1830 they were considered a serious problem there, taking scalps and captives, looting and burning small settlements, and running off large herds of horses and mules. The depredations continued for about forty years.

Although raiding parties were in style almost any month from February through October, the Comanches chose August as their favorite month for large forays. When the "Comanche moon" shone full and bright over the Mexican mountains in late summer, the frightened villagers huddled in their little huts while the marauders swept the unhappy countryside from Saltillo on the east to the Sierra Madre on the west, and south to the outskirts of Durango and Zacatecas. The Comanches delighted in senseless killings and the destruction of property before riding away to their home range with their captured prisoners and herds. They took only women and children, who might in a few years become Comanches if they lived through the hard times. Over the years such captives and their offspring were used to replace Comanche losses in battle and to disease, until they made up about half the entire Comanche population. Possibly half the captives each year were sold to traders in New Mexico or along the Arkansas.

One brief report by a traveler in Mexico described the Comanche terror visited upon the region each summer:

They are now overrunning the whole department of Durango and Chihuahua, and have cut off all communications, and defeated in two pitched battles the regular troops sent against them. Upward of ten thousand horses and mules have already been carried off, and scarcely has a hacienda or ranch on the frontier been unvisited, and the people have been killed or captured. The roads are impassable, all traffic is stopped, the ranchos barricaded, and the inhabitants afraid to venture out of their doors. The posts and express travel at night, avoiding the roads, and intelligence is brought in daily of massacres and harrowings.

A broad belt across the land, strewn with the whitened bones of slaughtered men and animals, marked the area of Comanche raids, a region that for many years was known as the "Desert of the Frontier."

When the United States Army finally set up posts to block the main trails to Mexico, the Comanches turned more and more to raiding the Texas frontier, gathering horses for their trading operations and taking a few captives to be turned over to northern army posts for $100 each. The problem of the Comanche raids was finally solved by wiping out the buffalo herds in the 1870's and penning all the warriors on a reservation.

18

The Diminishing Herds

ABOUT 1600 THE BUFFALO HERDS reached their widest distribution. They spread over all the pasture lands and through some of the open woodland from the Great Basin to the Virginia tidewater. Then the first colonists settled in Virginia and began ridding the land of buffalo, either driving them out or killing them off. This operation was necessary in farming areas to protect the fields and the cattle. By 1800 all the land east of the Mississippi had been cleared as the farming frontier advanced, but to the west the herds shrank rapidly too, for no apparent reason, retreating toward the center of the Great Plains from the entire perimeter of the former range.

In half a century, 1810–60, the grazing land occupied by the herds decreased by about one-half and the total number of buffalo decreased by about three-fourths, yet the yearly kill by hunters during this period was but a small fraction of the annual calf crop. Where did these millions of buffalo go? How much of the grasslands was left vacant because of smaller herds, and how much was abandoned because of increased pressure from hunters? It is worthy of note that as the buffalo crowded more and more into the central plains there was no mention by contemporary observers of any shortage of forage from the more intensive grazing.

One place where the retreat of the herds can be followed rather accurately from contemporary accounts is the broad strip of pasture land extending northward from Great Salt Lake through Bear Valley, the upper Snake Valley, and the upper Missouri Basin. The buffalo had come to this country in rather recent times, probably no earlier than 1600. The herds had been crowded up the Yellowstone Valley across Bozeman Pass and into the Missouri headwaters. Once this region was well stocked, the animals moved south across the continental divide through easy passes into the upper Snake country. Even slight pressure from the north against the herds would be sufficient to account for this movement.

After the Crows secured horses and guns, their hunting in the Yellowstone Valley increased. At the same time Blackfeet coming up the Missouri to Three Forks and the Columbia Basin tribes moving across from upper Clarks Fork pushed more and more animals south into Idaho, replacing the buffalo there as fast as they were being killed by the mounted Shoshoni and Bannocks. But after the smallpox epidemic of 1837 the Blackfeet stopped coming. The Crows could hunt more to the north. The new herds no longer came across Bozeman Pass, and some of those in the Three Forks area were pushed back by the increased hunting by the Columbia Basin tribes coming into the basin from the northwest.

In a few years the buffalo had all been cleared from the country west of the divide, and the Shoshoni and Bannocks had to travel far to hunt. Then the herds left the Three Forks country, and all the western hunters had to go to the central plains of Montana to find their game. The weakened Blackfeet were forced back toward Canada by the large bands of organized Columbia Basin hunters and had to allow the intruders to hunt even along the Sun River and in the Judith Basin.

During this period of change, in an unrelated development, the Blackfeet also changed some of their hunting practices, the most striking change being the abandonment of the piskin. It was abandoned, just as it was instituted, as the result of a dream.

In 1843 the Piegan band of Blackfeet was camped north of the Teton River, where they had built a strong piskin of the old type, a corral of timber just below a small cutbank in a coulee. After a successful drive in which 181 buffalo were trapped and killed, the camp was aroused in the night to find the piskin in flames. Then their buffalo caller, who had lured the herd to destruction the day before, stepped forth and confessed that he had deliberately destroyed the piskin, built with so much labor and in such a fine location. Early in the night a vision had come to him. His spirit had left his body and had traveled to a strange valley where a large buffalo bull approached him from some trees. The man and the bull exchanged peace signs, then the bull gave the buffalo caller a solemn warning that he and his people would suffer greatly if they continued to use the piskin, as it was too destructive.

When his spirit returned to his body, the man awoke. He knew he must burn the piskin at once and must persuade his people never to use one again. When he finished his story, the people agreed that the man was right to obey his vision, and forgave him for burning the piskin. This is rather dramatic evidence that some of the Indians along the fringes of the buffalo country were starting to worry over the absence of the herds from their old haunts. After this incident the Blackfeet moved much of their hunting to the north, around the Sweet Grass Hills, where they hunted from horseback.

Once the Blackfoot pressure had eased in central Montana, the Nez Percé and Flatheads used the short trail to the buffalo, from the Bitterroot Valley up the Big Blackfoot River and across Cadotte's Pass. Once on the east slope of the Sun River they engaged in sporadic fighting with the Blackfeet and kept this portion of Montana in a turmoil, to the detriment of the fur traders. It also closed the easy route west from Fort Benton to most travelers.

In 1853 when General Isaac Stevens traveled west to assume his duties as governor of the newly created Washington Territory, he was expected to survey a route for a possible railroad and to meet with the various Indian tribes along the way to arrange for future treaty councils, following the pattern developed at Fort Laramie in 1851. The trouble spot on the Sun River was one Stevens had to pass through.

When Stevens met with the Blackfoot chiefs and suggested a permanent peace settlement between their tribe and the western group, they were interested. They explained that the western tribes had come across the mountains and started the fights, and had forced the Blackfeet from some of their land. The Blackfeet were careful not to mention the many small raids they carried on against the Flathead villages across the divide, a practice they continued for the next two years.

In October 1855, Governor Stevens finally assembled delegations from the Flathead, Pend d'Oreille, and Nez Percé at the mouth of the Judith River, and a lasting peace with the Blackfeet was arranged. The Blackfeet agreed that the western tribes could hunt unmolested south of the Musselshell River and that the Blackfeet would stay north of that river. This reserved the Judith Basin for the Blackfeet, but western hunters often ranged there with tacit Blackfoot approval.

With the signing of this treaty and the resulting improvement in their relations with the Blackfeet, the Columbia Basin tribes stepped up their buffalo hunting, and the annual kill in this area, but the herds were not forced away from the Belt Mountains, for the Sioux at the same time were increasing their pressure on the herds from the east in Dakota. The triangle of the Montana plains between the Missouri and the Yellowstone as far west as the Belt Mountains continued as the home grounds of the northern buffalo herd until its complete destruction in 1883.

Meanwhile, on the eastern fringe the buffalo had no respite from the westward-moving farm frontier, even though the government's new Indian policy and new treaties eased tensions between red man and white. The course of national events kept the whole plains area in a state of constant flux, with steady pressure on the buffalo around the entire perimeter of the Great Plains crowding the herds toward the center. Corridors were opened up through the heart of the buffalo country from east to west, especially from the farmlands in eastern Kansas to the new mining camps in the Colorado mountains, a prelude to the later complete separation of the southern and northern herds.

The first large westward movement of farmers came in Kansas, against the heartland of the southern herd, which had its greatest concentration in the drainage basin of the Republican River. When slavery and antislavery forces clashed in Kansas, each side tried to outdo the other in rushing partisans to the territory, pushing the farming frontier westward about sixty miles in two years and crowding out the local Indians, who were forced from their small garden patches and villages and had to move south into Indian Territory. Although the new farmers spent most of their time and effort opposing one another, they effectively drove the buffalo from a wide belt of fine grassland that the herds had used for spring pasture.

Among the displaced Indian tribes the Pawnees suffered the most. As farms encroached on their lands, game became scarce and they finally gave up the struggle, surrendering almost all of their reservation and all their hunting grounds. The Indian Bureau moved them south into Indian Territory, displacing other tribes there to make way for the newcomers, who had to accept a much smaller reservation with poorer land than their former holdings, and had disgruntled neighbors besides.

As the conflict between pro- and anti-slavery forces died down in Kansas, the new settlers moved on up the valley of the Kansas River as far as Smoky Hill Fork, with a few scattered land claims farther west for about fifty miles. The frontier appeared to settle down for a time, but in 1858 it was stirred up again by reports of an important gold strike on Cherry Creek north of Pike's Peak. Small amounts of gold dust soon reached Kansas City, and the news received banner headlines in the papers. Excited people, hoping for another treasure spot like California, came rushing into towns all along the Missouri from Kansas City to Omaha to outfit for the 600-mile journey across the plains to the new mines. Each little village put forth its advantages as the jumping-off place. A letter to an Omaha paper commented:

> It is interesting to look over the papers published at different towns on the Missouri, below Omaha. Every town that can boast three houses, a well and a smoke house, are showing up their advantages as a place for outfitting; most of them have a military road leading to the mines, each one shorter than its neighbor— some of them save about one-half the distance. Well, now, that may be well enough, if they can make it.

This multiplicity of routes across the open plains was to be expected, for there were no large rivers and no mountains to cross on the way. At first travelers all chose one of the established trails for the first leg of the journey. The Santa Fe Trail would take them to the Arkansas River crossing, where a side road led upstream to Bent's Fort. From there the way was across trackless grasslands, but with Pike's Peak looming on the western horizon as a guide. Another good, well-traveled road led west from Omaha to Fort Kearney on the Platte, cutting off a toilsome stretch of the old Oregon Trail. From the fort the trail led up the south bank of the Platte to the forks, then directly up the South Platte to the mines. Both routes had good grass, water in the streams, and buffalo within hunting range.

Some adventurous men decided they could cut off fifty to a hundred miles by going west up the Kansas Valley and Smoky Hill Fork to its source, then west across the high plains to the mines. On this trail they would find some farms for 250 miles where they could get milk, butter, eggs, and vegetables. The drawbacks were that no road had been opened to the head of Smoky Hill Fork and that the last stretch was across dry country with poor grass, no game, and no water from July 1 until fall.

A fourth route, and probably the best, left the Missouri at Leavenworth and led straight west along the high ground between the Platte and Kansas drainage basins until it struck the Republican Fork of the Kansas, about 120 miles out, and followed that stream to its head, only a short distance east of Cherry Creek and the mines. This route offered easy traveling, good grass and water, plenty of game, and a direct road. Once it was opened, it became the favorite.

Compared to the trail to California, the distance to the new mines was quite short, only about a third as far. A good outfit could make the trip in six weeks, while people who knew the road and traveled light often made it in thirty days. On the long trail to California a train had to leave the Missouri by early June to have any chance of crossing the Sierra Nevada before the snows came. The Colorado-bound people could start as late as November, trusting to luck that they would not be trapped in a blizzard.

At Marysville, Kansas, the newspaper on November 4, 1858, carried this item: "Notwithstanding the lateness of the season, trains after trains continue to throng the road . . . bound for the new El Dorado."

As usual, many of the gold seekers started across the plains with rather skimpy outfits. On March 23, 1859, the *Missouri Republican* reported:

> There are now hundreds starting on foot with nothing but a cotton sack and a few pounds of crackers and meat . . . . Some men with mining shovels over their shoulders and their diminutive carpet bags on the ends of them. There were not five days' provisions in the whole party. One party of sixteen to twenty started with one old horse, and fifty pounds of hard bread. Their intention was to kill game on the road and sleep in barns at night. They appeared to think that the prairies were covered with barns and sheds, built by the Indians to shelter buffalo.

Next up the scale, as reported on November 6, 1858, by the Kansas City *Journal of Commerce*, was "the wheelbarrow man who left here a few weeks ago for Pike's Peak, taking his whole outfit in a wheelbarrow, passed several ox trains, and at Council Grove overtook the party he set out to go with. He traveled from twenty to thirty miles a day."

Then, according to a contemporary letter, came the handcarts: "A party left here [Leavenworth] yesterday on foot for the mines with a hand cart ingeniously contrived to ford all the streams like a boat."

There were carts and wagons of all kinds, drawn by horses, mules, or oxen. All these people planned to hunt some buffalo along the way, and indeed there seemed to be plenty of meat for skilled hunters, with some lucky kills by the greenhorns. At times the herds were so thick, especially along the Santa Fe Trail and the Republican River route, that they became troublesome, even dangerous. Horace Greeley, a New York newspaperman, went to the mines in 1859 and left several good items about the buffalo, each written the day it happened.

"I know a million is a great many, but I am confident we saw that number yesterday. Certainly all we saw could not have stood on ten square miles of ground. Often the country for miles on either hand seemed quite black with them."

He mentioned the dangers on three different occasions:

"We met or passed today two parties of Pike's Peakers who have respectively lost three oxen or steers, stampeded last night by herds of buffalo. The mules at express stations have to be carefully watched to preserve them from a similar catastrophe."

"A party of our drivers, who went back seven miles on mules last evening . . . report that they found the road absolutely dangerous from the crowds of buffalo feeding on either side, and running across it . . . that, the night being quite dark, they were often in danger of being run over and run down by the headlong brutes."

"A herd of buffalo north of the road . . . were stampeded by an emigrant train . . . . A slight ridge hid them from Mr. F's sight until their leader came full tilt against his mule, knocking him down and going over him at full speed." Both Mr. F. and his mule were shaken, but not injured.

The throngs of travelers on the four trails cutting through the heart of the buffalo country produced a great deal of disturbance among the buffalo. Each party had at least one hunter trying to kill an animal for meat each day or two, and most of the other people seemed to delight in shooting into the herds even when they did not expect to kill anything. The shooting and other activities of the travelers produced a great many stampedes, some of them involving many thousands of animals. It is probable that the large herd that came from the Republican River range and crossed to the north bank of the Platte had been started north by just such a stampede, for no large herd had crossed the Platte since the big California rush had scared the buffalo out of the Platte Valley.

The little town of Wood River Center on the north bank of the Platte was almost overrun by this buffalo herd. The local paper carried the story:

> As we sometimes since predicted, our beautiful town site has been rudely trampled upon by those ugly-looking wild beasts known as buffalo . . . . We intend to keep some weapons handy, so that, should they kick up too much dust around our office, or rob the porkers of their accustomed slop, we shall not be responsible for their safety. We are determined not to be bit by the ugly scamps, at all hazards, and should the ECHO fail to make its accustomed visit, it may be inferred that either ourself or some huge buffalo has fallen, and perchance, editor, printer and devil may for the moment have forgotten their duty, whilst regaling upon the finest broiled ribs.

A month later the buffalo were in town again. They broke into a garden and ate up all the corn. The townspeople shot a large number just across the Wood River. Even though they saved the hides and some of the meat, enough carrion was left to ripen in the summer sun and send a powerful stench across the stream into town.

This visit in 1860 marks the last recorded passage of a large herd of buffalo across the Platte in either direction. The separation of the buffalo into the southern and northern herds was complete.

The huge volume of travel along the Platte in 1849 and the following years had annoyed and troubled the Indian tribes near the trail, but for the most part the wagon trains had been confined to a corridor between tribal holdings. This new rush into Colorado, starting in 1858 and increasing greatly in the next two years, not only put more people along the old Oregon and Santa Fe trails but also opened up two new trails in the buffalo country. These travelers, instead of going on to distant places, stopped and occupied the foothill country that the southern Arapahoes and the southern Cheyennes had used for a winter range for fifty years or more. Here were sheltered valleys, plenty of wood, and buffalo nearby. A miner on Cherry Creek in January 1859 wrote that immense herds of buffalo ranged there during severe winters.

The Indians were forced to move south of the mines, but they stayed in the foothills. A traveler on the Santa Fe–Bent's Fort trail observed, "The Arkansas from Bent's Fort up to the mountains is one vast Indian camp—the Comanches, Kioways, and Arapahoes are all banded together and unless the government does something to protect the emigrants, many will never reach this place."

That same winter another miner wrote home, "The Indians have sent us word that we must leave the country." Two months later a warrior band told some miners that they would need all their logs for forts in the spring to protect themselves from Indian attacks. They identified the hostiles as Kiowas, Cheyennes, and Arapahoes.

In spite of this continued unrest among the tribes, there was no serious trouble for a time. Along the trail some of the Indians did stop wagon trains to beg from the drivers or to levy a toll on a train wanting to cross Indian lands.

Near Council Grove a typical sight was reported: "Near us a band of about 400 Kaw [Kansas] Indians . . . they are a miserable, lowlived set who live by thieving."

Horace Greeley, near the head of the Republican River, encountered a large band of Indians who stopped the train and demanded a toll. "Arapahoes . . . not hostile to us but intent on begging or stealing, and stopping the wagons peremptorily until their demands are complied with." Greeley, like other whites, would not admit that the Indians had any right to collect tolls from intruders on their lands.

The friction between the trains and the tribes increased year by year as the Colorado mining camps continued to grow and regular express runs, stage coach lines, and freight trains joined in the traffic. Here was a potential trouble spot with a short fuse, needing very little to produce an outbreak.

Buffalo cows graze with their calves. Although buffalo grow for six or seven years, they are considered adults in their fourth. (U.S. Bureau of Sport Fisheries & Wildlife, photo by E. P. Haddon)

An average adult bull weighs sixteen hundred pounds and stands six feet tall. Buffalo grow dark brown, almost black, hair on the foreparts; the shorter hair on the hindquarters changes color with the seasons. (U.S. Bureau of Sport Fisheries & Wildlife, photo by Wesley D. Parker)

19

Buffalo Country Troubles,
1860–65

IN 1860 THE NATIONAL GOVERNMENT was so involved in the slavery question and the presidential election that it could pay little heed to the trouble spots developing along the fringes of the buffalo country, where delays in negotiating and ratifying treaties and irregularities in treaty payments caused much unrest among the tribes. The problems were greatly aggravated by the arrogance of the settlers who invaded the Indian reservations, ignoring or deliberately defying specific treaty provisions.

The outbreak of the Civil War in 1861 drained the western military posts of the better officers and troop units. They were replaced by less able officers commanding poorly trained and equipped men. These officers often were from the east or midwest and knew very little about dealing with Indians.

Many of the men in the new boom towns and mining camps were another source of trouble. They were out west to avoid war service, or they had left the east one jump ahead of the sheriff. Local volunteer units were composed largely of these two classes, who sometimes deliberately tried to stir up Indian troubles to justify their continued presence on the frontier.

When a number of these causes were at work in one locality, serious trouble soon developed, and in some instances broke out into open conflict between red men and white. The first of these was the Sioux War.

The Minnesota border had a difficult Indian problem as the result of the rapid settlement following establishment of the Minnesota Territory in 1849. At that time more than 90 percent of the territory was held by various tribes of Indians—Sioux, Winnebago, Fox, Sauk, Menominee. All the white settlers were concentrated around Fort Snelling at St. Anthony's Falls, which marked the head of steamboat navigation on the Mississippi. Settlers moved in rapidly to occupy the new territory. The Indian commissioner sought new land for them by securing a new treaty, which would permit him to move the Indians out of the lower Minnesota Valley and the lands just to the west.

Once the Sioux had signed the treaty, they were defrauded of their treaty payments by the officials, who paid the money, not to the individual Indians, but to any traders who claimed the Indians owed them for goods bought on credit. The resulting scandals and investigations so delayed further payments that white settlers occupied much of the land before the payments for it were made. The Sioux finally broke loose with a large war party and in August 1862 wiped out 700 whites whom the Sioux sincerely believed were stealing Indian lands.

Troops marched out at once against the warriors. After two months of bloody fighting, the Indians were subdued and the army had 1,500 Sioux prisoners, mostly women and children. General John Pope, commander of the forces in Minnesota, backed by the local population, wanted to execute at least 100 of the captive men, but in the end had to be satisfied with hanging only thirty-four of them before President Lincoln intervened.

The next spring, 1863, General Henry Hastings Sibley marched out with 3,000 men to clear all the Sioux out of their homes, where they had lived for more than 200 years. This was accomplished in two months after two large battles and several small fights. The Sioux leader, Little Chief, was killed and cut up for souvenirs by the soldiers. They took his scalp, skull, and wrist bones.

Several thousand seminomadic Sioux were affected in this mass expulsion. They were driven from their wild-rice swamps and fishing lakes, and were forced to turn more to buffalo hunting to supplement the crops they began to grow along the Missouri. This sudden large increase in hunters in the Sioux buffalo country forced the tribe to

[167]

expand westward, at the expense of the Crows. The Powder River Basin, which included most of the land between the Black Hills and the Bighorn Mountains, became the Sioux's prized hunting ground. When the whites tried to put a road through and protect it with military posts, the Sioux responded with a full-scale war.

On the central plains the southern Cheyennes and the southern Arapahoes also came under heavy pressure from white intruders on their lands in the 1850's. The treaty they had signed at Fort Laramie defined the boundaries of their land and promised them large annual payments from the government, but the Senate never bothered to ratify the treaty. The tribes could not understand the Indian Bureau's failure to keep the promises made in writing at Fort Laramie.

The massive stampede to the Colorado mines in 1858 and 1859 pushed the tribes toward open resistance. Their plight was described in the Indian agent's report for 1859:

> I estimate the number of whites traversing the plains across the central belt to have exceeded sixty thousand during the present season. The trains of vehicles and cattle are frequent and valuable in proportion. Post lines and private expresses are in constant motion. The explorations of this season have established the existence of precious metals in absolutely infinite abundance and convenience of position. A concourse of whites is, therefore, constantly swelling an incapability of control or restraint by the government.

The lack of government control in the mining camps and the reckless breed of men there were felt at once by the Indians. No effort was made to keep the whites from further encroachment on Indian lands, or to punish the men who shot an occasional Indian, but before the breaking point was reached, the Indian Bureau held a meeting with the tribes at Bent's Fort in 1861 and induced the southern Cheyennes and the southern Arapahoes to give up claim to most of their hunting grounds in Colorado and western Kansas. They accepted a small reservation in the southeastern Colorado sand hills.

After three years of comparative quiet, the border was stirred up by a rather small complaint that through bungling became a serious incident. A settler reported to the officer at Camp Sanborn that some Indians had stolen cattle from him and his neighbor. As he guided a lieutenant and forty men toward the spot, they met about seventy Indians traveling with a small herd of horses, but no cattle. The settler then asked the officer to take some of the horses, which the settler claimed belonged to him, although he had not reported any stolen. The Indians would not submit to the settler's demands and beat off the troops, with small losses on each side.

In retaliation for this Indian resistance, troops attacked a Cheyenne village 135 miles to the north, and not implicated in the trouble. The peaceful village was caught by surprise and lost sixty, mostly women and children, in the attack. The troops then destroyed the tipis. This incident angered the Indians over a wide area. The Cheyennes, Arapahoes, Kiowas, and Comanches put on their war paint and made the western plains a dangerous place for whites. They ran off stock, wiped out stage stations, and for a time cut off Colorado from the east. The troops were helpless against the raiders, being unable either to prevent or avenge attack. One frontier officer stated the problem:

> It is conceived that scattered bands of mounted hunters, with the speed of a horse and the watchfulness of a wolf or an antelope, whose faculties are sharpened by their necessities; who, when they get short of provisions, separate and look for something to eat, and find it in the water, in the ground, or on the surface; whose bill of fare ranges from grass-seed, nuts, roots, grasshoppers, lizards, and rattlesnakes, up to deer, antelope, elk, bear, and buffalo, and who have a continent to roam over, will be neither surprised, caught, conquered, over-awed, or reduced to famine by a rumbling, bugle-blowing, drum-beating town passing through their country on wheels at the speed of a loaded wagon.
>
> If the Indians are in the path and do not wish to be seen, they cross a ridge, and the town moves on, ignorant of whether there are fifty Indians within a mile or no Indians within fifty miles. If the Indians wish to see, they return to the crest of the ridge, crawl up to the edge, pull up a bunch of grass by the roots, and look through or under it at the procession.

This fruitless chasing of the Indian raiders inspired Governor John Evans of Colorado Territory to send word to all the Indians that they had to come in and settle at Fort Lyons or their families would be exterminated. Several important Cheyenne chiefs went to Denver to talk with the governor, but he would not make peace with them. General S. R. Curtis, in command of the Department of Kansas, had sent out word: "I want no peace until the Indians suffer more . . . . It is better to chastise before giving anything but a little tobacco to talk over. No peace must be made without my directions."

This harsh attitude on the part of the general and the governor encouraged Colonel John Chivington of the Colorado volunteers to march out with 1,100 men and make a surprise attack on the peaceful Cheyenne village of Chief Black Kettle, who had set up camp for his people at Sand Creek, near Fort Lyons, as he had been ordered to do. Chivington attacked the unsuspecting village at dawn on a snowy winter morning.

Later a government commission, in the report of its official investigation, included this commentary: "Fleeing women holding up their hands and praying for mercy were brutally shot down; infants were killed and scalped in derision; men were tortured and mutilated in a manner that would put to shame the savage ingenuity of interior Africa." From a village of 700, over 500 were massacred and the camp was destroyed.

This senseless slaughter of the peaceful Cheyennes proved costly to the people of Colorado and to the whole border. An experienced army officer remarked later, "But for that horrible butchery it is a fair presumption that all the subsequent wars with the Cheyennes and Arapahoes and their kindred might possibly have been averted."

Instead, the Plains Indians from the Canadian border to the Red River went out on a war of revenge that 8,000 troops could not quell, and took the lives of several hundred whites, mostly in small groups at widely spaced spots over the region.

Public indignation over the Sand Creek massacre forced the army to end the war with a treaty. Although the southern Cheyennes escaped further attacks by the troops for a time, they had to give up all their lands north of the Arkansas and move south. This left the heart of the buffalo country, from the Arkansas to the Platte and west to the Rockies, free of any Indian claims and opened the way for new settlers and the railroads.

The initial attack on a Cheyenne village had stirred up the tribes to the south. Some of the Cheyennes joined with the Comanches and Kiowas to form a formidable force of about 3,000 fighting men, with their camps in the Texas Panhandle along the Canadian River. Here Kit Carson with troops from New Mexico fought them in a desperate battle at Adobe Walls the same week Colonel Chivington was massacring the Cheyennes at Sand Creek.

Adobe Walls was the ruins of a trading post built on the Canadian River by William Bent in the 1830's to supplement his post on the Arkansas. He wanted the Comanche trade but did not want them coming to his Arkansas post, where they might get into fights with the Cheyennes and Arapahoes to the north. After the Comanches joined with those tribes in a peace treaty in 1840, they could come to the Arkansas post to trade, and the post on the Canadian was abandoned. After twenty-five years it had fallen into ruin, but about five or six feet of the thick abode walls were still standing, offering a strong defensive position for Carson and his troops.

Carson had 300 men and two howitzers to hold off 3,000 Indians, and even with the protection of the walls he had to fight desperately to stave off disaster. Finally toward night the Indians withdrew and Carson retreated to the west.

This was an indecisive fight, with Carson getting a little the worst of it. He was unable to advance against the Indian camp, while the Indians were unwilling to pay the price in lives that an all-out assault on the little force would have entailed. This fight did show that the Indians on the southern plains were able to collect a formidable force when they thought their existence or their hunting grounds were in serious danger.

20

Cattle and Railroads in the Buffalo Country

IN THE 1860's the buffalo found that their pastures on the Great Plains were being invaded by a newcomer, also a grass eater: Texas longhorns were coming up the trail each year in a seemingly endless procession.

Among the chaparral and mesquite thickets of southern Texas the longhorns could survive and multiply where buffalo would starve or die of thirst. This large desert range was extended rapidly as more settlers moved into Texas and the Indians were pushed back. Then the good range land near the settlements was cleared of buffalo, and the longhorns took over that pasture too, until their range covered about half of Texas. During the Civil War the herds increased rapidly in a practically wild state as most of the cowhands went off to war and there were not enough left to round up the cattle. When peace finally came, there were perhaps 3 million or more cattle waiting for the roundups, too many for the Texas market. Herds were driven north along the trail in hopes of reaching a market somewhere. For several years, each spring saw a steady stream of cattle on the way to northern markets.

These trail herds were beset by many dangers—floods, stampedes, hostile Indians—but the most disastrous, and the most difficult to protect against, was a large herd of buffalo across the trail. The longhorns, like the horses, mules, and oxen along the Santa Fe and Oregon trails, seemed to take special delight in breaking away from the cowboys and scampering off across the plains with the buffalo. Once they mixed with the buffalo, it might take a week or so of hard work to cut them out and get them back on the trail, and even then the herders were lucky if they recovered three-fourths of their animals.

Beyond the wild country the herds found new obstacles, the settlers, who turned out en masse to prevent the range cattle from spreading Texas fever among their own stock. They blocked the direct route across Missouri to St. Louis and forced the herds to move farther west into Kansas. A newspaper item in 1867 from eastern Kansas, quoted by E. S. Osgood, describes the movement:

> The entire country, east, west, and south of Salina down to the Arkansas River and Wichita is now filled with Texas cattle. There are not only cattle on a thousand hills but a thousand cattle on one hill and every hill. The bottoms are overflowing with them and the water courses with this great article of traffic. Perhaps not less than 200,000 of them are in the state, 60,000 of which are within a day's ride of Salina, and the cry is, "Still they come."

The herds from Texas moved along the eastern side of the buffalo country and occupied the grassy belt of land from the edge of the herds to the farming frontier all the way from Indian Territory to the Dakota line. This open belt grew wider each year as the buffalo were pushed back even more rapidly than the farming frontier advanced.

At the same time the buffalo range was being nibbled away on the western side. The pastures along the foothills of the Rockies were filling up rapidly with Texas cattle on their way to market in the mining camps and towns. At first some of the herds were pastured for a few weeks until they were needed by the butchers, but in a short time surplus animals were put on the ranges as breeding stock.

In the early 1850's, freight teams had discovered that their stock could survive the winters on the western ranges in the foothills, where there was some protection from the storms. A large train, caught in an early snow, turned out all its stock to rustle for themselves. In the spring the teamsters were surprised to find that the animals had survived in very good shape and were ready for work again. The oxen fared well on the cured nutritious grasses of the high plains without any hay or grain supplement.

The stockmen in Colorado decided that their range stock could do as well as the oxen from the freight teams. They found that the cattle, tired and worn from the long drive from Texas, quickly recuperated on the open range, survived the winter in good shape, and needed little care beyond protection from rustlers and a rounding up after each bad storm.

Another invader, meanwhile, was inching its way into the buffalo country: the iron horse. California led the west in demanding railroad ties with the eastern seaboard. Cattlemen moving into Kansas from the south, farmers flocking in from the east, and the continued growth of the Colorado mining districts emphasized the necessity for better transportation.

In 1865, the Union Pacific started west from Omaha. This line up the Platte was of great national importance but had little impact on the buffalo, for by this time the herds had learned to avoid the whole Platte Valley. The new steel ribbon merely underlined the fact that the great buffalo herd of the plains had been divided permanently into northern and southern segments.

The first railroad to invade the buffalo homeland in western Kansas and to dispute the right of way with the dark-brown masses was the Kansas and Pacific, which came from Kansas City to Salina, then up Smoky Hill Fork toward Denver. By the time this new line had reached Hayes City, Kansas, it was among herds grazing in large numbers on every side.

The railroad construction gangs around Hayes City in 1867 numbered about 1,200 men and required a great deal of fresh meat each day, which the contractors bought from various market hunters, the most famous being William F. Cody. Bill Cody had a good buffalo horse, Brigham, which he had bought from the Utes, and a new-model 50-caliber breech-loading rifle, beautiful and deadly, christened Lucretia Borgia. With these two, and teamsters and wagons to haul in the meat, Cody contracted to supply twelve buffalo to the cook tents each day.

With his fine horse and good rifle, Cody could easily kill buffalo by running them, but for his regular kill he shot from cover and thus secured his animals without disturbing the rest of the herd. He would select a small band on the edge of the main herd and drop the chosen animals in a small area, handy for the teamsters, who also doubled as butchers. In eighteen months as a market hunter Cody brought in meat from 4,280 buffalo to the construction camps and to the Hayes City market.

Bill Cody earned his name "Buffalo Bill" in a hunt with a small party of army officers. He was at the construction camp at a time when the cry "Buffalo!" was raised. Slipping a bridle on Brigham and grabbing his rifle, Cody rode off bareback toward the small band, eleven animals, approaching at a distance. Soon he was joined by five army officers out for a hunt. Evidently they thought the young man was a laborer on the work crew, riding one of the work horses. They kindly offered to give him everything of their kill except the tongues and tenderloins.

As the party moved slowly toward the unsuspecting buffalo, walking down a gentle slope, Cody moved away and circled to approach the animals from the rear. Then he gave Brigham the signal, unlimbered Lucretia, and in a short ride had killed all eleven buffalo with twelve shots before the amazed officers could come within range. He offered the tongues and tenderloins to them, and they presented him with his title, Buffalo Bill.

When word of the incident spread, friends of Billy Comstock, chief scout at Fort Wallace, on the Colorado-Nebraska line, claimed their man had an earlier and better claim on the title. They demanded a contest between the two. The newspapers played up the challenge, and the Kansas and Pacific saw an opportunity for good publicity and ran an excursion train from St. Louis for the big event. Referees were appointed, the field was chosen, and the big show was on.

Buffalo were plentiful near the railroad. On the first run Cody outscored Comstock quite easily. Then they had lunch and made two shorter runs in the afternoon. For the third run Cody stripped the saddle off Brigham's back and rode out bareback. To wind up his day he chased a huge buffalo bull toward the crowd of spectators and, the women screaming in excitement and alarm, dropped it with one shot almost at their feet. Then the kills were totaled and Cody was declared the winner, with sixty-nine to Comstock's fifty-seven.

The Kansas and Pacific had the 126 buffalo heads mounted and distributed them throughout the country for their advertising value. Several more excursion trains were run out to the end of the track, with round-trip tickets at $10. To stimulate more interest in the new line, the railroad promoters proposed that a carload of buffalo bulls be rounded up and sent on an eastern tour.

A crew of top hands was organized and sent out into the herds. These skilled workers worked in pairs, one coming up on each side of the quarry, with their ropes settling in place almost simultaneously. Then the ropers let the bull run, but each kept his rope taut and his horse away from the animal so that it could not charge either one.

After the bull was choked down, it was hogtied and loaded on a railway car with block and tackle. Of twenty-four bulls roped and tied down, only three survived. The rest died at various stages during the struggle; usually the noose damaged the thorax and suffocated the animal. The three survivors created a great deal of interest on their journey through the eastern cities.

During the late summer and fall the excursion trains ran at fairly regular intervals, stopping overnight at Ellsworth, Kansas, before going on to the end of the line. Trains did not travel at night through this country, for the Indians had learned that a log or two on the rails could derail the iron monster. On the daylight runs there was less danger. Each train carried twenty-five good rifles and an ample supply of ammunition for the crew, and most of the passengers were loaded down with guns.

West of Ellsworth buffalo could usually be found near the tracks, often galloping alongside the cars. Passengers were encouraged to shoot at them from the moving train, which rattled along at about fifteen miles an hour, a pace the buffalo could match for some distance. If one of the animals was downed, the train would stop to allow the passengers to harvest whatever portions of the animal they wanted, but most of the huge carcass was left as carrion. However, there is this interesting item from the local press: "On the down train the other day a buffalo was killed by the conductor, rolled upon a flat car, and taken to Ellsworth to feed the community."

Once the trains left Hayes City, they could be in real trouble with the moving herds. Buffalo often had a powerful urge to dash in front of the engine, racing even more madly if the whistle tooted and the bell rang. The engineers soon learned not to drive into an animal on the tracks, for their engine would be derailed or overturned.

On the new Atchison, Topeka and Santa Fe line along the Arkansas, trains were derailed twice in one week by buffalo, and the engineers were given orders to stop and let the herds go by when the situation looked dangerous. At times this meant a wait of several hours, but on at least one occasion waiting for the herd was not enough.

A train was trapped by a large herd moving across the tracks both to the front and to the rear. Suddenly the herd took fright and started to stampede in a solid mass right for the cars. The engineer blew the whistle, rang the bell, and let up clouds of steam, but to no avail. Passengers fired from the windows and the platforms, but the herd came on, piling up in a great mass against the cars. Some of them jammed their heads under the carriages, and three cars were overturned, with the buffalo still piling up against them until a few animals managed to scramble across the pile and the cars, leaving one of their number with its legs caught in a broken window.

In a year or so the buffalo became more wary of the trains and ranged farther from the right of way. Then the hunters were deposited at stations along the way where they could rent horses and guns for the chase. They usually preferred the new Winchester carbine, 44-caliber, a "saddle gun," for it could be carried in a scabbard. It held twelve shots in the magazine. Many an excited hunter rode up to a buffalo and pumped the whole dozen shots into the quarry, then had to stop and reload in order to finish the job, while the wounded animal stood there, braced and bleeding but unable to run.

The most glamorous sportsman among all the thousands shooting buffalo in the west was Grand Duke Alexis, son of the Russian tsar, a tall, handsome, young bachelor. General Philip Sheridan met the young prince at a White House dinner, and invited him to a buffalo hunt in Nebraska. Although it was midwinter, Alexis accepted at once, and off they went by rail to the North Platte, then south on horseback to the watershed of the Republican River.

The army supplied a military escort to ward off any possible Indian trouble, and a cavalry band to furnish music in camp. To add a colorful touch, sixty Sioux warriors and their families, led by Chief Spotted Tail, were invited to join the party. Tents, ambulances, a carriage, a light wagon, and a large herd of good riding horses were also furnished.

The hunt was staged on the high plains of southwestern Nebraska in the middle of January, but the young prince seemed untroubled by the weather, which was milder than that of a Russian winter. He rode out to the chase, and with the able assistance of Bill Cody he killed a fine bull with Lucretia Borgia, then returned to camp to a band concert and some entertainment by the Sioux. On the hunt the next day, the Sioux surprised the prince by downing a buffalo cow with a single arrow from what Alexis had considered a toy bow. The prince then bought the bow and a quiver of arrows to add to his imposing list of trophies.

After a few days visiting in the Colorado mining towns, Alexis asked for another hunt. This one was near Fort Wallace, and was equally successful. Then Alexis, loaded with trophies and gifts, boarded the train and rode east to a succession of gala receptions, and Bill Cody went back to scouting for the army.

Riders drive buffalo into pens where certain of the animals will be selected for slaughter. Now individuals may purchase live buffalo or carcasses from government stock and surplus animals from private herds. (U.S. Bureau of Sport Fisheries & Wildlife, photo by E. P. Haddon)

Once roaming North America in uncounted millions, buffalo now graze on pastures at the Montana Buffalo Preserve. By simulating conditions under which buffalo once lived, officials hope to maintain a truly wild herd in Yellowstone National Park. (Montana Historical Society, U.S. Fish & Wildlife photo)

21

The Last Stand of the Plains Tribes

THE INDIAN TREATIES OF 1865 brought an uneasy peace to the central plains, but north of the Platte troubles increased. Three big gold strikes in southwestern Montana set off new stampedes and the growth of new camps, Bannock, Virginia City, and Helena, all far from any of the established trails.

Two long, roundabout routes led to the new mines. The first was by steamboat 2,400 miles up the Missouri to Fort Benton, Montana, then overland another 170 miles to the nearest gold diggings, at Helena. The second route followed the old Oregon Trail to Fort Laramie, Wyoming, and on across the mountains to Fort Hall, on the Snake River in Idaho, then north another 200 miles across the desert and the continental divide, about 1,500 miles in all.

In 1865 an old mountain man, John Bozeman, blazed a shorter, easier trail, with better grass and water along the way. This trail branched off at Fort Laramie and went north to Powder River, around the northern end of the Bighorn Mountains, and on up the Yellowstone. It crossed into the upper Missouri Basin through Bozeman Pass, ninety miles short of Virginia City, 120 miles from Helena. But this new trail had one very serious drawback: it led through the heart of the Powder River and Tongue River basins, the prize buffalo country of the Sioux and their northern neighbors, the northern Cheyennes and the northern Arapahoes. In 1855 Sir St. George Gore on his western hunt had met with friendly treatment throughout the region. In 1866 travelers could expect serious trouble.

At a treaty council in 1865 Red Cloud, war chief of the Oglala Sioux, had threatened war if any attempt was made by the army to open a trail across their lands. He also insisted there must be no forts on the buffalo range. When his protests and threats were ignored, Red Cloud stormed out of the meeting. The commissioners later decided that they had pacified the Sioux after this episode by giving them a huge pile of presents, then on receiving reports of further Sioux threats, called another council with the chiefs at Fort Laramie in June 1866.

Early that summer, before the council convened, travelers along the trail reported trouble with the Indians along a stretch of 200 miles, and as soon as the council ended, the chiefs returned to their bands and reopened hostilities. But during the latter part of June, while the chiefs were at Fort Laramie, trains along the trail had no trouble. The travelers were nervous and on their guard when Indian bands approached their trains, only to find the visitors friendly. Here is the experience of one train, as told in letters by Ellen Gordon Fletcher, a bride on the trail:

Wed. June 27, 1866. . . . Tongue River was crossed in the morning. We drove until about the middle of the afternoon, when the head teams came rushing back with the cry of "Indians." . . . A good many of the men were still out [hunting buffalo]. The two teams ahead had only women, and one little boy driving, and they were very badly frightened. Said that there were two hundred Indians down at the foot of the hill. This looked like hostility . . . . The Indians stood in line down at the foot of the hill. Instead of 200, there were about 80. They were armed with bows and arrows, and a few of them had guns, and some of them long spears . . . . They gave the Indians some bacon, flour, etc. . . . These Indians were Rappahoes.

Thurs. 28th. . . . The Indians led the way around for us to cross another bad stream, and rode along with us nearly all the forenoon trying to swap . . . one old chief made the captain of the train a present of a nice buffalo robe.

July 1st. Sabbath. We found plenty of Indians over on the other side [of Bighorn River]. . . . They all wanted to swap . . . One old squaw brought me a pair [of moccasins] and wanted a cup of sugar . . . Dell got a pair of plain ones for Chell. Mine only have a few pink, blue, and white beads.

At the time this train was crossing the Bighorn among the friendly Arapahoes, Colonel H. B. Carrington was encountering hostile Sioux on the trail between Fort Laramie and Fort Reno. He was coming up the new trail to build two new posts, one on Powder River, one on Bighorn River, to protect the trail, hoping in this way to keep the section peaceful. He had about 700 soldiers for the task.

There would be no peace. When the Sioux chiefs returned to their villages from Fort Laramie they called out the war parties and began new attacks, a raid on the Fort Reno horse herd and an attack on a wagon train at Crazy Woman Creek, where six people were killed.

On July 15 Carrington began building his first post, Fort Phil Kearney, between the forks of Big and Little Piney, away from water and miles from good timber logs or adequate firewood. He sent two companies on to the Bighorn crossing to build Fort C. F. Smith, a much smaller post.

The Sioux swarmed around Fort Phil Kearney like a violated nest of yellowjackets. They swooped down, wounding a man here, killing another there, stealing or killing cattle and horses, attacking wagon trains, and always escaping with loot. The post was on a constant alert, expecting attacks at any hour of the day or night.

December 21 dawned crisp and clear. A large party of wood cutters moved out to the west, with an armed guard for protection. Scarcely had they begun their work when the Sioux warriors attacked in force. Captain W. J. Fetterman was sent out at once with a relief force of fifty infantry, twenty-seven cavalry, and two junior officers, eighty men in all. He had strict orders to relieve the wood detail and escort it back to Fort Phil Kearney. Under no circumstances was he to chase the Indians across the ridge to the north. But Fetterman did chase the decoy group across the ridge, just as a cold northern storm blew in. A second relief force found eighty frozen bodies across the ridge where the ambush had been set.

The harassments continued for months. Then in late July Chief Red Cloud mustered two large forces, sending one against the haying crew at Fort C. F. Smith on August 1, the other against a wood detail on

Big Piney on August 2. From behind a log barricade the haying crew and its guard, nineteen men in all, beat off the warriors with considerable losses.

On Big Piney, Major J. W. Powell had his men place wagon boxes on the ground in a tight rectangle before starting to work. When the Sioux charged, some of the men escaped to the post, but thirty-two of them took refuge in the wagon boxes and stood off about a thousand Sioux for a long time, inflicting heavy casualties on the attacking masses. The decisive factor in both these fights was the troops' new breech-loading rifles, a weapon that came as a complete surprise to the Indians, and more deadly than any firearm they had ever faced.

Although Chief Red Cloud knew that his men had suffered defeat in both the hay-meadow fight and the wagon-box fight, he soon found that he had won the war. In the face of the continued Sioux opposition, government officials decided to abandon the new posts and turn the country back to the Indians. In the spring of 1868 they met with the chiefs and drew up a new treaty, which the Sioux willingly signed, for it gave them what they had been demanding for three years. In early summer as the troops marched out from the abandoned posts, the red men were waiting to put a torch to all the hated buildings. Their buffalo were safe again.

South of the Arkansas, Indian problems continued. After the Sand Creek massacre in 1864 and the resulting border war, the Cheyennes in 1865 had signed a treaty for a new reservation, but were induced to give it up in a new treaty negotiated at Medicine Lodge Creek in 1867. Chief Black Kettle, who had survived the Sand Creek attack, was again the leader of a large Cheyenne band, peaceful and settled on the Wichita according to the terms of the treaty.

Some of the officials gave the band a good deal of trouble, withholding the ammunition needed for hunting buffalo. This had been promised to them, but Black Kettle had to turn to an old friend, Indian agent Wyncoop, for help before he was allowed to buy the necessary ammunition. His band then went out on a successful fall hunt and set up a winter camp on the bank of the Washita to dry their meat, make their robes, and relax.

But Lieutenant Colonel George A. Custer was on the prowl with his Seventh Cavalry. With the approval of General Philip Sheridan, Custer was hunting Indian villages to destroy, shooting or hanging all the Indian men he could capture, destroying the lodges, food, and camp gear, shooting the captured ponies, and bringing in the surviving women and children as captives.

Custer could be more certain of success in a surprise attack if he picked a peaceful village that was expecting no trouble. He approached Black Kettle's village in a snowstorm, then traveled the last few miles at night after the storm had stopped. His dawn attack came as a complete surprise to the Cheyennes. They lost over a hundred men killed, and a much larger number of women and children. Custer then burned the lodges, the winter stores, and shot 850 captured horses. For this attack Custer was known among all the Plains tribes as the "squaw killer."

Up in Wyoming along Powder River all was serene as the winds scattered the ashes of the burned posts, the rains washed the ground clean, and weeds covered the ruins. Their victory over the army and a new treaty to their liking made the Sioux feel secure again. They settled back in their old pattern, relaxed and happy.

This idyllic interlude lasted only three years. Then surveyors with their strange instruments moved through Sioux country leaving little wooden stakes to mark their passage. The alarmed Indians protested to their agents, only to learn that the fine new treaty specifically provided for a railroad, which the government was sponsoring. The Northern Pacific, similar to the Union Pacific up the Platte, was to cross the Missouri at the Mandan villages, cut across Dakota into Montana, then follow the Yellowstone Valley west. The Indians were sure this new line would bring them new troubles and would damage their buffalo grounds.

In August 1872 war parties attempted to wipe out the surveying crews on the Yellowstone, only to be pushed back by a large force of cavalry. Then they assailed the new Fort Abraham Lincoln at the Missouri crossing, and were beaten off five times before they gave up. Skilled as they were as daring raiders on the open plains attacking wagon trains and small army units, the mounted warriors were helpless against soldiers with cannon behind strong walls. Even in the open, the Sioux were defeated again in 1873 on the Yellowstone, this time by Colonel Custer, the hated "woman killer."

That same year, 1873, far to the west in the lava beds of northern California, a small band of lowly Modocs wrote a bloody page in western history and gave all the western tribes new hope that the white menace could be beaten back. About fifty Modocs and their families had forted up in the lava beds, where they held out for weeks against an army that grew to 1,800 men before the fight was over. The soldier dead totaled more than the whole Modoc fighting force, which lost only three men.

News of the fight spread through all the western tribes. If the Modocs could make such a stand, perhaps a great army from all the buffalo-hunting tribes of the northwest, with 10,000 warriors striking at once, could wipe out the whites group by group or drive them out of the buffalo country entirely. The Sioux chiefs set up a council to discuss the plans, inviting tribes even from the Columbia Basin, 600 miles to the west. They all came together in the lower Yellowstone Valley early in 1874, with most of the tribes voting for war, but the Nez Percé and Flatheads refused to join. The fight was too far from their own country, and they did not like to join with their enemies, the Sioux.

The activities of General Sheridan forced the Sioux to hasten their plans. Sheridan had decided he needed a strong military post in the Black Hills in order to protect the new railroad. He knew he was acting in open violation of the treaty of 1868 when he sent Custer to the Black Hills to reconnoiter and to select a suitable site for the fort. Custer returned with the news that the Black Hills were full of rich placer gold deposits, a report confirmed by another survey party. This led government officials to summon the Sioux chiefs and offer to buy the Black Hills from the tribe. The chiefs refused to sell, and prepared to fight.

A mad stampede of gold hunters soon filled the valleys of the Black Hills with several thousand men, 11,000 in Custer City alone. The Sioux could not stem this mad rush into their sacred hills. They could wipe out small parties of prospectors and cut off many stragglers, but they could not carry out a large-scale attack against a mining camp. Other western tribes had faced this same problem. In all the history of the western mining rushes, no attack was ever attempted against a large mining camp. The tribes lacked the traditions, skills, and discipline necessary to train their men for such fighting. Instead, they planned to fight again on the open plains against the army.

In the face of the obvious Indian unrest the army prepared for trouble. All the Indian bands were ordered to settle on the reservations by January 31, 1876. Any laggards would be classed as hostile and would be subject to attacks on their villages. On March 17 the first attack was made. Colonel J. J. Reynolds struck a combined Oglala and Cheyenne village on Little Powder, but the outcome was indecisive. A month later Sitting Bull, of the Hunkpapa Sioux, called a great war council on the Tongue River for all the tribes.

The council reached a decision to fight that summer, but first they needed some reserve supplies. The whole gathering scattered out in many small bands to make up packs of dried meat. Once the soldiers came, the hunters would be too busy fighting to kill buffalo for fresh meat. The hunting was good, and day by day new warrior bands came from faraway places into the Yellowstone Valley anxious to help in the big fight.

Army scouts soon reported the large-scale preparations of the tribes, and the army massed its troops for action. General Alfred A. Terry, the field commander, marched west from Fort Abraham Lincoln with 400 men, Colonel John Gibbon came down the Yellowstone from the west with 450, while General George Crook moved north from new Fort Fetterman on the Powder River with a column of over 1,000.

Crook's advance was halted on upper Rosebud Creek on June 17, 1876, by about a thousand warriors led by Crazy Horse. All day they fought, with the warriors more than holding their own against the troops, blocking the line of advance and inflicting fifty-seven casualties while suffering seventeen of their own. After the fight Crook retreated about forty miles to the Tongue River, where he had left his wagon train. Here he rested his men and reorganized, and was too late for all the action to the north.

Terry and Gibbon reached the mouth of Rosebud Creek a hundred miles to the north of Crook, unaware of his fight and delay. Their scouts found a broad Indian trail, trampled by countless hooves and scarred by dragged lodge poles, crossing from Rosebud Creek over an open range of hills to the Little Bighorn.

At once Terry planned to encircle the Indians on Little Bighorn and force them to fight. He sent Custer with the Seventh Cavalry to follow the trail the Indians had made, while he and Gibbon moved up the Yellowstone and up the Bighorn to the Little Bighorn Fork. The forces were to be in place by June 26, and would mount a joint attack that day.

But Custer, the glory hunter, could not wait. If he struck the camp before Terry and Gibbon arrived, he could win another overwhelming victory like that against Black Kettle on the Washita. Once his scouts had located the camp on the river bottom, Custer did not even wait to estimate its size. He divided his forces, sending Major Marens A. Reno to charge the camp from the south while he, with 225 men, rode behind the bluffs to the east of the river and struck from the north.

Major Reno led his men in a bold attack, but found himself badly outnumbered. He lost twenty-nine men in the first few minutes and was forced to retreat across the river and take refuge on a hill with Major Fred Benteen and the pack train. Here they beat off the attackers for a day and a night before the warriors finally withdrew.

Custer rode off down the "glory trail" and, like Fetterman at Big Piney, found too many Indians. Also like Fetterman, Custer and all his men died quickly, trapped and hopelessly outnumbered, but not massacred. They died fighting. Terry and Gibbon kept their rendezvous, arriving promptly on June 26 just in time to bury the dead.

After their great victory the Indian forces regrouped in small bands, hunting meat and robes for the winter and seeking new pasture for their horses. They had no reserves of food, supplies, or ammunition, and no steamboats or supply trains on the way. While the Indians could assemble 2,000 or 3,000 warriors in one group for a week or so, they could not keep a large force in the field.

Having been so victorious, the Indians expected the army officers to call another peace council, perhaps would even offer to return the Black Hills to satisfy the Sioux. Instead, the army pursued them with new vigor, hunting down every band they could find, attacking villages in winter, killing the women and children, burning the lodges, destroying the meat and robes, killing the horses. When the pressure forced Sitting Bull north across the Yellowstone, he fought once more in October, then escaped across the border into Canada with about 700 people, but the other Sioux could not evade their pursuers. By May 1877 all the other hostile bands had surrendered and had been penned on reservations. Four years later Sitting Bull, his welcome in Canada worn out, had to come back. With his surrender the resistance of the northern tribes ceased. Two years later the last of the buffalo herds were slaughtered on the Sioux hunting grounds.

22

The Great Slaughter

THE MARKETING OF BUFFALO ROBES and tanned hides from the central and northern plains areas, begun about 1764 by traders working out of St. Louis, brought rather meager profits per pound of skin. The robes and hides could be carried to market successfully by the traders only if they could be purchased along a stream and taken out in canoes or boats. There is no indication that the traders at that time made any special effort to buy skins, but seemed to buy from the various tribes only to keep the Indians happy and to ensure that the Indians would then sell them their better furs. For a long period the number of skins marketed through St. Louis each year remained constant, at about 5,000 a year, with no estimate of the number of robes compared to the number of hides. There is no record of any untanned skins being handled before 1870.

When Americans took over the western fur trade, the number of robes and hides brought to the St. Louis market increased rapidly as the traders competed with one another along the Missouri. At the end of the Napoleonic Wars, with the population of Europe increasing rapidly and the United States expanding, the traders had a greater potential market, which they were quick to exploit.

The supply of buffalo robes coming to market increased again when the market for beaver declined in the 1830's, the traders turning to robes to make up for their losses in beaver. At the same time the Blackfoot country on the upper Missouri was opened to American traders.

Steamboats ran upriver to Fort Union at the mouth of the Yellowstone, and keelboats and mackinaw boats could be used on both the Missouri and the Yellowstone above that point. With this kind of transportation, the traders could handle all the robes the tribes could produce, and sell them at a profit.

With the Blackfeet supplying from 15,000 to 20,000 robes each year, and the Crow, Gros Ventre, and Assiniboin combined adding a like number, the shipments from the Montana country through Fort Union totaled about half the entire number reaching market. The Hidatsa, Sioux, Cheyenne, Arapahoe, and Pawnee brought in the rest, except for a few thousand from the Osage and Wichita. Until the railroads were built into the buffalo country, almost the entire supply of robes, as many as 100,000 a year, came from the Missouri River country, from the northern half of the buffalo range, a pattern determined largely by the presence of good water transportation.

The 100,000 robes a year represented about as many as the Plains Indian women could possibly produce in addition to the robes and hides needed for their own families, for each robe represented many hours of back-breaking work. When the railroads came to Kansas, the Indians could not bring in any more robes even if the traders wanted them, but large quantities of buffalo meat and tongues were available, and these shipments increased rapidly. Any dramatic increase in buffalo hides had to wait on some new tanning process. This came from Germany, and its effect was soon felt in Kansas. A young man from Vermont was an important factor in developing the new market.

In the fall of 1870 young Josiah Wright Mooar arrived in Hayes City, Kansas. He and a partner cut firewood on contract for the military post at Fort Hayes that winter, but in the spring he was ready for more interesting work. He secured a small outfit and began to hunt buffalo, selling the meat locally or shipping it out on the railroad. In butchering his animals he placed the carcass prone, split it down the middle, and took the saddle and hindquarters with the hide still on them. The rest was left on the prairie. This meat found a ready market in Kansas City and St. Louis, and was distributed to local butcher shops and restaurants, usually as buffalo, but quite often as beef.

In this kind of hunting the waste of hides was appalling, but there was no market for them. Buffalo hides tanned by the usual commercial process produced a soft, spongy leather with a rather limited use. Then a bundle of hides shipped to Germany inspired a tannery to try some new methods, which soon produced a better grade of leather. As word of the new leather-tanning process spread, other tanners borrowed it or developed similar ones. By the spring of 1871 the demand for dried hides had grown to the point that one buyer in Kansas City offered to buy any number brought to him.

That fall a buyer in Leavenworth received an order from an English firm for 500 hides. He turned to Hayes City for the hides, and young Wright Mooar helped fill the contract. After delivery was made, Mooar found himself with fifty-seven good hides on his hands. These he shipped to his older brother John in New York City to sell for him.

John Mooar knew something about advertising. He loaded the hides onto an open wagon and hauled them up Broadway on the way to the storage shed. One of the spectators, a tanner from Pennsylvania, promptly bought the lot at $3.50 each, as he wanted to experiment with them. The results were so satisfactory that he sent an order for 2,000 hides to John Mooar, who promptly left New York to become a hide dealer in Kansas.

Once the tanners found they could handle buffalo hides at a profit, orders poured into Kansas from all over the east and from England. Competing buyers showed up at every railroad shipping point near the buffalo country, most of them ready to pay cash on the spot for hides as they were hauled into town, and piling their purchases along the railroad sidings until they could be shipped.

All these dried hides were shipped with the hair on. Those taken in the fall and early winter had fine, thick coats and could be made into robes, but most of the late winter hides and all the summer ones were tanned into leather. Thus the nearly bare "summer" skins, once of little value, were now in great demand, and the hide hunter was able to work the year around for greater profits. Hides were easier to secure and deliver in the summer months, but none of the fresh meat could be marketed, so it was left on the carcasses.

At first Hayes City was the center of the hide trade, but as the railroads pushed west and the Kansas and Pacific line was extended, new shipping points, such as Dodge City, were established. After two years, when the supply of hides dwindled, some of the buyers went out to the hunting camps and took delivery of the hides there.

With a single hide worth a week's wages for a laboring man, the rush of new hunters to the Kansas plains resembled the stampede to a new gold strike. Wild-eyed fortune hunters were all over the place, for yonder were millions of buffalo, each with a valuable hide waiting to be harvested. Why, with a little luck a man could make $20 or $30 or even $50 a day, and be rich in no time. So in they came in 1871 and 1872, buying up all the wagons, teams, and supplies, and heading out in all directions. In the fall of 1872 when the construction crews for the Santa Fe Railroad were laid off for the season, hundreds of them joined the rush for easy money. That winter marked the all-time high for the number of hides brought in, and the number of hunters out, an estimated total of 10,000 to 20,000 men of all classes—hunters, skinners, drivers, cooks, and helpers—in the field at one time.

The usual outfit consisted of a hunter with two to four helpers, makeshift gear, vague plans, and a vast ignorance about how to kill buffalo and process the hides. They carried any kind of a gun that would shoot, whether it could kill a buffalo or not, and drove any kind of rig with wheels, drawn by any kind of animal that could be found quickly. These men were inefficient in their skinning and careless in their handling of the hides afterward, but in the aggregate they managed to bring in enough hides to swamp the market and drive prices as low as 25 cents a hide, hardly enough to pay for the bullets used to kill the buffalo that had worn it. Thousands of the men went broke and drifted on to other fields. The price of hides rebounded by the next summer, and several thousand hunters remained to continue the slaughter until the herds were wiped out.

For fifty years artists depicting western scenes had favored action pictures of Plains Indians dashing into the buffalo herds and attacking the galloping beasts with lances and arrows. In the late 1860's Buffalo Bill was usually shown as running the buffalo, although most of those he killed for the construction crews were shot from a distance. From all these pictures most Americans concluded that the best way to kill buffalo was from the back of a fast horse. The new hunters expected that they too would make their kills in this exciting manner.

Once on the plains easterners and westerners alike learned the hard way that while a chase might be exciting, it was not profitable. It was dangerous to both horse and rider, it produced too few hides for each hunter, and it left the carcasses scattered all over the plains.

Smart hunters decided it would be more efficient to kill the buffalo as it stood or grazed, thus avoiding the dangers of the chase and the scattering of the kill. Hunters could easily get within effective range of a small band and shoot several of the animals before the rest became alarmed, if the shooting was carefully done. The buffalo were particularly vulnerable to this type of attack because of their strong herd instinct, poor eyesight, and stupidity.

In a short time the hunters learned that this new method worked best against a small band of five to twenty head feeding at the edge of the main herd, preferably in a hollow or draw, where they were partially out of sight of the others. Because the hunter did all his shooting from one spot, this kind of kill was called a "stand," to distinguish it from the chase. The men who chased buffalo had long been known as buffalo hunters, so the men who shot from a stand, to set themselves apart from the common crowd, insisted on being called buffalo runners, to the confusion of many people.

A good hunter looking for a stand liked to scout the buffalo herd in the evening just as the animals were settling down for the night. He picked out the band he would attack, and planned his approach. Then an hour or so before dawn he eased into position about 300 yards away, downwind, his horse picketed out of sight. He liked a little cover—sagebrush, a clump of grass, or the edge of a buffalo wallow— for he usually shot from a sitting position and had to move around a little, swabbing out his rifle and reloading after each shot.

The hunters found the buffalo so easy to approach that at first they moved in too close, perhaps within fifty yards or less, before they began shooting, but they soon learned that even the stupid buffalo took alarm at a gunshot so near and often ran away at the first shot, with even a fatally wounded animal able to run a mile or more before dropping. By using accurate, long-range buffalo guns, the hunters found it easy to kill any animal they chose at a distance of 300 yards, and at that distance the buffalo paid little attention to the sound of the gun.

Once the hunter was in position, his rifle loaded, his ammunition laid out within easy reach, he waited until dawn broke and he could clearly distinguish the animals. Then he chose the wise old cow that was the leader and waited until she had moved into position for a good shot, a disabling shot that would not kill at once, either through the lungs or in the spine near the hips. As the cow started to bleed and act sick, the others would gather around, pushing at her with their heads, pawing at her, disturbed by the smell of blood. When one of them turned and started to walk away, a shot caught it in the heart or at the base of the neck, killing it instantly. This usually threw the rest into hopeless confusion, and they milled helplessly about as the hunter chose his targets with care and shot them down until he had wiped out the entire band or, if it was a large band, until he had killed all that his skinners could handle that day, for any animals left unskinned overnight would have their hides ripped by the wolves. Usually two skinners were expected to handle twenty-five to thirty hides, although if they had been resting for a few days because of poor hunting, they might be able to skin out forty or fifty.

If the first stand was a small one, as was usual, the hunter moved on at once to another and continued shooting until he had his quota, or until the herd became alarmed and moved off. When the buffalo were plentiful and feeding quietly, the killing was dull, tedious work—shoot, swab out the gun, let it cool, reload, and shoot again. Sometimes a single stand produced a kill of fifty or sixty, with the record being 120. This hunter had several skinners working that day.

As soon as he had finished his kill, the hunter signaled to the skinners, who came up in their wagon and set to work. They took the hide off in one piece, leaving the head and lower legs unskinned. On a well-run outfit they took the tongue, which was put into brine, then packed in a barrel. It was worth 25 cents at the shipping point. The hides were taken to camp and spread out, flesh side up, with strong wooden pegs driven through slits all around the edge to keep them from shrinking or curling as they dried.

Barring rain or snow, the hides were dry enough in a few days to pack. Then they were folded, hair side in, stacked in piles of ten, and bound together with green thong, or they were rolled into bundles of ten each, flesh side out. The fresh skins as they came from the buffalo averaged about 75 pounds for adult cows, and as much as 150 pounds for an old bull. In drying they lost about two-thirds of their weight. Thirty-five bundles or packs made up a full load for a big wagon, about 8,000 to 9,000 pounds, for the haul to the railroad, and represented about two months' work for the crew. In a good season they could expect to bring in three or four loads, plus a few barrels of tongues. Toward the end of the period, when buffalo were scarce, they would also save the best heads for trophies.

Skinning was hard, slow, dirty work, with hands and clothes covered with grease, the hot sun beating down, and swarms of flies all over. Some skinners tried to work out a method in which a draft animal would do most of the work. They drove a big iron stake through the buffalo's head and into the ground, cut the skin loose around the neck, and hitched up a mule to peel off the hide, but too often a chunk or two tore out, ruining the hide. A horse or mule could be a real help in turning a carcass or pulling a skin from under the animal once it was free from the body. Usually the hitch was made on the tail.

When the hides were brought into camp, ignorance, carelessness, insects, and bad weather could spoil many of them. With a poor crew and heavy rain, this might be as many as three out of four. Even with the most skilled, careful handling, the loss seldom could be kept at less than one in five. Any hides put into bundles before they were dry would soon rot, and the hair would slip off. Some hides became infected with beetles.

In the face of such difficulties, plus occasional Indian trouble and periods of poor hunting, most of the outfits did well to break even, and only a few of the best showed a profit. There is no verified record of any hide hunter getting rich, although some of the men in later years told of great success in the old days. One man, Fred Meyer, considered by his contemporaries as one of the very best, kept careful books on his operations for several years. After deducting expenses and interest on his investment, he found that he had averaged about $125 a month for all his work, supervision, and planning. He did admit that he might have squandered about that much more, but with this top man, in his best years, averaging $2,600 a year including his squanderings, it is evident that few fortunes were made from buffalo hides, although a hundred or so might have ended up with a modest stake. This man made his profits by handling the skins carefully, saving and marketing the tongues, and, toward the end, marketing a good deal of meat and some trophy heads, all items neglected by the average outfits.

Tongues and meat for the eastern market had to be cured, smoked, and carefully packed. One hide buyer moved out onto the plains near the hunting camps and bought tongues and meat as well as hides. He preferred the hindquarters, which the old mountain men had scorned, for each one would yield three good solid chunks of meat without any bone, and in nice shape to handle and to market, for they had much the size and shape of the standard cured hams.

To cure the meat, pits about four feet deep were dug in the ground, and each lined with a green buffalo hide from a large bull. The pit was filled with the pickling solution, and the well-trimmed tongues and chunks of meat were put in it for several days, then taken out and smoked. The tongues were packed in barrels for shipment. Each piece of cured meat was sewn into a tight-fitting canvas wrapper. The cured meat found a ready sale in the eastern markets.

Good buffalo outfits were expensive, and wore out within three or four years from hauling the large loads over roadless country. All the wagons and camp gear were very high priced in 1871 and 1872, at the height of the rush, with newcomers bidding up the prices. A good large wagon, capable of hauling four tons of hides at a load, cost $600 or $700. It had steel wheels with nine-inch-wide steel rims and a flatbed of steel plate. Loaded, it needed six span of mules to haul it. The camp wagon was about half as large, also with nine-inch wheels. It had a steel box for hauling camp gear and supplies, and needed three span of mules. Wagons with wooden boxes and wooden wheels wore out too rapidly under the rough work in the very dry air.

The amount of ammunition carried by an outfit for one season is rather astonishing. One outfit with two hunters took a ton—1,600 pounds of lead and 400 pounds of powder, enough for about 25,000 rounds. The brass cartridge cases were used over and over, being reloaded in camp each night after a hunt. A first-class hunter could get by with half as much ammunition. He figured on downing eighty to ninety buffalo for every 100 rounds fired.

Although almost every kind of gun was tried on the buffalo, the hide hunters needed very good rifles, both powerful and accurate. At least three-fourths of all the commercial hides taken were from buffalo downed by either the large-bore Sharps single-shot breechloader or the equally large Remington, also single-shot. Many of these fine guns were made to order, so they varied in bore, weight of ball, and powder charge, but they were about 50-caliber and shot a ball weighing about an ounce (437.5 grains), with some hunters using all the way from 320 grains to 550 grains. Such a gun was accurate to 800 yards, and with a good telescopic sight was deadly against even the toughest bulls at 300 yards. It weighed from twelve to eighteen pounds, with the sixteen-pound weight very common, and could be fancied up to suit the heavy spender with double triggers, 20 power scope, and beautiful chasing on the stock and barrel. The plain model sold on the frontier for about $125, but the extras could easily double the price.

In the spring of 1872, when the hunting camps lined the north bank of the Arkansas and the hunters, lying in wait, caught the herds as they came up from swimming the river, the constant booming of the big guns sounded more like a battle than a hunt.

At the height of the hunting, as hundreds of large wagons rolled in from the plains to the railroad loading points, and the long trains of boxcars, each crammed to the roof, rolled east to the tanneries, no one seemed interested in keeping a grand total of all the hides going from the several stations, although records were saved of the number shipped from any one station by the larger buyers. Each firm tallied its own shipments, and some of these accounts have survived, giving the basis for a reasonably sound estimate.

At Dodge City during the winter season of 1872–73, the peak season for hide shipments in all history, one firm reported handling 200,000 hides, 1,617 pounds of meat, and $2.5 million worth of bones. It has been estimated by totaling such reports, and including some allowance for the many small buyers not reporting, that 1,491,000 hides were shipped in 1872, 1,508,000 in 1873, and only 158,000 in 1874—a grand total of 3,157,000 hides shipped to market in these three years. To arrive at the number of buffalo killed to furnish these hides, one should add an allowance for those killed but not skinned, mostly old bulls, and for the many skins spoiled in handling before they ever reached the buyers, perhaps 2 million in all. During these three years the various tribes of Plains Indians were credited with killing over 400,000 a year, for an added 1.2 million. Thus in western Kansas and south into Texas over 6.3 million buffalo were slain in three years, changing the face of the plains with dramatic suddenness, for all the big herds had been destroyed, leaving the vast pastures empty except for the rotting carcasses and whitened skeletons.

Abandoning the empty plains of Kansas, the buffalo hunters moved on south into Comanche territory, and into trouble. They had no intention of honoring the terms of the Medicine Lodge Treaty, which reserved all the lands south of the Arkansas for the exclusive use of the Indians. Although the Comanches promptly protested the invasion, federal officials and army officers alike deliberately overlooked the treaty violations, and the few Indian agents who attempted to keep the hunters and whisky peddlers out of Indian lands were threatened with violence, not only by the invaders, but by respected newspaper editors in Kansas towns. In Washington, President Grant agreed with a delegation of visiting chiefs that the treaty ought to be enforced, but he gave no orders to that effect.

The Comanches formed war parties to oppose the hunters, picking off a man here, another there, stealing horses, plundering camps, burning the grass. They staged full-scale attacks against some of the smaller camps and succeeded in wiping out several small groups, but the large camps resisted so bitterly and effectively that the Indians gave up on mass attacks. They found the buffalo hunters to be tough, capable, experienced men, armed with long-range guns, well supplied with ammunition, and difficult to catch off guard. Attacking them in force meant the Indians would lose warriors and horses, and still might not win.

The most famous fight of the period took place at Adobe Walls on the Canadian River, where Kit Carson had his troubles with the allied Indian force in 1864. Now in 1874, when the first invasion wave reached the Texas Panhandle, the Comanches gathered their allies and, about 700 strong, decided to wipe out the new trading post at Adobe Walls, deep in Indian country 150 miles from Dodge City and the nearest help.

This trading post was an interesting attempt to adapt to the new hunting conditions. At the end of the fall hunt in 1873, many outfits knew that they had to find new ranges if they wanted more buffalo, and the only herds left south of the Platte were those on Comanche lands in the Texas Panhandle. Not only would they have a much longer haul with their hides to the railroad, but they would also be in serious danger from the Indians.

A sharp hide buyer, A. C. Myers, offered a solution that appealed to many of the hunters. If they would all go south together, he would load their empty hide wagons with his trade goods and pay them to haul the outfit to a permanent camp that he planned to establish. Then he would take their hides there in trade for supplies at Dodge City prices. If they all traveled together, they would be strong enough to beat off Indian attacks.

The hunters hastened to sign up for this adventure, and in a short time a caravan was formed, with fifty men, thirty wagons, and a few saddle horses in addition to the draft animals. One of the wagons carried a full load of whisky to stock a saloon at the new camp, considered more necessary by the hunters than an eating place.

Among the crumbling adobe walls of Bent's old post they built a saloon with sod walls and a dirt-covered roof. A house with picket walls served as a store, another as a blacksmith shop. A strong picket corral was built to protect the stock at night. The post always contained a minimum of nine men; blacksmith, saloon keeper, storekeepers, and helpers. The other forty-one men formed the hunting outfits.

On June 26, 1874, after the killing had been going well for some time and the hides were stacking up at the little camps, it happened that nineteen hunters from several different outfits came to the post at one time, bringing in hides to trade for supplies. A wild party in the saloon kept them up until about midnight, but they were all bedded down when, about 3 A.M., the ridgepole of the saloon cracked with a loud report, awakening everyone. They rolled out and scurried around in the dark, scraping dirt off the roof, cutting and fitting props, and making temporary repairs. At dawn they had finished, and some of them crawled back into their bedrolls while the rest prepared to pack up and get an early start back to their camps.

Just then all hell broke loose as 700 painted braves charged in a yelling mass straight for the little post, capturing or killing all the horses and carving up two teamsters who had slept in their wagons out by the corral. The rest of the men quickly holed up in the blacksmith shop, the store, and the saloon, some barefooted and in their underwear, too rushed to bother with clothes. Instead, their first grabs were for guns and ammunition, and they had no time for seconds.

By the time the charging Indians had crossed the open ground and reached the post, a matter of perhaps ninety seconds, several of the rifles were ready and took their toll, each shot downing a brave or a horse. This immediate strong resistance took the attackers by surprise. Their great medicine man had convinced them that his spells would keep all the whites in a deep sleep and permit them to be killed before they could move. Also he had charmed most of the warriors, at a price, so that no bullets could harm them. Neither the medicine man nor the warriors knew in time that one of the allies, not realizing the enormity of his deed at such a time, had killed a skunk just before dawn, thus ruining all the magic and bringing death to several men.

Skunk or no skunk, the brash warriors could not withstand those one-ounce slugs designed to drop a buffalo bull. They paid with their lives for their boldness and their belief in their invulnerability, their broken bodies littering the hard-packed earth, almost touching the muzzles of the smoking buffalo guns. Then their comrades were shot down as they tried desperately to retrieve the bodies, until the attack was blunted and the disheartened, disillusioned survivors rode sadly away. Their bold, well-planned attack against a force they out-numbered twenty-five to one killed only the two men caught in the wagons and one other.

After the Indians left, the post was cleared of the dead men and horses. In a few days the hunters returned to their camps for more hides, and when they returned from Dodge City the next spring they had large reinforcements anxious to help wipe out the remaining herds. For the next four years the hide wagons, loaded to the top, rolled out on their way to market, many of them now going to a new shipping point, Fort Worth.

There was much bitter fighting with the Indians for years, full of gore and glory for both sides, but the continued attacks could not keep the hunters out. By 1880 the southern Indians had lost all their buffalo and the plains lay open to the cattlemen.

23

Gleaning the Leavings

DURING THE YEARS OF THE GREAT SLAUGHTER the wolves and coyotes prospered greatly. They never needed to hunt, or to go hungry. Instead, when they heard the buffalo guns booming, they gathered at a safe distance and waited for the skinners to finish their task, then they moved in to the prepared feast. Even when there were skinned carcasses lying all about, the predators would usually tear open any animal left unskinned, for they liked the warm entrails. As the hunters increased the number of their kills, the food supply became much greater than the capacity of the distended stomachs of the scavengers, and much of the meat rotted, fouling the air for miles around.

With an abundance of food, the wolves and coyotes multiplied rapidly. What would this savage horde do for food once all the buffalo had been killed and starvation stalked the plains? This never became a serious question, for the wolves and coyotes vanished with the buffalo, but not as completely. Each animal had a hide worth a dollar or two in cash at the nearest trader's station, enough to attract a new breed of hunters, the wolfers, whom the buffalo hunters considered a dirty, drunken mess, much lower than themselves on the social scale—and the buffalo hunters had been characterized by Colonel Richard Irving Dodge, who knew them well, as "fearless as a Bayard, unsavory as a skunk."

A wolfer could manage with just a pack horse, a gun, a bedroll, and a bottle of strychnine crystals, but more often he had two pack horses, or a team pulling a small cart or wagon. He followed after the buffalo hunters, and at each kill poisoned every carcass within a mile or so of his central point. Then he went away for a few days to let the wolves and coyotes have plenty of time to eat their fill and die. He then came back and collected the skins, but if a cold spell came along, he might have to pile up the bodies and wait for the next thaw before skinning them out. He made no fortune at this work, and he was looked down on by everyone else, but wolfing provided a living of a sort for several hundred men, and kept the predator population on the ranges within bounds.

When the wolfer had gone and the last vestiges of decayed meat had fallen from the bones, storms washed the skeletons until they gleamed clean and white in the fresh, uncropped grass. Then came the bone pickers for the final harvest.

Homesteaders in Kansas, Nebraska, and the Dakotas had a tough time just staying alive on their claims during the mid-1870's. The Panic of 1873 and the resulting hard times drove many prospective homesteaders west with very little money or supplies. Money was tight, especially in the debt-ridden west, while hail, drought, and grasshoppers laid waste the grain fields. To get any money at all for a little food for the winter, these men turned to the buffalo ranges.

In the early 1870's the homesteaders could still go out with their wagons in the fall, expecting to come back with a full load of buffalo meat in a week or two, but by the fall of 1873 the range was empty. Then they turned to gathering bones, after they learned that buyers would take all they could haul to the railroad shipping point and would pay good cash money, $4 to $12 a ton. And when drought, hail, or grasshoppers struck, the time allotted for harvesting went for gathering bones instead of grain.

Many of the seminomadic Indians along the farming frontier also turned to gathering bones when they could no longer deliver any buffalo robes to the traders. Freighters returning from some distant point after delivering supplies to an army post or a small settlement found it profitable to pause and load their wagons with bones, thus adding to their profits, for hauling empty wagons back for a hundred miles or so resulted in nothing but a dead loss. From all these sources the bones poured into the shipping points by millions of pounds a year, to be shipped to the eastern sugar refineries or fertilizer plants. Some of them ended up in bone-china dishes for the carriage trade.

Thus for about two decades the bone market was an important

factor in the plains economic structure, supplying work for the destitute and ready cash to a debt-ridden economy. A few statistics help round out the picture. In 1872 the Santa Fe Railroad shipped over 1 million pounds of bones; in 1873, 2,740,000 pounds; and in 1874, over 7 million pounds. Other railroads were also hauling vast amounts of bones during this period.

Bones exposed to the dry air of the high plains remained in good condition for commercial use for twenty years or more unless damaged by a grass fire. This gave the bone pickers plenty of time to complete the harvest, which finally ended about 1890 in western Dakota and eastern Montana, where both the end of the buffalo and the arrival of the railroads lagged about a decade behind that combination of events in Kansas. One of the Montana bone buyers found out toward the end of the harvest that he could increase his profits by grinding the bones and shipping them east in sacks for $18 a ton, whereas the whole bones were selling for $12. This was the delivered price in the east, not the price paid to pickers at the Montana buying point.

The southern buffalo herd had succumbed under great pressure from the swarms of hide hunters and homesteaders, both groups entirely dependent on the new railroads for profits and for attracting recruits. As long as the main southern herd was far from the shipping points, it survived, but once the rails cut into its range, the buffalo were doomed.

During the rapid destruction of the southern herd, the northern herd suffered very little in comparison. In 1870 it was distributed from central Dakota on the east to the Rockies, and from the Powder River Basin north into the prairie provinces of Canada. No important overland trail crossed the entire expanse in any direction, no railroad even approached its boundaries. The only important route for trade was by steamboat up the Missouri to Fort Benton, with a belt of rugged badlands along both banks from Fort Union to Fort Benton, making access to the buffalo plains slow and difficult.

Another important difference between conditions on the northern and the southern ranges was in the distribution of the Indian tribes. In the south the Indians lived away from the railroads and did not block the approach of the hunters to the herds. In the north a broad belt of land occupied by strong, rather hostile nomadic tribes protected the herd from the approach of white hunters from any direction. The Sioux, Assiniboin, Gros Ventre, Blackfoot, and Crow held an unbroken ring around the range.

Since the 1830's, the fur traders had shipped a large number of robes each year from the Fort Benton area, 15,000 a year at the start, and growing to 25,000 a year by 1875, with 75,000 green hides added. In addition, a substantial number came down from the Yellowstone posts.

Then in a few years the whole pattern changed drastically. Early in January 1870, Colonel E. M. Baker left Fort Shaw on the Sun River, Montana, to punish the marauding Blackfoot band led by Mountain Chief, but the guide led the soldiers to the friendly village under Chief Heavy Runner which was camped on the Marias River. At daylight on January 23, the troops surprised the village and killed 173 Indians of all ages and captured 140 women and children.

The Baker massacre crushed the fighting spirit of the Blackfeet. The hostile Sioux, meanwhile, were penned on their reservations by the army, and the Northern Pacific Railroad began inching its way westward across North Dakota from Bismarck to Dickinson, then to Miles City, Montana, bringing good transportation to the buffalo range.

With the Indians leaving and the railroad coming, the hunters flocked in by the thousands to repeat the pattern of slaughter that had been so effective in Kansas. At first they found very good hunting around Dickinson and on west to the Powder River. Here the herds were almost helpless in the severe winter storms when northern winds drove the fine snow and the temperature dropped well below zero. "Yellowstone" Kelly, frontiersman and army scout, mentioned finding a large herd huddled near the mouth of the Powder River so numbed with snow and cold they scarcely moved when he and his companions approached within a short distance and began shooting into them.

By 1880 the hunters were out in force north of the Yellowstone. In that high, dry, cold country the carcasses sometimes lay on the ground for months during the winter with very little spoilage, and by the next summer had become so desiccated they decomposed very slowly. In the spring of 1880 along Porcupine Creek a few miles north of the Yellowstone, carcasses littered the ground for miles. A similar condition was reported near Dickinson that same year.

About 1870 the Sweetgrass Hills on the Canadian border sixty-five miles north of Fort Benton were the central point of the range for a herd of several hundred thousand buffalo that wandered from the Marias River in Montana to the Bow River in Alberta, and eastward from the Rockies to the Cypress Hills. Most of the 100,000 hides shipped annually from Fort Benton came from this herd, with hired hunters from the fort supplementing the work of the Blackfeet and Gros Ventres. These tribes now lived north of the border most of the year, but they came south each summer to hunt and trade. The constant pressure exerted on the herd by these several thousand hunters in the course of a few years drove the herd across the Missouri and into the Judith Basin. A few small bands came back from time to time as hunters moved up from the south, but the good hunting around the Sweetgrass Hills was gone forever.

As a result of the combined attacks on the outlying bulges of the range, when the big rush of hide hunters arrived in 1880 they found the buffalo confined to a strip about 180 miles wide, extending from the Wyoming border north to the Missouri, and from the Little Belt Mountains in central Montana eastward into the Dakotas, with the heavy concentration in the triangle between the Missouri and Yellowstone rivers.

At first the hunters concentrated on the herds nearest the shipping points, Dickinson and Miles City. Then as more outfits took to the plains, a cordon of camps formed along the northern border, attacking any herds moving toward Canada and burning off a wide belt to prevent the buffalo from straying out of the country. This intense activity to the north and west left a temporary gap to the southeast, and in the fall of 1880 a few thousand head broke through and moved off toward the Sioux reservations. As they approached the Cheyenne River reservation, the whole Indian population turned out for a big hunt. Off they went to the northwest, meeting the advance guard of the herd in October and finishing the kill about Christmas. They returned with 2,000 hides and hundreds of horses loaded with meat from this, their last, buffalo hunt.

Three years later a larger herd broke through to the southeast and wandered east of the Black Hills, about 10,000 head in all. Hunters both red and white flocked in as soon as the word went out of the herd's approach. About 9,000 hides were taken in a few weeks, and the remaining 1,000 head were annihilated in a grand two-day hunt staged by several hundred Sioux led by Sitting Bull and joined by a crowd of white hunters. This was the last big buffalo hunt staged by any of the Plains tribes.

While this herd was being wiped out in South Dakota, about 5,000 or more white hunters were at work on the Montana herd, estimated at about 75,000 animals. When the hunters had finished their work and moved out to market in the spring of 1884 with their hides, they left only a few hundred, widely scattered buffalo, most of them in small bands of five to ten animals, in the badlands of eastern Montana.

The hunters did not realize how few were left. They all outfitted again in the fall of 1884 and moved north to the grazing grounds, but found no buffalo. Assuring one another that the herd was out to the west, they kept moving in that direction for a couple of months, each day expecting to find buffalo, but by the time they reached the Little Belts they knew the worst: the buffalo were gone. With their season a total failure, and many of them deeply in debt for their outfits, the hunters went broke and moved on to other pursuits.

By this time even Congress had begun to take notice of the dwindling herds, but a large majority of the Congressmen approved of the situation. When the first restrictive measure was proposed, a government official pointed out, "There is no law which human hands can write, there is no law which a Congress of men can enact, that will stay the disappearance of these wild animals before civilization. They eat grass. They trample the plains. They are as uncivilized as the Indian."

One man favoring the legislation discussed the problem of the sportsmen, many of them foreigners. "I was told that they went to the plains and shot down these animals, not even desiring to take their tongues or their pelts . . . . We allow them to come here and kill the buffalo wantonly and wickedly, but at the same time we afford them the protection of our arms." And a colleague added, "Not only that; but they are furnished horses by the army to go out and kill the buffalo."

Army officers in general were in favor of exterminating the buffalo as a means of solving the Indian problem. At some posts hide hunters were supplied with thousands of rounds of free ammunition so to increase the rate of kill.

In spite of the opposition, a mild bill was finally passed and sent to President Grant near the end of his term. He took care of it with a pocket veto. The next Congress tried again; a bill passed the House but died in the Senate committee. After that no bill was needed, for the herds had vanished.

By 1880 it was apparent that the buffalo was doomed. Sportsmen planning to kill one for the thrill of the kill or to secure a trophy head were urged by the press to act quickly or it would be too late. This advice stimulated hundreds of men to grab their guns and dash out to the attack. The desire to kill a buffalo increased rapidly as the animals

[2 0 5]

became scarce. A few sportsmen even hoped to achieve a sort of historical recognition by killing the very last buffalo. At the same time, these same men were deploring the slaughter wrought by the hide hunters, who at least made some use of their kills.

An account of one hunting trip illustrates the attitude of the sportsmen. In an article for a sports magazine, *The American Field*, George O. Shields wrote that he had fulfilled his fondest dream: to hunt buffalo on its native range, to shoot antelope, elk, and coyotes as they roamed the unspoiled wild country of the west.

Shields outfitted at a military post, Camp McIntosh, in the Dakota Badlands, where the officer in charge furnished at no cost a military escort and wagons and teams to haul his camp gear. The first day out, the party sighted several small bands of buffalo, and shot into each of them, but this was not quite what Shields had come for. That night in camp he was delighted to learn from a scout that a herd of about 200,000 head was just twelve miles away. With this delightful prospect in store, Shields mused about such noble animals being killed by hide hunters, calling it "a burning shame and a disgrace to any civilized citizen," and urging Congress to restrict the hide hunters by law.

In the morning he rolled out of his sleeping bag and managed to kill two old bulls before breakfast. Then he ate and went out after the main herd, shooting indiscriminately at any buffalo within range. The high point of his hunt came when his party stampeded a large band over a seventy-foot cutbank, leaving the animals in a writhing, surging mass about ten feet deep to die at their leisure. On this hunt the recorded kill was sixty-four buffalo, several antelope and deer, and some small game, of which the party used a little of the meat and a few hides. This score does not include the many wounded or the pile of cripples at the foot of the jump.

Shields wrote that this was "a most pleasant and successful hunt in every respect," and advised his readers who wanted to kill a few buffalo for sport to hurry out to the range before the herd was wiped out completely by the hide hunters.

Another hunter from the east, William T. Hornaday, had a different objective in hunting down some of the last strays in the Badlands. In 1886 he was head taxidermist for the National Museum in Washington, D.C. When the directors decided that the museum needed a good buffalo group, Hornaday found that there were no good specimens in stock. He wrote to various places in the west in an attempt to locate a small herd.

He was told of six animals in South Dakota, perhaps a hundred in the rough, remote places in the Texas Panhandle, and a few strays north of Miles City. He decided on Miles City, and set out in the spring to investigate. After a determined hunt, his party found three bulls and killed two of them, only to find that the pelts were of poor quality at that time of year. His guides were sure that he could find more buffalo deeper in the Badlands.

In the fall of 1886 Hornaday returned to Miles City and outfitted for a long hunt. In two months of steady hunting, involving much difficult travel, he killed twenty-six animals of diverse sizes and ages. From these he selected six of the best for a family group in the museum exhibit, and shipped grass and sage from Miles City to make the setting as authentic as possible.

In his report of the project Hornaday gave a fairly comprehensive history of the bison and the destruction of the herds. His interest in the subject aroused, he began working for the preservation of the species and enlisted the assistance of several other people dedicated to the cause. By 1905 he was able to organize the American Bison Society, with President Theodore Roosevelt as the honorary president. This society, with the support of many other groups, finally persuaded Congress to establish the National Bison Range in western Montana and to provide breeding stock to the national parks.

24

The Dying Flame

THE SLAUGHTER OF THE BUFFALO HERDS left a void in the Plains Indians' culture complex far greater in consequence than the economic loss. The buffalo had been the central figure in the Indians' whole pattern of existence, and its disappearance left a spiritually disturbed people, socially disorganized, and lacking a meaningful pattern for a new way of life. Overwhelmed by the winds of change, which they were powerless either to modify or evade, they turned to the mystical world.

At this time of need there arose in the western desert a red messiah who brought a ray of hope, a promise of supernatural aid that would blot out the whites and destroy all their works. And like many a desert prophet before him, this new messiah, Wovoka, came from a small, weak tribe, the Paviotso, living in a remote area of western Nevada.

Wovoka was a sincere young man, trained in the tribal pattern of a medicine man by his father. He was subject to trances in which he traveled to the spirit world and there received visions and instructions that he believed came from the Great Spirit, the Creator, and that he was obligated to share with all Indians.

After years of minor visions and minor miracles, and some acceptance among his own people as a prophet as well as a medicine man, Wovoka had his great vision as he lay seriously ill with a high fever. On January 1, 1889, during a total eclipse of the sun, Wovoka fell into a deep trance that lasted for several days. When he revived, he gave his people a detailed account of his visit to the spirit world: "When the sun died, I went up to heaven and saw God and all the people who had died a long time ago. God told me to come back and tell my people they must be good and love one another, and not fight, or steal, or lie. He gave me this dance to give to my people." He had also been given appropriate songs for the new dance.

Most ritual dances among the Plains tribes were for men only, but west of the Rockies women often were included in these important ceremonies. Wovoka's new dance and its songs were for all the people, men, women, and children, and could last for five days at a time. With its inspiring message, it fired the imagination of the people of the Great Basin, and spread like a range fire in a high wind. Soon it had reached the western rim of the Great Plains.

The Plains tribes, in their disturbed and distressed condition, turned eagerly to the west to receive Wovoka's message. Several tribes sent delegations of their respected leaders to see Wovoka and to determine if he was indeed a real prophet. Greatly impressed, the delegations returned sincere believers and spread the dance and the teachings among their own tribes.

Wovoka was not above sprinkling his spiritual teachings with a little sleight-of-hand, as was customary among the medicine men of the desert tribes. His most impressive performance was staged one night under a towering cottonwood tree by the flickering glow of a campfire. Standing on a tanned skin and wearing a white cotton shirt of new design adorned with magic symbols, he had a trusted follower blaze away at his breast with a large-bore shotgun from a short distance. When the cloud of black smoke from the powder charge cleared away, there stood Wovoka, smiling, unharmed, with a handful of buckshot scattered at his feet. Seemingly his magic shirt had stopped the bullets. In that emotionally steeped setting, who among his devoted followers would suspect that the buckshot had come from the prophet's hand, not from the gun barrel?

As news of this miracle spread, followers from all over the desert and eastward into the plains clamored for the charmed shirts, soon called "ghost shirts" because of their color. Wovoka supplied the shirts, at a good price, putting on each one for a moment to endow it with magic power. With each shirt he gave a solemn warning that it was not to be used for war, as all his followers should be peaceful, but this admonition was easily forgotten by many of the purchasers.

On the plains the new dance soon became known as the ghost dance, from its connection with the ghost shirts. And along with the dance, the songs, and the shirts went a message that promised deliverance for all red men in the near future. When the Indians had proved their sincerity by ritual dancing and improved behavior, the Great Spirit would destroy the white man and his works by a great flood. Then the earth would be renewed, as it had been long ago, with all the buffalo and other game restored. Indians who had died and gone to the spirit world would return, for this was to be a new heaven where there would be no death.

On the plains the dancers wore two feathers in their hair, by which they would be lifted up into the new world. Instead of a flood, they expected a new earth to come out of the west, dropping down and blotting out the old. All the good Indians would be lifted up by their feathers, while all the whites would be buried. In every variation of this regeneration theme, the whites were to be destroyed by the Great Spirit and the Indians would not need to fight.

All through the summer of 1890 many thousands throughout the plains joined in the ghost dance, the mass frenzy providing a dramatic release of their pent-up frustrations. All this furor among their charges went unnoticed or was ignored by the Indian agents on the many reservations until one among the Sioux at Pine Ridge, South Dakota, more alert than the rest, took notice of the meetings and banned the ghost dance among the 6,000 Sioux under his care, but the dancing still went on out in the Badlands, far from the agency.

That summer the Sioux were more restless than usual, closely confined to their reservations, their ranks reduced by wars and disease, their buffalo gone. Government rations of beef, their basic food supply, had been cut in half by Congress, and a new cut was rumored. The Sioux were in the mood to listen to any teachings that might lead to a better future. When they heard of the red messiah in the Nevada desert, they sent reputable men to investigate. These all returned true believers, deeply committed to the new religion. In a short time some of the Sioux medicine men were falling into trances and receiving visions.

In the midst of the growing excitement, the Indian commissioner announced a further cut in the beef rations just as a severe drought was destroying the few crops planted by the more progressive Sioux. At the same time, the experienced Indian agents and agency employees were replaced by inexperienced men, but politically more acceptable to the new administration in Washington. One of the poorest of the new men was given the critical post at Pine Ridge, with its 6,000 restive Sioux. By his timidity and poor judgment he invited disorder, then made matters worse by calling for soldiers to help him keep his unruly wards in line. This was in mid-October 1890.

By this time accounts of the ghost dance and the general unrest had reached Washington, disturbing both the army officials and the Indian Bureau. They moved quickly to prevent the possibility of another Little Bighorn debacle by sending in General Nelson A. Miles with 3,000 troops. Then the high officials sent out an order to seize the old medicine man Sitting Bull and lock him up. When Sitting Bull resisted, he and several of his men were shot down.

Other Sioux bands camped near the agency heard rumors that this attack was the first step in a plan to wipe out all the Sioux. They scattered like frightened quail, seeking shelter in the Badlands. General Miles did his best to calm their fears and soon induced most of them to return to the neighborhood of the agency, where they could be fed and supervised. A few of the bands were very slow in returning, stopping now and again to talk things over. Troops were sent out to escort and speed up the laggards.

One band returning under escort camped for the night on Wounded Knee Creek, setting up their tipis in the dry creek bottom. In the morning they discovered that many other troops had joined their escort during the night and that the camp was entirely surrounded. Next, all the men and older boys were ordered from the tipis and made to sit on the open ground wrapped in their blankets; the frightened women and children remained huddled in the tipis. The morning was cold and gloomy, December 29, 1890.

Troops then began searching the tipis for hidden guns, pushing the women about, tearing open the packs and scattering everything on the ground. As the women began wailing, a medicine man sprang to his feet and began the ghost dance among the seated men, blowing on a war whistle of eagle bone. When an officer ordered a soldier to stop the dancer, a young Sioux pulled out a revolver and shot the officer. At the sound of the shot, the troops all started firing into the crowd.

For a few minutes a hail of fire from the army rifles swept the camp ground, tearing the sitting men to pieces, piercing the tipis, and whistling across the circle to strike some of the troops on the other side.

Then it was all over, and as the Indian men, women, and children died on Wounded Knee that morning, the whole ghost-dance movement died with them, for about half the dead men wore the magic ghost shirts, torn to tatters by the bullets.

The flame of hope that had burned so brightly in the early autumn flickered out at Wounded Knee. The buffalo would never return.

25

Crossbreeding Buffalo and Cattle

THE MANY ATTEMPTS of the early Spanish colonists to raise
buffalo along the Rio Grande in New Mexico were unsuccessful, They
were able to capture the calves in the buffalo country, some 200 miles
to the east, in the late spring, and could raise them using cows or goats
as foster mothers, but they could not control them after the first year
or so. The young buffalo became unruly and dangerous during their
third year and could be kept only in strongly fenced enclosures, which
the Spanish could not afford in that treeless country. Although the old
records do not give the details, it is probable that all the buffalo had
to be killed by the time they were three years old. It is also probable
that the tradition of a few buffalo being seen along the Rio Grande
in the seventeenth century traces back to these captives.

Quite a large number of people have tried to raise and tame buffalo
over the years, but all records since 1800 indicate that every attempt
to domesticate the animal has failed. The handlers mention that the
calves are friendly and easy to handle when caught young, not more
than a month old, but that they become bad-tempered and unruly later,
the bulls as two-year-olds, the cows sometimes not until they are three.
Then they attack their handlers without any warning. Several people
have been killed in this way. Ernest Thompson Seton, who hunted and

studied big game for many years, rated the buffalo as the wild animal most dangerous to man. He included these captives in his reckoning, for he considered them truly wild even though they had been raised in captivity.

Many of the people who engaged in attempts to domesticate the buffalo were interested in crossing them with domestic cattle, hoping to secure a good beef animal more docile than buffalo and hardier than cattle. Since 1890 it has been the custom to call all such crosses cattalo, a name given them by Colonel Charles Jesse "Buffalo" Jones when he produced his first hybrids in Kansas.

As early as 1701 a colony of Huguenots in Virginia tried their hand at raising buffalo. They settled on the James River above Richmond and were able to capture several buffalo calves in the vicinity, but had to kill them off in two or three years because they had become unmanageable. At about the same time, Pierre Le Moyne, Sieur d'Iberville, governor of the new colony of Louisiana, proposed bringing buffalo from the plains to the lower Mississippi so that they could be raised for wool and meat. There is no record that this project ever went beyond the planning stage.

In 1786 farmers in West Virginia tried crossing buffalo and cattle. According to Albert Gallatin, they succeeded in producing several hybrid calves. Stockmen farther west in the Ohio Valley also tried crossbreeding, with indifferent results. Robert Wycliff, near Lexington, Kentucky, began his program in 1815 and carried it on for thirty years. He induced at least one neighbor, Thomas Corneal, to help him for a while.

The next well-documented attempt to produce cattalo was that by Sam L. Bedson at Stony Mountain, Saskatchewan. In six years he had a herd of twenty-five hybrids with his fifty-eight buffalo. He then sold all his buffalo to Buffalo Jones, who by that time had a herd of fifty-seven in Kansas, some of them old enough to breed. Jones sold off part of his herd from time to time, sending five pairs of buffalo to England, and selling twenty-six buffalo and eighteen cattalo to Michel Pablo. In spite of experiments over a period of twenty years, Jones was never able to produce a hybrid that could reproduce itself.

During this same period Charles Goodnight, who had a small buffalo herd on his cattle ranch in the Palo Duro Canyon, bred some cattalo. In 1896 Mosson Boyd, of Bobcaygeon, Ontario, secured some buffalo and bred hybrids for nineteen years, producing about one live animal a year. Then he quit and shipped all his stock west to the National Bison Range at Wainwright, Alberta.

One difficulty confronted the breeders from the first: buffalo bulls were reluctant to serve domestic cows, and domestic bulls showed little interest in buffalo cows. Only when the bull in either case had been raised with the cows away from his own kind could he be induced to cover the strange cows. Once they were properly served, both the buffalo cows and the domestic cows produced calves.

This brought to light a second difficulty: about two-thirds of the domestic cows aborted or produced stillborn calves, and more than half the cows died. In western Montana the ranchers were convinced that the heads of the buffalo calves were too large, while others insisted that it was the hump that caused the trouble. However, closer study revealed that the heads were really quite small at birth and that the hump did not start to develop until the calves were several months old. To add to the confusion, the buffalo cows bred to domestic bulls, usually Hereford or Angus, had no trouble in calving and produced healthy calves.

After the Canadian government had its buffalo herd well established at Wainwright, it instituted a scientific program of crossbreeding that was carried on for twenty-one years, 1920–41. The careful, detailed work here showed that the domestic cows died of an excessive amount of amniotic fluid produced during pregnancy and that it was not desirable ever to cross a domestic cow with a buffalo bull.

The healthy calves produced by the buffalo cows grew well and produced a good grade of meat. All the females were fertile and could be crossed with either buffalo or domestic bulls, but hybrids bred back to buffalo bulls had a high rate of abortions and stillbirths. All the male hybrids were found to be completely sterile, incapable of producing any sperm cells. Hybrid males with $\frac{3}{4}$ domestic breeding could produce some weak and imperfect sperm cells, but to secure males with normal, healthy sperm cells it was necessary to dilute the buffalo strain until the hybrid was $\frac{31}{32}$ domestic breeding. The offspring of such hybrids showed practically no advantage of any kind over the pure domestic breeds, and were of no interest to the cattlemen. The Canadian experimenters concluded after their twenty-one years of work that crossbreeding of buffalo and domestic cattle was biologically feasible but economically undesirable.

The buffalo, then, is an interesting wild animal, unfit for domestication or crossbreeding. It can thrive on the open range with no more attention than being protected from men. The species is picturesque, an important feature in our western parks, but of little economic value to civilized man even though it was the staff of life for many thousands of hunters on the western plains for 10,000 years or more.

26

Preservation of the Species

THE INITIAL PROBLEM in the effort to save the buffalo from total extinction was learning how to handle the animals on a controlled, protected range. Many different men over a period of 350 years had determined that the buffalo could not be domesticated, nor could it be successfully crossed with cattle. Buffalo had to be handled like animals in a zoo, and it would be difficult to get enough initial breeding stock from the open plains to stock the fenced ranges.

The first attempts to manage buffalo as domestic stock were made on the plains east of the Pecos River by pioneer settlers from the Rio Grande Valley who expected to become wealthy stockmen overnight, with their great herds fattening on the free grass of the Great Plains. They expected to choose their initial range stock from the immense herds of wild "cattle," the cibolas, which, they reasoned, should need only to be corraled and supervised. A well-organized party of mounted men should be able to round up enough buffalo in one day to stock a large ranch, an initial herd of perhaps 10,000. In 1599 sixty men set out for the plains on just such a mission, and soon found the buffalo herds. Don Juan de Oñate gave this account:

> Next day they went three more leagues in search of a convenient and suitable site for a corral, and on finding a place, they began to construct it out of large pieces of cottonwood. It took them three days to complete it. It was so large and the wings so long they thought they could corral ten thousand head of cattle, because

they had seen so many, during those days, wandering so near the tents and houses. In view of this and the further fact that when they run they act as though fettered, they took their capture for granted. It was declared by those who had seen them that in that place alone there were more buffalo than there were cattle in the three largest ranches in Spain.

The corral constructed, they went next day to a plain where on the previous afternoon about a hundred thousand cattle had been seen. Giving them the right of way, the cattle started very nicely toward the corral, but soon they turned back in a stampede toward the men, and, rushing through them in a mass, it was impossible to stop them, because they are cattle terribly obstinate, courageous beyond exaggeration, and so cunning if pursued they run, and that if their pursuers stop or slacken their speed they stop and roll, just like mules, and with this respite renew their run. For several days they tried a thousand ways of shutting them in or surrounding them, but in no manner was it possible to do so. This was not due to fear, for they are remarkably savage and ferocious, so much so that they killed three of our horses and badly wounded forty, for their horns are very sharp and fairly long, about a span and a half, and bend upward together. They attack from the side, putting the head far down, so that whatever they seize, they tear very badly . . . .

Seeing that the full grown cattle could not be brought alive, the sargente major ordered that the calves be captured, but they became so enraged that out of the many which were being brought, some dragged by ropes and others upon the horses, not one got a league toward the camp, for they all died within about an hour. Therefore it is believed that unless taken shortly after birth and put under the care of our cows or goats, they cannot be brought until the cattle become tamer than they are now.

This attempt was made in the middle of October, when the calves were five or six months old and well grown. About thirty years later men from the same Spanish colony had improved their methods of capturing and raising buffalo: "They were not cattle that let themselves be rounded up, though as a means they take among them some of our tame cattle. And so, at the time of calving, the Spanish go to catch the little calves and bring them up with goats."

[2 1 8]

About 200 years later in the Red River Valley near Pembina, Alexander Henry found the young calves very easy to capture.

> I killed four calves, of which I took only the thighs, and brought two calves home alive; they no sooner lost sight of the herd than they followed my horse like dogs, directly into the fort. On chasing a herd at this season, the calves follow until they are fatigued, when they throw themselves down in the high grass and lie still, hiding their heads if possible. On coming to them, they start to run, but seeing only the person and his horse, they remain quiet and allow themselves to be taken. Having been handled a little, they follow like dogs.

George Catlin at Fort Union reported that he would sometimes catch a very young calf, and breathe into its nostrils. Then when the calf was turned loose, it would follow him closely, attracted by his now-familiar scent. A hide hunter in the Texas Panhandle, Charlie Jones, reported taking young calves in the same manner.

Usually a captured calf would be killed for food within a day or two, for the men around a trading post had neither the means nor the inclination to raise such a pet. It is probable that the calves behaved gently only during the first month or so of their existence; Horace Greeley reported from Kansas in 1859:

> A calf two or three months old is tied to a stake just beside our wagons. He was taken by rushing a herd up a steep creek bank, which so many could not possibly climb at once; this one was picked out in the melee as most worth having, and taken with a rope. Though fast-tied and with but a short tether he is true game, and makes at whatever goes near him with desperate intent to butt the intruder over.

The docility of the very young buffalo calves was a big factor in establishing small captive herds in various parts of the country after most of the wild herds had been killed. About eighty calves furnished the breeding stock for most of the buffalo alive today.

The first of the modern breeding herds was started in northwestern Montana almost by chance. In the fall of 1872, long before there was any serious concern about the survival of the buffalo, a young Pend d'Oreille Indian, Walking Coyote, went from the Flathead reservation to hunt buffalo in the Blackfoot country some 300 miles to the east, across the Rockies. Along the Milk River about where it crosses from Canada into Montana, Walking Coyote joined a friendly band of Piegans who were wintering there in good hunting country.

In the spring after the new calves arrived, the band staged a successful hunt, but which left some of the calves wandering, motherless and friendless, looking for company. Some of the strays joined a horse herd, and there Walking Coyote found them the next morning, among his horses. He decided to take them back to the Flathead country alive and start his own buffalo herd. He must have had some recently foaled mares to feed the calves, for there was no other possible source of milk.

The Indian agent at Browning was interested in the plan. He suggested that the calves be taken first to a ranch on the Sun River where a rancher friend would help. A hundred miles later the strange little cavalcade showed up at the ranch near Haystack Butte, Montana. The rancher took them in, and turned the calves in with his own cows to rest them up for the trek across the mountains.

From Sun River a rather easy trail led across the open range to the head of the Dearborn River and across the continental divide by way of Cadotte's Pass. On the west side the trail followed down the Big Blackfoot River to Hell's Gate, then northwest across the hills to the Flathead country, about 150 miles in all. Six of the calves, two bulls and four cows, survived the long journey in good condition and were placed on good range land on the Flathead reservation. In eleven years they had increased to thirteen head. Obviously there were some losses.

Buffalo calves for the second breeding herd were captured across the Canadian border about 300 miles to the northeast of where Walking Coyote discovered his strays. Some Indian hunters from the Winnipeg area found the calves in Manitoba and brought them back alive, one bull and four cows. They traded them to Tonka Jim McKay, a trader who must have had others, for he had twenty-three to sell to Sam L. Bedson in 1882, too many for just natural increase. Bedson kept the animals at Stony Mountain, Manitoba, and used some of them to crossbreed with domestic cattle. By 1888 he had a herd of fifty-eight buffalo and twenty-five hybrids. That November he sold all the buffalo to Charles J. Jones, later known as Buffalo Jones, of Garden City, Kansas, but a few of the tough old bulls escaped while they were being driven to the railroad shipping point.

The third breeding herd was started on impulse in the Palo Duro

Canyon of the Texas Panhandle. Charles Goodnight moved into the canyon and started a cattle ranch in the 1870's, when there were still a few small bands of buffalo in the area. One day his cowboys brought in a buffalo calf with the range stock. Mrs. Goodnight had a special little pasture fenced for it. The cowboys brought in several more buffalo calves in the next few years to put in the pasture.

The fourth breeding herd was started according to a definite plan for the purpose of trying to cross the buffalo with cattle. Buffalo Jones had been a hide hunter around Dodge City in the 1870's, but quit hunting to become a prosperous rancher and businessman at Garden City. A hard winter, 1885–86, killed off some of the range cattle and inspired Jones to try to produce a more hardy breed of beef animal for the plains.

Jones went out with a good outfit and some helpers to rope buffalo calves in the summer of 1886. He was an expert roper and tied up fourteen calves for the wagon to pick up. The calves were fed condensed milk until they could be hauled back to the ranch, 300 miles away, where they were turned over to milk cows to raise. Four of the calves died on the way home, and Jones decided he would drive the foster-mother milk cows along on the next hunt. The cows and captive calves had little trouble adjusting to one another, and Jones returned with seven more calves in 1887.

His greatest success came in the summer of 1888. He expected to make a good catch and took along twenty cows, but soon he had thirty-two calves to feed. He found twenty more cows at a ranch in the area, which he bought at a rather high price, and all thirty-two calves survived the trip to the home ranch.

The next spring he was out on the range early and followed a small herd of cows, capturing the little calves as they were born, and ended with seven. He and his men roped and tied down seventeen buffalo cows in an attempt to take them back, but the cows fought themselves into exhaustion and all died within an hour or so after being roped. Jones then had his men follow a herd of twenty-one for about six weeks, keeping close to the buffalo day and night. When the animals had become accustomed to the horsemen, other riders came up with twenty-five tame buffalo from the home ranch and mixed them with the wild ones. The herd moved along easily until they approached the first ranches, then the wild ones broke and ran. Although the herders followed them until the buffalo had such sore and bleeding feet they could scarcely walk, they would not allow themselves to be driven and had to be left on the range.

At the end of this summer, 1889, Jones had fifty-six buffalo he had captured, plus a few calves born that year to his first catch. In addition he had the fifty-eight purchased from Sam Bedson, and a number of hybrids, which he called cattalo. Added to his colorful character, Jones had a flair for publicity and became known to the nation's press as Buffalo Jones.

In western Montana, Walking Coyote had become discouraged with his buffalo herd and talked of selling them. A neighbor living on the Flathead reservation, Michel Pablo, was interested at once. Pablo was the son of a Mexican father and a Piegan mother, and had been raised in Montana. He and a part-Indian friend, Charles Allard, who also liked buffalo, entered into a partnership, scraped up the $2,000 in gold coin that Walking Coyote demanded, and took over the herd of thirteen.

Under Pablo's skilled management the herd increased more rapidly than before, even though some animals were lost to buffalo rustlers in spite of Pablo's watchfulness and his promise of a reward of $100 for the capture of the rustlers. In 1893 the partners bought twenty-six head of buffalo from Buffalo Jones, bringing in two new breeding strains, one from Manitoba, the other from the Texas Panhandle, to mix with the Milk River stock.

When Charles Allard died in 1896, the herd was divided, one-half, 150 head, going to Pablo, the other 150 being divided among Mrs. Allard and her four children. Mrs. Allard sold her share to Charles Conrad of Kalispell, Montana, who later supplied most of the initial stock for the National Bison Range. The daughters and one son sold their shares to Howard Eaton, who later supplied the first eighteen cows for the Yellowstone Park herd. The other son sold to Judge Woodrow, who later shipped them to the 101 Ranch in Texas. As a result of this dispersal, it was estimated that in 1900 more than 80 percent of the buffalo in the United States could be traced to the Pablo-Allard herd.

Once Michel Pablo had sole charge of his herd, it increased at a rapid rate, from 150 in 1896 to more than 600 in 1906, and he had sold more than fifty head to various zoos. The large herd outgrew the pasture, and Pablo asked the federal officials for a long-term lease on public range lands nearby. They refused, and Pablo learned that they were planning to open the Flathead reservation to homesteaders, which would mean the end of his present range. He then petitioned the federal government to buy his herd. While President Roosevelt and many conservationists favored the purchase, Congress balked at appropriating the money. Pablo then applied for grazing rights in Alberta.

By then the Canadian government was deeply interested in the problem of buffalo survival. After the Canadian plains had been cleared of buffalo and the Montana herd was slaughtered in 1883, the only important herd left consisted of possibly 300 or 400 head of wood buffalo in northern Alberta, too few and too far away to attract the hide hunters. In 1889 the Canadian government placed a permanent closed season on all its buffalo and delegated the Northwest Mounted Police to protect the Alberta herd, which had grown to about 600 animals. Under this protection the herd increased steadily.

When the Canadian government established Banff National Park in 1897, T. J. Blackstock of Toronto purchased three buffalo from Charles Goodnight and donated them to the park as a tourist attraction. The following year brought the gift of another animal, and a few young buffalo were brought in from the north. In twelve years of good management this herd had increased to over a hundred head and needed new range.

When Pablo had asked for grazing land in Alberta, the officials refused, but offered to buy his entire herd at $200 each for all animals delivered to a railroad station in eastern Alberta where a new large range had been set aside for buffalo. During this same period the Canadians also bought thirty buffalo from Charles Conrad.

The roundup of the Pablo herd attracted widespread interest throughout the west. For a period of five years buffalo were rounded up each summer for shipment, but in the end several of the stubborn old bulls had to be left behind. The driving and loading of the buffalo was a wild and woolly affair with plenty of excitement, especially for the riders. A good roper on a first-class roping horse had little trouble if he knew when to run away for a time. Even with twenty-two hands to help, Pablo had his hands full shipping out the first 200 of the tamer animals and loading them in specially reinforced stock cars. One of the big bulls even broke through the side of the car after he had been loaded, and was allowed to go back to the range.

This purchase of the Montana buffalo for shipment to Canada and the publicity given the roundup helped spark interest in the United States in establishing herds in the west. First Congress set aside 20,000 acres in the Flathead country for the National Bison Range. Although this was across the Rockies from the original buffalo country, it had proved suitable for the Pablo herd and the buffalo have prospered there. Another herd was started in Yellowstone Park and gradually merged with the few wild buffalo that had survived on the upper Lamar River.

By 1915 it was obvious that the buffalo as a species had been saved. From the available breeding stock any desired number of animals could be raised, the only limitation being the amount of pasture that could be set aside for their use. At the present time, 1969, private individuals may purchase either live buffalo or carcasses from the government herds each year, and there are quite a number of private herds with surplus animals to sell.

To help the herd in Yellowstone Park when it was small and adjusting to the new range, hay was furnished each winter, but this feeding of the herd in one spot was finally considered undesirable and was discontinued. Now the herd is allowed complete freedom on its range, and if the winter feed is short or the snows extra heavy, the weaker animals are allowed to die. In this way the park officials hope to preserve a truly wild buffalo herd under conditions very close to those prevailing on their ranges before the coming of the white man.

Appendix

Where to See the Buffalo

SMALL BANDS OF BUFFALO can now be found in most of the larger zoos, on many stock ranches, and in pens at several filling stations along western highways, so it is comparatively easy for an interested person to find specimens to observe from a short distance. Animals kept in these small pens are often a disappointment to the viewer, for they appear unkempt and dull and sleepy, but they do give a good concept of the large size and the distinctive shape.

To get a glimpse of the monarch of the plains still clothed in some shreds of his former majesty it is necessary to visit one of the larger herds living on the open range in a national or state park or game refuge. The animals will appear at their best in late summer and fall, after they have finished shedding their old coat and have grown the new one. Any visit to one of these larger herds will be more rewarding if the visitor finds out beforehand from the local staff the exact location of the herd at that particular time and any special regulations or precautions to be observed.

Casual visitors usually find the National Bison Range in the Flathead Valley in western Montana a satisfactory place to visit without advance planning. On this range 400 buffalo roam freely over 20,000 acres of rolling range land decorated with scattered groves of yellow pine, but during the summer they spend most of their time grazing on a half-mile-wide strip along the northern boundary fence. A surfaced road parallels the fence for a few miles, giving the motorist easy access to a good viewing spot. Adjacent to the range headquarters a pasture of about 600 acres holds a small band which is always close to the fence in some spot for the camera fan to take pictures. A few elk mingle with these buffalo.

In Yellowstone National Park a herd of 800 buffalo roams an unfenced range between the Yellowstone and Lamar rivers. During the summer this herd usually stays in the higher country, well away from the highway. An observer must either rent a horse or hike in for several miles to reach a good viewpoint.

The largest buffalo herd in existence contains over half of all living buffalo. It is in the Wood Buffalo National Park near the Great Slave Lake in northwestern Canada. There about 16,000 animals occupy 11 million acres of wild land. The best view of this park and herd can be obtained from a light plane.

The second largest concentration of buffalo is in the Black Hills of South Dakota. A herd of 1,300 is in Custer State Park and another herd of 370 is in the adjoining Wind Cave National Park. In each case a good road provides easy access to park headquarters.

The Wichita Mountains Wildlife Refuge in Oklahoma occupies a rough, wild country in the Panhandle, and holds a herd of 900. A special attraction for spectators is the roundup each fall to cut out the surplus stock for market.

New parks and new refuges, such as the Theodore Roosevelt Memorial National Park in western North Dakota badlands and the Charles M. Russell National Wildlife Range in the breaks of the Missouri in north central Montana, are being stocked with buffalo. Many small herds are being placed on national monuments and in state parks throughout the west, and more than a hundred stock ranches now have buffalo herds under private ownership. The number of such herds is increasing rapidly. Up-to-date information on them can be secured from the travel information bureaus of the various states.

Selected Bibliography

FOR A COMPREHENSIVE BIBLIOGRAPHY of material on the buffalo, consult Frank Gilbert Roe, *The North American Buffalo*, Toronto, 1951. This large volume contains many quotations from primary sources.

Quotations of translations from early Spanish documents used in this work were taken from the following:

T. BUCKINGHAM SMITH, *Relation of Álvar Núñez Cabeza de Vaca*, Washington, D.C., 1851.

GEORGE PARKER WINSHIP, "The Coronado Expedition, 1540–42," in the *Fourteenth Annual Report of the American Bureau of Ethnology*, Washington, D.C., 1896.

HERBERT EUGENE BOLTON, *Spanish Exploration in the Southwest, 1542–1706*, New York, Charles Scribner's Sons, 1908.

The Memorial of Fray Alonso de Benavides, 1630, translated by Mrs. Edward E. Ayer, annotated by Fredrick Webb Hodge and Charles Fletcher Lummis (privately printed), Chicago, 1916.

REUBEN GOLD THWAITES, ed., *The Original Journals of Lewis and Clark Expedition, 1804–06*, 8 vols., New York, 1904–05, was used for cited passages by Meriwether Lewis.

Material quoted by Frémont came from two of his works: John Charles Frémont, *Memoirs of My Life*, New York, 1887; and his official report, John C. Frémont, *Report of the Exploring Expedition to the Rocky Mountains and to Oregon and North California in the years 1843–44*, Washington, 1845.

After his trip to the Colorado mines Horace Greeley published his account, *An Overland Journey from New York to San Francisco in the Summer of 1859*, New York, 1860.

Many details on buffalo and Plains Indians are found in *Pacific Railway Survey Reports*, 36th Cong., 1st Sess., Ex. Doc. 56, 12 vols. Volume XII,

Book I, contains the material by General Isaac I. Stevens, while his treaty council is described by Lawrence Kip, *The Indian Council in the Valley of the Walla Walla, 1855* (printed, not published), San Francisco, 1855.

RUPERT N. RICHARDSON, *The Comanche Barrier to South Plains Settlement*, Glendale, Calif., Arthur H. Clark Co., 1933, contains some early accounts of Indian troubles.

Interesting journals of travel on the overland trail to California are: J. Goldsborough Bruff, *Gold Rush,* ed. by Georgia W. Read and Ruth Gaines, New York, Columbia University Press, 1949; Irene D. Paden, ed., *The Journal of Madison Berryman Moorman, 1850–51*, San Francisco, California Historical Society, 1948; and LeRoy R. Hafen and Ann W. Hafen, eds., *To the Rockies and Oregon, 1839–1842*, Glendale, Calif., Arthur H. Clark Co., 1955.

For the introduction of cattle to the western plains, E. S. Osgood, *The Day of the Cattleman*, Minneapolis, University of Minnesota Press, 1929, is recommended.

ROBERT STUART, *The Discovery of the Oregon Trail*, ed. by Philip Ashton Rollins, New York, Charles Scribner's Sons, 1935, furnished comments on early travel on the Platte River. Other books on the fur trade for recommended reading are: Hiram Martin Chittenden, *The American Fur Trade of the Far West*, Elmira, New York, Wilson-Erickson, Inc., 1935; Bernard DeVoto, *Across the Wide Missouri*, Boston, Houghton Mifflin Co., 1947; Elliott Coues, ed., *New Light on the Early History of the Greater Northwest: The Henry-Thompson Journals*, New York, 1897; Josiah Gregg, *Commerce of the Prairies*, 1842; Alexander Ross, *Red River Settlements*, London, 1856; and George Catlin, *Indian Tribes of North America*, 1847. Alfred Jacob Miller, *The West of Alfred Jacob Miller (1837)*, Norman, University of Oklahoma Press, 1967, contains a large number of sketches and paintings of the buffalo country done from life, as do the works by DeVoto and Catlin. Paul Kane, *Wanderings of an Artist among the Indians of North America*, London, 1859, also deals with the fur trade.

For a good overview of the buffalo hunting tribes the best is Robert H. Lowie, *Indians of the Plains*, New York, McGraw-Hill Book Co., 1954. Many good books on the various tribes have been published by the University of Oklahoma Press, and the reader is directed to the complete list, especially in the Civilizations of the Americas series.

The slaughter of the buffalo herds has been handled well by Wayne Gard, *The Great Buffalo Hunt*, New York, Alfred A. Knopf, Inc., 1959, and by E. Douglas Branch, *The Hunting of the Buffalo*, New York, D. Appleton-Century Co., 1929. A first-hand account of the killing is given by Frank Mayer and Charles B. Roth, *The Buffalo Harvest*, Denver, Alan Swallow, 1958.

Index